CONSTRUCTING IDENTITIES

CONSTRUCTING IDENTITIES

The Social, the Nonhuman and Change

Mike Michael

SAGE Publications
London • Thousand Oaks • New Delhi

© Mike Michael 1996

First published 1996

 SAGE Publications Ltd
6 Bonhill Street
London EC2A 4PU

SAGE Publications Inc
2455 Teller Road
Thousand Oaks, California 91320

SAGE Publications India Pvt Ltd
32, M-Block Market
Greater Kailash – I
New Delhi 110 048

British Library Cataloguing in Publication data

A catalogue record for this book is available
from the British Library

ISBN 0 8039 8951 2
ISBN 0 8039 8952 (pbk)

Library of Congress catalog record available

Typeset by M Rules
Printed in Great Britain by Redwood Books, Trowbridge, Wiltshire

Dedicated to the memory of my father

Contents

Acknowledgements

Many people have contributed in one way or another to this book. Colleagues and students at Lancaster University have provided a richly fecund intellectual environment. My thanks go particularly to Susan Condor, Robin Grove-White, Gavin Kendall, Celia Lury, Kath Smart, Vicky Singleton, John Wakeford and Brian Wynne. Further afield, I have benefited immensely from conversations and collaborations with Lynda Birke, Rob Briner, Alan Irwin, Rosemary McKechnie, Arthur Still, Chris Todd and Carol Youngson. Light in those inevitable moments of darkness was shed by Sue Armistead, Lynda Birke, Susan Condor, Celia Lury and Marios Michael. Bethan and Aneirin Rees provided the final, glorious spur to completing this text. Finally, I would like to thank all those participants who so graciously gave of their time. Parts of the research reported here were funded by the ESRC/SPSG programme on the Public Understanding of Science and by the ESRC/NCC programme on the People, Economies and Nature Conservation, as well as by the *New Scientist*, Cancer Research Campaign and the Universities Federation for Animal Welfare.

1

Introduction

I was going to start this introduction with a specific metaphor about the constitution of social psychology. I was intending to liken social psychology to a chimera. I might have said rude things like: the large, over-fed body is bloated with the fiery wind of experimentation; the soft paws of the front feet and the talons of the back, alternately grooming and savaging the body, might be those approaches that take a sympathetically critical view of the experiment (social representations or, perhaps, rhetorical social psychology); the head is attached to the shoulders by the thinnest of necks and is full of the cognitions and representations of social constructionism; finally, I would locate myself and my allies, whoever they might be, in the tail, desperately trying to wag the beast. The whole would, of course, be a parasite: parasitical on positivism and hypothetico-deductivism, classical sociology, sociology of science, social theory, philosophy, literary theory, etc.

However, such an image could do justice neither to the mutability nor to the stability of that thing that some of us call social psychology. Perhaps a better metaphor would be that of the amoeba. But even that is too bounded. So, I will give up on such unsavoury metaphors and begin with a more prosaic mapping of the relation between this book and (some aspects of) social psychology. What follows is intended as a critical contribution to the growing literature on the social construction of identity (e.g. Shotter and Gergen, 1989; Sampson, 1988; Henriques et al., 1984; Gergen and Davis, 1985; Harré, 1987). This body of work has been concerned to demarcate the epistemological, methodological and political distance between itself and orthodox experimental social psychology, with its embodiment of what might be termed the modernist Western cosmology (which includes such elements as individualism, cognitivism, realism, narrative linearity and intellectual progressivism). In contrast, one of the aims of this book is to place this blooming tradition (or, perhaps more precisely, range of endeavours) in the context of wider social theory. This is partly an exercise in critical reflexivity – that is, my heart belongs to social constructionism, but my brain is constantly throwing up doubts, confusions and criticism (or is it the other way round?). More importantly, this volume begins to point to some of the aporias that follow in the wake of the 'linguistic turn' upon which so much of social constructionism in social psychology putatively rests.

In essence, the prioritization afforded 'the linguistic' and, more generally, 'the social' can be embedded in a particular historical narrative that suggests that the 'bracketing' of non-linguistic, nonhuman and non-social entities as the constructions of social, linguistic, intersubjective, intertextual, etc. activity is not unproblematic. Indeed, underlying the rhetoric of much social constructionism is a tacit promise: what we social constructionists do (i.e. reveal the processes by which such and such is socially constructed) is an improvement on the works of our misguided predecessors – the cognitivists, the intergroup theorists, the social representation theorists. They failed to take language seriously enough: we take it very seriously and in so doing we reveal the real processes that underpin such social psychological 'topics' as racism, sexism, heterosexism, conservatism, fascism, etc.

Now, this is a caricature. Nevertheless, it does touch upon something, namely, the tendency to treat the emergence of social constructionism in intellectualist terms. The tradition which social constructionism attempts to overhaul or replace was an intellectual mistake. This is the implicit story that grounds the social constructionist case. And yet, such stories are themselves constructed. What happens if, in the spirit of social constructionism, we introduce another story?

This book suggests a number of other stories: historical, political, pragmatic, philosophical. One of my primary goals is to find within social constructionism a conceptual space for the 'nonhuman' – it is not a matter of setting out fatally to undermine social constructionism. From within this space, the 'nonhuman' acts relatively 'autonomously' and 'efficaciously'. As such, the aim is to look at how the nonhuman impacts upon the production of identity. In doing this, I draw heavily upon an approach that sits uncomfortably within the sociology of scientific knowledge, that of actor-network theory (ANT). I treat this as a heuristic, and will, in addition to introducing this perspective in some detail, point to some of the serious problems that it has to contend with. Nonetheless, it does furnish an analytic skeleton from which to hang a story of identity which regards the process of construction as heterogeneous. Before this, and the outline of the chapters, it would perhaps be useful to have a brief and all too scanty introduction to social constructionism in social psychology.

Constructing Social Constructionism

In trying to trace the rise (or advocate the adoption) of social constructionism in social psychology there are various textual techniques one can use. It is possible to narrate the history of the discipline and in so doing excavate the problems that were faced in the 'old' social psychology and how they were (or are in the process of being) overcome by more recent social psychology whether that be cast as critical (Wexler, 1983), generative (Gergen, 1982) or deconstructionist/Marxist (Parker, 1989) social psychology. These problems are usually a mixture of the political (how can we pursue experimental social psychology when it is oppressive?), the epistemological (how can we say we have accessed the phenomena that orthodox social psychology claims to study – phenomena such as attitudes, stereotypes, identity – when these phenomena are constituted by the very practices and commitments of psychologists?), and the ontological (how can we say that social behaviour and thought rest upon cognitive process when it is really cultural/linguistic convention that structures these?).

So our historical vignette might begin with the 'crisis in social psychology', perhaps most recognizably signalled by the volumes edited by Israel and Tajfel (1972) and Armistead (1974) and by Gergen's (1973) paper on social psychology as history. In the aftermath, much energy has been expended on formulating the 'social' in such a way as to preserve certain elements of orthodox social psychology (e.g. Taylor and Brown, 1979; Forgas, 1983; Hewstone and Jaspers, 1984; Farr, 1978; Jaspers, 1983). Since then, the debates within that broad spectrum of approaches that might be called the social constructionist camp have presupposed not merely the importance of the 'social', but its essential priority in understanding human conduct (primarily talk and texts). The arguments are no longer about how we integrate the 'social' and the 'individual', but concern how we are to conceptualize the social in its production of the individual. The sorts of questions that flow from this key shift of focus are: Is the social simply equivalent to language? Do we take certain material practices as givens? What about institutions? But are these not also the products of language? Do we look for the constitutive 'social' at the performative, local, interactional level, or do we seek it in the domain of ideology or in the dynamics of cultural condensation and change?

These debates, which I will consider in greater detail with specific reference to the social construction of identity, reflect the disparate sources upon which social constructionist social psychology has drawn. With this last sentence I would like to think that I neatly and seamlessly begin to fulfil the typical requirement of academic writing of demarcating the history and development of one's field. Usually this takes the form of some sort of literature review. Thus, to ground my account of social constructionism, I could produce various genealogies. I could, like Gergen (1985), point to various and manifold roots through which the 'social constructionist movement in modern psychology' has been nourished. I might identify such bodies of literature as the philosophy and history of science (e.g. Kuhn, 1962; Feyerabend, 1975) which show us that science is not the value-free enterprise we once believed, but that empirical observation is through and through theory-laden. I could point to what one might call the 'disciplines of difference' – anthropology and history. These provide us with accounts which reveal the contingency and situatedness of phenomena that we modern Westerners supposedly see as absolutes – such phenomena as childhood (Aries, 1962), psychological process (Heelas and Lock, 1981) and personhood (Mauss, 1985).

I might, as Kitzinger does in her now classic volume on the social construction of lesbianism (1987), claim descent from, or at least a family resemblance to, another social constructionist tradition – that manifested in the sociologies of knowledge and scientific knowledge which show us how knowledge of the everyday world and of nature is constructed through processes of social interaction and the mobilization of disparate rhetorical/representational resources (e.g. Garfinkel, 1967; Berger and Luckman, 1966; Collins, 1985; Lynch, 1985; Latour and Woolgar, 1979; Knorr-Cetina, 1981 – this is despite the fact that the lineage between the sociology of knowledge and the sociology of scientific knowledge is not unproblematic, cf. Sismondo, 1993. Indeed, as we might expect, these sociologies by no means form a coherent tradition.) I might like, Potter and Wetherell (1987) in their pathbreaking social constructionist text on discourse and social psychology, critically identify as foundational Austin's (1962) speech act theory, ethnomethodology and Barthes' (e.g. 1972) semiology. And, as I have alluded to post-structuralism, I could say that some recent social psychological endeavours, which might be herded under the banner of social constructionism, have drawn directly upon such post-structuralists as Foucault (e.g. 1979b, 1981; Henriques et al., 1984; Rose, 1985, 1989b) and Derrida (e.g. 1976, 1978, 1982; Parker and Shotter, 1990; Parker, 1989; Sampson, 1993).

Of course, this list is by no means exhaustive: for example, such eminent figures as Billig, Harré and Shotter are strikingly absent. Nevertheless, the aim here is to indicate what a broad spectrum of sources social constructionist social psychology draws upon. As such it seems a trifle futile to attempt to generate some simple origin story for this 'movement'. Indeed, it might even seem dubious to seek out one's various and disparate intellectual precursors, forebears and ancestors. This is, in part, because such origin stories are themselves constructions and need to be treated with appropriate circumspection (cf. Ashmore, 1989) lest they begin to read like discovery accounts. Discovery accounts, in constituting particular events as points at which the 'new' emerged (e.g. pulsars or Mendel's law, cf. Woolgar, 1976; Brannigan, 1981), serve the immediate concerns of the person claiming the discovery (or the discovery of a discovery – as accounted by Brannigan's analysis of the construction of Mendel's work as the foundation of genetics by Correns in his priority dispute with De Vries; or the discovery of discovery accounting – as narrated by Mulkay, 1985, who reflexively deconstructs Brannigan's work on the social construction of discovery). Likewise, for social constructionist social psychologists to point to the 'discoverers' of post-structuralism or ethnomethodology or speech act theory and to align themselves with them, that is, to trace out an intellectual lineage, is to ignore the local legitimatory function that such histories and origin stories serve.

An alternative would be to be more positive about one's choice of forebears and, like Billig (1987, 1988a), opt for those that seem most amenable, challenging, different, etc. In the process, one might perhaps try to articulate, in however contingent a way, the criteria that guide one's intellectual opportunism and instrumentalities (rather than tacking oneself onto the tail-end of a tradition). Moreover, and this is the central point here, such tradition-construction, while in a sense inevitable – both for legitimation purposes and to furnish the reader with the textual and intellectual background which they might subsequently critically scrutinize – tends to reproduce an intellectualist account of the historical trajectory of which one's work is a part. Later on I will be doing this, but I will also be legitimating my perspective in terms of its potential political and pragmatic value. In the process, I will suggest that the accounts of the intellectual roots of social constructionist social psychology tacitly argue for a qualitative advance over traditional forms of social psychology (with its attendant epistemology and ontology). As such the resemblance to a discovery account is reinforced, and the message reads something like: '"social constructionism" has improved on what went before; we have a better way of understanding the person, society, and our own understandings'. What this misses out on are the local historical and political conditions that led to the emergence of these proto-social constructionist perspectives. This does not necessarily compromise the value of the social constructionist approach – it simply means that we need to be more circumspect about the epistemological and political claims we make about it.

Having said all this, it is nevertheless valuable to provide some general or minimal definition of social constructionism. The 'value' of this is manifold. For example, it gives a narrative focus to this volume and will help guide the reader (or rather, invite the reader into an appropriate subject position). Of course, this can be recast in more instrumentalist terms: such a definition sets up a narratively and morally convenient target which in due course, and with appropriate aplomb, will be thoroughly critiqued. Further, it can be used to indicate again the variety of approaches and agendas that make up the 'movement'. More importantly, it serves to flag some of the tensions and conflicts that will be addressed in subsequent chapters. In essence, we may say that all the above approaches have in common the following general assumption: *social practices constitute givens which have consequences.*

Now, each of the constituent terms of this phrase can be problematized, variably interpreted and multiply realized. For example, 'social practices' might be regarded as face-to-face linguistic interaction as with the more ethnomethodologically tinged forms of discourse analysis (e.g. Potter and Wetherell, 1987) or such discourse/practices of institutions as the panoptic gaze as with more Foucauldian treatments (e.g. Henriques et al., 1984). 'Constitute' might place the stress wholly on the linguistic determination of givens (e.g. Potter et al., 1984, p. 23) or incorporate some non-linguistically determined real that also contributes the process of construction (e.g. ecological positioning of the person in relation to the physical and social world, Parker, 1992; the reality of the situated human conversation, Davies and Harré, 1990; Harré, 1992; Knorr-Cetina, 1988). 'Givens' signifies the range of entities from objects through events and on to categories which would otherwise remain routinely unproblematized; these are the entities which would in the 'natural attitude' (Schutz, 1967) be perceived as, indeed, 'natural' – that is, assumed, part of our (or the particular group's) cultural backdrop which would normally require great effort to interrogate. Such entities would include: ostensibly concrete objects such as nature-in-general (Merchant, 1980; Michael, 1991; McNaghten, 1993), specific 'facts of nature' like brain peptides (Latour and Woolgar, 1979), technological artefacts like bicycles (Pinch and Bijker, 1984) or commonly accepted medical conditions like syphilis (e.g. Fleck, 1979); everyday phenomena and categories such as lesbianism (e.g. Kitzinger, 1987), race

(Wetherell and Potter, 1992), political entities such as a riot or a community (Potter and Reicher, 1987) or gender and employment opportunities (Wetherell et al., 1987); or broadly academic concepts such as mind (Coulter, 1979), the self (Sampson, 1989), emotion (Harré, 1986) and memory (Middleton and Edwards, 1990; Edwards and Potter, 1992). The critical dimension here comprises, at base, a desire to reveal that things could be other than they are, that the current state of affairs – institutional, political, ideological, cultural and social – are not inevitable. However, the partial context of the reproduction of these 'givens' is the consequences that they yield, and such consequences can range from the local accomplishment of a particular impression of self (e.g. Potter and Wetherell, 1987), through the complex mediation of ideologies (e.g. Billig et al., 1988; Parker, 1992) to the (re)production of certain sorts of subjecthood (e.g. Sampson, 1983), institution (Edwards and Mercer, 1987; Rose, 1985) and society (e.g. Bowers and Iwi, 1993).

Despite the many differences signalled in the above list, it is nonetheless fair to say that there is one rather broad but still coherent theme that runs throughout, namely, the privileging of the social (however that is defined and deployed in its specificity). The 'social' structures the production of givens that critical social psychologists, amongst many others, disassemble in order to reveal the social, cultural, linguistic, etc. dynamics upon which such production rests. The point here is that the 'social' in which these analytic processes are embedded remains underscrutinized: its priority is not simply a matter of progress, or of the transcendence of past concerns about the biological or cognitive bases of human conduct. Rather, if one draws upon the same range of parameters that are used to analyse others' (i.e. the human objects of study) social practices and applies them to the form of that analysis itself (which is, of course, simply another social practice), the following sorts of questions emerge:

1. What are the institutional and local bases of the privileging of the social, language, culture?
2. What are the academic products and textual consumables that have facilitated the entrenchment of social constructionism? How might we understand the 'work' that has to be done in order to convince others of the value of social constructionism? In other words, what resources and processes have had to be mobilized in order to 'sell' social constructionism, to alter the identities of those who were once 'other' – experimentalists, empiricists, realists?
3. Broadening the above question a little: how do we get a handle on the dynamics of change in identities in general?
4. What contemporary historical and epistemological problematics lead to the questioning of this privileging of the social, of language, of culture?
5. What might the form and content of the non-social and nonhuman take? How do we formulate the technological and the natural in such a way as to admit of their constructed-ness while permitting them to have autonomous truth-effects vis-à-vis identity?

6. What are the implications of this for wider social theory and the traditions that are drawn upon in social constructionist social psychology?

Each of these questions will be addressed in the course of the book. However, two broad themes in particular (questions 3 and 5), precisely because they are relatively neglected, will receive special attention. The first theme concerns the problem of theorizing change in identity: How do identities shift from one recognizable sort to another? What would be a good way of narrating such innovations, transitions and transformations of identity? The second theme relates to the role of nonhumans and the non-social in the construction of identity. In attempting to do these themes justice, I turn to actor-network theory which has been developed over the last decade to unpick the movement, entrenchment and impacts of nonhumans as they change human actors and social arrangements.

Before providing an overview of the rest of the book, I should forewarn the reader that nowhere in the text will they find a simple, overarching definition of 'identity'. There will be no such definition in relation to orthodox social psychology, to social constructionist social psychology, or to the actor-network theory I present and promote. This is deliberate for two reasons. Firstly, it is very difficult to find any consensual definition of identity in the relevant traditions – if one were wanting to be provocative, one might say that it is this very definitional amorphousness that gives the concept of identity its resonance. Secondly, and more importantly (or less cynically), given this lack of rigour, it seems important to me to interrogate the discursive practices (as opposed to definitions) of social constructionists through which this thing 'identity' emerges. If the practice of social constructionism has primarily taken the form of tracing the reproduction of identity through texts, representations and verbal exchanges, the present volume aims to supplement this practice. As noted above, this supplementation attends, on the one hand, to how particular representations, texts and exchanges come to be replaced over time, and, on the other, how nonhumans might contribute to these representations, etc. and their turnover.

Overview

Chapter 2 looks specifically at the social construction of identity, and pays particular attention to the way that this general perspective has focused upon the uses of various texts – be they discourses, linguistic repertoires, rhetorics or narratives – to construct identity in given contexts. It is often claimed that these – let us call them, 'textual commodities' – should be treated as topics – the objects of research (e.g. Potter and Wetherell, 1987). The aim is to uncover how they are put together and deployed in micro-situations to achieve particular ends, often self-presentational. However, how such discourses managed to get in place – that is, to become part of people's repertoires – is left unexplicated. There seems to be a tacit assumption that they are just there – in the tradition, in the culture, in the milieu. The chapter argues that part of the analysis of the construction of identity should be the tracing out of how such textual commodities are 'sold', and, in being sold, generate changes in the identities of some group, collective or constituency. Actor-network theory is one means of getting at this process.

Chapter 3 presents another critique of the social constructionist perspective. This will involve looking at (some of the) historical, political and aesthetic roots of the prioritization of the social. Unsurprisingly, social constructionism emerges as actually able to accommodate a role for the nonhuman and non-social. Equally unsurprisingly, it is discovered that it is actor-network theory that can best theorize such a role.

So Chapter 4 introduces actor-network theory. Here you will find details of the central concepts of enrolment, association, black-boxing, immutable mobiles, translation, obligatory points of passage, intermediaries. These are illustrated with case studies from the literature. In addition, I link ANT to some ongoing concerns of the social sciences: the notion of agency, the status of marginality, the theorization of power, the relations of the micro- to the macrosociological. Chapter 5 then applies ANT to the production of human identities. Drawing in particular on the talk of scientists, I show how their talk in defence of animal experimentation generates a range of identities for relevant audiences and a corollary social world. Chapter 6 extends this to a consideration of the way that the official spokespersons of science, and their social science intermediaries, have attempted to define the identity of the lay public, in terms of both scientific literacy and citizenship. However, I also trace some of the means by which people can accept, accommodate or resist these constructed identities.

In Chapter 7 I begin at last to consider how the nonhuman can play a part in the processes of construction of identity. While ANT has tended to focus on technological artefacts as instrumental in the (re)production of social orders, I concentrate on 'natural' nonhumans. Using the examples of companion animals and local environments, I tentatively suggest actor networkish ways of narrating the ways that these might shape human identities. Finally, in the concluding chapter, I list some of the problems, issues, aporias and obfuscations that I have managed to detect in the main body of this text. It goes without saying that I transform these from devastating flaws into fascinating research opportunities.

2
Constructing Socially Constructed Identity

This chapter considers the variety of perspectives that can be said to fall under social constructionist social psychological approaches to identity. That there is a wide spectrum of such approaches is obvious, and I will engage with a number of them in order to contrast some of the differences in emphasis and to explore the central issues, at least in my mind, that arise from such differences. My narrative aim is to set up the primary context for the discussions in future chapters. My intellectual purpose is to focus upon the problem, to the extent that it is a problem, of the (albeit contingent) origins of the various linguistic, social, cultural resources through which identity is constituted. In other words, I will consider the ways in which such resources are variously imposed, adopted, appropriated or resisted in the process of 'doing identity'. Contrary to much of the literature on the social construction of identity, my immediate goal is to emphasize the 'storied-ness' of our academic accounts of the construction of identity – to flesh out a narrative and articulate a history: Who promoted identity X? Where and when, how and why? What linguistic, social, cultural tools did they use? Who was 'persuaded'? Who resisted? And how do we as analysts, and the participants we consider, variously construct these various 'whos'?

But why should these be interesting questions? Well, because it is at these specific historically situated junctures that we see identities formulated, mediated and reproduced. More importantly, we might begin to excavate the local processes by which new identities emerge – the dynamics of the evolution of identity. This is, hopefully, not some sad, anachronistic attempt to write origin stories. Rather, it is to acknowledge that it is possible to construct accounts in which, in the evolution of identities, there are more or less (narratively) specifiable junctures at which 'texts of identities' come to be 'markedly (re)articulated' and 'newly disseminated'. The issue is: how do we go about addressing these moments of formulation and avenues of transmission?

However, before I go on to this, I want to unpack the issues that I address a little more. A good starting point is Shotter and Gergen's (1989) edited volume, *Texts of Identity*, which stands as a landmark in social constructionist social psychology's approach to identity. It collects together a wide variety of perspectives and themes. A number of the chapters can be very unsatisfactorily summarized as follows. Harré's and Shotter's chapters are concerned with the role of pronouns in the social constitution of the person as agent; Gergen addresses the rhetorical payoffs of an expanding vocabulary of psychological

terms; Slugoski and Ginsberg as well as Wetherell and Potter consider the
way that psychological texts are both reflections of, and resources for, lay
texts of psychological health and violence respectively; Tololyan traces the
way the fundamental narratives of Armenian community and struggle structure both the writings of Armenian terrorists and their reception in the
Armenian Diaspora; Young's chapter is on the use biographical stories told
by an Auschwitz survivor to his physician in order to reintroduce the subjective self into what, in the examination phase, is being treated as a mere
objective body; Murray shows how the narrative forms of comedy and
romance serve to insert a decision to travel or run a marathon in the context
of a desire to distance oneself from the social order and thereby achieve a
sense of the self; Kitzinger documents the way that the ideology of liberal
humanism, expressed in both academic writings and the talk of lesbians, in
laying stress upon self-actualization and romantic love, depoliticizes lesbianism. To list the units in this sample, we have: pronoun, vocabulary, theory,
narrative character, local narrative, biographical story, narrative form, ideology. Clearly there is much overlap here. But it is also important to consider
their inter-relations. To what extent might we expect these disparate units to
cohere as integrated or functional wholes? If we find 'contradictions' between
them, what are the likely effects?

We can flesh out these questions by looking at the mutual impact of the
Gergen and Tololyan papers. Gergen's chapter considers how our mental
interiority has assumed the form and contents with which we are familiar, and
how reference to these warrants voice, that is, privileged attention. Gergen's
thesis is that the extension of the self through the elaboration of mental furniture and the corollary mastery of an increasing vocabulary of the self – a
knowing how to talk about oneself – affords a rhetorical edge. In all this, psychology has been a major source of terminology and as such the provider of
a range of warranting devices. While Gergen presents this process of elaboration as a broad historical movement, it is unclear to what extent its local
rhetorical potency generalizes across situations. In Tololyan's chapter, one of
the central organizing narratives of Armenian terrorism, the story of the
Martyrdom of Vartan and his followers, serves as a model of heroism. This is
one of the narratives to which terrorist acts are reduced and under which they
are subsumed, and it is through this narrative that terrorists (and indeed
their critics) gain voice. On the basis of this brief comparison, one might
ask: How does the textual or discursive reduction of complex terrorist acts in
terms of a grand narrative stand in relation to the warranted voice that hinges
upon an expanding psychological vocabulary? Under what circumstances do
these strategies negate one another, thereby perhaps setting up the space for
new forms of discourse to emerge?

Clearly, one of the prime values of *Texts of Identity* simply is that it serves
as a survey of the terrain. Yet the juxtaposition of chapters (with their respective units of analysis) throws up issues of tension and contradiction. This is
not simply at the level of theoretical incompatibility, where the epistemological baggage entailed in these units leads to conflict between approaches (for

example, most obviously between a critical notion of ideology and a constitutive conception of discourse – cf. Kitzinger's and Rose's chapters, Michael,
1989). Over and above this, there are contradictions at the heart of identity
itself – that is, in the very dynamics of its reproduction through the various
linguistic processes described in these chapters. By side-stepping the possible
contradictions or tensions between the various textual units, or, indeed, by
focusing upon one or two texts rather than paying attention to the ways that
the multiplicity of texts of identity might generate tensions and contradictions, there is a danger of too functionalist a reading of the role of a particular
text. To neglect these possible contradictions is to make the study of changes
in identity all the harder.

This chapter is not concerned to overcome these tensions. Rather, the main
point I want to make is that the work evidenced in *Texts of Identity*, reflecting
as it does the multitude of ways of analysing identity, alerts us to a number of
questions about the constitution of identity that have not been fully – or, at
best, only obliquely – addressed. These can be tentatively formulated as a
nexus of issues in the following way:

Generally, what exactly is being attended to (or constructed) when we talk
of the social construction of identity and self?

Specifically,

1. What is the historical frame, the unit of analysis and the context of medi-
    ation? Crudely, we might say that there are two ends of an analytic
    spectrum. At one end, there are those microsociological, ethnomethod-
    ology tinged approaches. These focus on the situated reproduction of
    identity through local discursive interaction. At the opposite end of the
    spectrum are those approaches which consider the representations of
    identity, how they are mediated (say by certain institutions), and how
    they come to constitute individuals. The purpose here is to uncover the
    historical (or genealogical) evolution of these representations and to
    probe the means by which they are imparted to, or 'inscribed upon', per-
    sons (cf. Parker, 1990a, b; Potter et al., 1990; Fairclough, 1992; Michael,
    1994).

2. The first corollary to the preceding question asks: what level of identity
    are these different analytic postures oriented towards? Again a spectrum
    of selves emerges, from the local to the institutional to the cultural to the
    global.

3. The second corollary issue concerns ontology: are we dealing with an
    analytically decentred self or a historically 'decentred' self or both?
    'Decentring' generally refers to the idea that we can no longer assume that
    the self is some coherent, unitary, discrete entity. Rather, it is constituted
    through, and from, various linguistic resources that are mobilized accord-
    ing to the exigencies of particular times and places. If such is the case, is
    the job of the analyst simply to look at the development and deployment
    of these in the production of a sense of a coherent self? Or do we take seri-
    ously some of the treatments of postmodernity which suggest that such

     coherence is no longer a motive force for the typical postmodern? Do postmoderns revel in incoherence and fragmentation?

4.   The third corollary addresses the issue of where these constitutive resources come from. Often the impression one is left with is that these things float around in some linguistic or discursive or cultural ether. The point is that these are specifically embodied in particular textual and representational forms, realized in specific and particular social contexts or patterns of social contexts. How do we as analysts come to understand these? Further, if we want to identify, however contingently, sources of such resources, we need to attend to how these resources are distributed. Are these resources 'successfully' imparted, imposed, sold and so on? Are they duly adopted, are they appropriated or, indeed, are they resisted? What is the best way to construct and warrant such an analytic narrative?

5.   Finally, we might ask, what is left out of this melange of perspectives, units of analysis, levels of identity, time frames and so on? The answer is, of course, the non-social. If much of the emphasis of social constructionism has been upon the 'intertextuality' of the linguistic resources that serve identity, perhaps we can now begin to talk about 'intercorporeality' – a concept with which to get a handle on the process by which the 'embodiment' of identity is an echo of other embodiments – in technologies, in architectures, in 'natures'.

In what follows I will be considering the above nexus of issues. In the next section, I will attend to the issue of the differences between, broadly, the 'representational' and 'interactive' formulations of identity. This will be folded into a discussion of the different levels of identity that we find and the resources that structure the processes by which such identities are (re)produced. After considering these different levels of 'identity', I ask the obvious question: what is the relation between them, and how do we bring them together analytically?

    It should be noted that while I aim to pick out some general themes and traditions in the following, I do not claim to be comprehensive. For example, I do not address the construction of self through autobiographical narration (Freeman, 1993) or its mediation through material possessions (Dittmar, 1992). Nevertheless, I can say that each of these could be accommodated within the crude schema I present below. Thus, Freeman's concern with the (re)construction of the self through narrative texts can be seen as dealing with some of the big historical narrative resources people have available to them in order to 'go on'; Dittmar's 'symbolic-communicational model of possessions and identity' (p. 88) in which material possessions serve as symbolic expressions of who we are rests on a version of 'accomplishment' in what I call acontextual situations that is evident in discourse analytic treatments of identity. In sum, the aim is simply to present some overarching trends in order to show how each neglects something that the other does not, and in tentatively attempting to integrate them, to see what, if anything, we can say about the constitution of identity that is new.

Historical Frames: Units of Analysis

This section is essentially concerned with the multiplicity that is the social construction of identities. We have seen already at the start of this chapter that there are a number of approaches that can be said to constitute social constructionist social psychology. Sorting out the morass is beyond the scope of this chapter (and book). Nevertheless, and despite the temptation to gloss the situation with a thoughtful 'well, let a thousand flowers bloom', there are certain patterns and traditions that can be teased out. As I mentioned above, there seems to be an analytic spectrum. At one end one might locate those microsociological, ethnomethodology tinged approaches. I say eth-nomethodologically tinged because ethnomethodologists would argue that their micro-studies are foundational to macrosociological theorizing; indeed, some like Button (1993) would dispute whether ethnomethodology can prop-erly be counted social constructionist. At the other end of this spectrum one finds a concern with representations of identity, the historical (or genealogi-cal) evolution (or, rather, emergence) of these representations, and the means by which they are 'inscribed upon' bodies and thereby constitute persons of particular sorts.

Now, this is not a mono-dimensional spectrum and it can be decomposed in various ways. However, here I will concentrate on one aspect – the histor-ical frame. What time-period do the materials we consider occupy? Is it the conversation? Is it the history of an institution? Is it a civilization? In each case one can say that there is a social construction of identity but the type of identity might be radically different and its 'consequences' or 'functions' likewise.

Big History

The work of Muhlhausler and Harré (1990) addresses the role of particular pronouns in the construction of selves – in particular, following Wittgenstein (1953), they suggest that grammar is the expression of norms. Some norms are so deeply embedded that they are 'grammaticized', such that they cannot easily be reflected upon. Thus, in Japanese the 'social order is fully function-ally embodied in the grammar' (p. 8). To unpick this embeddedness requires what we might call 'long-wave' historical analysis. According to Muhlhausler and Harré,

> It is largely through pronouns and functionally equivalent indexing devices that responsibility for actions is taken by actors and assigned by them to others. . . . [this] moral order of speaking [is] rooted in the Judeo-Christian tradition of individual moral responsibility, elaborated and modified by the necessities of scientific culture in which we have been embedded since the Enlightenment. (p. 89)

The main point is that this is culturally specific – in Japan, the usual index-ing of location in a moral order is 'to a relevant group rather than to the speaker as an individual', though 'there are weak pronominal resources for indexing individual responsibility' (p. 93). Here, we have perhaps one of the widest historical frames in which the self is constructed (another would be gender-related, cf. Spender, 1980; Muhlhausler and Harré, 1990, Ch. 9). It is the large-scale historical changes to which we must look in order to under- stand how such models of the person arose and how they are maintained, in part, through the pronoun system and its use. In effect, within their Wittgensteinian framework, Muhlhausler and Harré's prime concern is with moral responsibility and with 'going on' – that is, maintaining one's status as a 'person' per se (per se for the relevant culture, that is) and sustaining the attendant sociality or form of life.

Another approach to the long-wave constitution of self – of Western selves in general – can be found in the work of Sampson (1993). Developing from his sustained critique of orthodox psychology's formulation of the self (e.g. 1981, 1983, 1989), Sampson's project is the 'celebration of the other' which entails a transcendence of the confines of self-celebratory monologism in which there is a 'construction of a serviceable other, one constructed on behalf of the particular needs, interests and desires of the dominating group' (p. 4). The upshot is the (re)production of a model of the self as self-con- tained, individual, the owner of one's own capacities. In contrast to this monologism, Sampson recommends a genuine dialogism. This requires that we recognize that 'we gain a self only in and through a process of social inter- action, dialogue, and conversation with others in our social world; that the only knowledge we can have of ourselves appears in and through social forms – namely, others' responses' (p. 106). The upshot is that we 'are fun- damentally many, never just one . . . because we are members of diverse conversational communities, with various perspectives on the world, our- selves and others with which to frame our experiences and render them, us and others meaningful' (p. 125). From this model, Sampson derives a dia- logical ethics: dialogism 'recasts the meaning of freedom: we are free jointly to construct our lives together, and are therefore of necessity responsible beings by virtue of this feature. "I" cannot be free, only "We" can be free"' (p. 171). However, to actually realize this dialogism, one needs 'a democratic and egalitarian context' for 'not only does democracy issue from dialogism, but without a genuinely democratic and egalitarian society, dialogues themselves are not possible' (p. 187).

Sampson's rich text does many things. However, in the present context, I will focus upon the way that it provides us with an, albeit necessarily frag- mented, narrative of the predominance of an untruth – that of self-celebratory monologism – that has usurped the (ontologically) rightful place of dialogism. In the process, Sampson draws upon the work of feminist authors to illustrate how dialogism has been suppressed and how the 'other that is woman' is excluded from, for example, representations in which what passes for the universal human gaze is actually the male gaze. The point is that there is an implicit long-wave history here. Monologic identity or, rather, representations of identity as monologic – free-standing, hermetic and so on – have arisen historically, at numerous sites (Sampson also points to the

African-American as other) and that it is implicitly possible to recover, in part, this history by close scrutiny of monologic texts (psychology furnishing some of these). While an old-fashioned origin story is avoided, there is an implicit appeal to one: once there was a dialogic arcadia (or one day there will be, or might be, a dialogic utopia).

This historicity can be brought into relief if we consider how 'Woman' has recently been introduced into poststructuralist discourse – a process Jardine (1985) calls 'gynesis' – and the problems and contradictions that such a process generates (is it a genuine evocation or a colonization?). Here, we see that there is an admittedly problematic problematization of the deployment of woman-as-other. The question we might pose is: What are the historical conditions which have enabled such a recognition and attempted incorporation of woman-as-other? Indeed, what are the conditions which have enabled Sampson and the writers he draws upon, to identify and then to question several of the forms of self-celebratory monologism? At the same time, we might ask, what others continue to be others? Sampson's others are derived from a particular implicit history: the oppression of women and blacks in particular, though Sampson, of course, notes that there are many others. However, one is left with the impression that these oppressions – or 'other-izations' – pertain only to what from a left-liberal perspective are 'good' others. There are some others which I for one would be more than happy to 'oppress' – fascist and cannibalistic to name but two. In other words, different tacit constructions of a relevant history, say fascistic or cannibalistic, would yield different suppressed others. Now, there is no simple cause and effect process here: the identification of the other constitutes the history and vice versa in a process that resembles the operation of a hermeneutic circle.

What is at stake here, and in the account of the work of Muhlhausler and Harré, is the fact that the construction of identity is embedded in a long-wave historical account. We see the reproduction of such identities at local sites (say particular texts or the situated use of pronouns), but the potency of these modes of realization of self (as 'personally responsible' or 'self-contained') lies in their, for want of a better term, 'historical gravitas'. Now, this is all rather amorphous: historical gravitas is, after all, pretty vague (and possibly tautologous). My main concern is to convey the idea that some aspects of identity, while constantly realized and reproduced, have been long-time facets of individuals and their intersubjective exchanges. To excavate these requires a reading (and, therefore, construction) of long-wave or big history, with an attendant construction, no doubt circumspect, of an origin story. But this implicit origin story lies at some remove from the processes of interaction where we find such identities-in-action, where these selves are mediated. If these broad social processes yield selves, how do they infiltrate, and come to characterize, the innumerable local interactions that, some might say (e.g. Knorr-Cetina, 1988), make up the 'social'? One cannot help feeling that it is almost as if these sites of local interaction are the sites of reproduction where the same old identities are dusted down, aired and polished. In contrast, change takes place elsewhere – at the level of the macrosociological where history sweeps out (however dialectically) the old and somehow, magically, colonizes those infinite, little interactions with the new.

We find another example of the long-wave historical account of the construction of a new(er) identity in Gergen's (1991) *The Saturated Self*. Here, the actual break-up (and intellectual problematization) of the sorts of long-standing features of Western, patriarchal, modernist selves are grounded in a reading of contemporary history, but, in this case, one which is ostensibly realized at the level of the local.

Gergen contrasts the postmodern or saturated self with the romantic and modern selves. The romantic self hinged on a vocabulary of 'passion, purpose, depth and personal significance' (p. 27) and the 'romantic individual was forever a mystery – the vital essence quixotic and out of reach' (p. 47). By comparison, the modernist self is infused with reason – it is 'reliable, self-contained and machine-produced' (p. 44–5) and as such it is fundamentally knowable and measurable. However, in the wake of what Gergen calls the 'Technologies of Social Saturation' (p. 49) – that is, the variety of high technologies such as air travel, video and television and new information technologies such as electronic mail, faxes, satellites and computers – there is a population of the self which opens 'relationships to new ranges of possibility' and renders 'subjective life . . . more fully laminated' (p. 71). Indeed, 'we find a profound sea change taking place in the character of social life during the twentieth century . . . . We engage in greater numbers of relationships, in a greater variety of forms, and with greater intensities than ever before. With the multiplication of relationships also comes a transformation in the social capacities of the individual – both in knowing how and knowing that . . . . A multiphrenic condition emerges in which one swims in ever-shifting, concatenating and contentious currents of being' (p. 79–80).

Gergen contrasts this fluidity to the strictures and constraints of pre-postmodern everyday conventionality. Where the postmodern entails serious play in which the rules are changeable, rules circumscribe modernist everyday life. As Gergen puts it:

> Although the finite games of daily relatedness are essential, when their implications are fully extended they become exclusionary, hierarchical and potentially deadly. It is when we rise above the finite game, open ourselves to the possibility of an infinitely changing array of rules . . . that the game of human existence finds greatest promise. (p. 197–8)

Of course, Gergen is fully aware of the possible drawbacks of this postmodern scenario, especially for the way that such a transition threatens our perception of personal authenticity. Nevertheless, Gergen's postmodernity points to the potential 'flowering forms of relatedness, a growing consciousness of interdependence, an organic relationship to our planet, and the withering of lethal conflict' (p. 259).

Ironically, Gergen's account extends from a modernist historical reading of contemporary change, in which the latent or emergent characteristics of the present epoch can be read off more or less unproblematically (cf. Michael, 1992a). Now, Gergen clearly recognizes that such a reading is itself a representation and a construction: as an instance of academic work, it is clearly also prone to the 'bursting of postmodern consciousness into the academic sphere' in which 'attention [has been] removed from the "world as it is" and centers instead on our representations of the world' (p. 16). Nevertheless, within his own narrative of the rise of postmodernity, and its realization in, and impact upon, such 'postmodern' academic trends as the sociology of scientific knowledge, ethnomethodology and post-structuralism, we find an albeit dispersed framework of causes that have led up to the condition Gergen calls postmodernity and its human corollary, the saturated self. As such Gergen does not differ from many other treatments of the 'postmodern' – treatments which do not overly problematize the histories, or rather historiographies, out of which the postmodern emerges. This contrast between a concern with new (postmodern) epistemologies and methodologies for the doing of social science and a concern with an emergent social real (the postmodern) is articulated by Featherstone (1991) in terms of a postmodern sociology versus a sociology of postmodernity. Gergen's representation fits in with a series of works in the sociology of postmodernity that have considered in detail, for example, the relations between modernity and postmodernity, transitions in patterns of consumption and production, and the phenomenological facets of the postmodern epoch such as the experience of time and space (e.g. Harvey, 1989; Lash and Urry, 1987; Featherstone, 1991; Turner, 1990; Giddens, 1990, 1991). The common feature of these approaches is their deployment of a more or less traditional, that is to say, modernist, analytic armoury to narrate the supposed rise of postmodernity (or less disjunctive epochs such as late or high modernity).

Thus, for example, Lash and Urry (1987) analyse the postmodern world under three headings. Firstly, there is the semiotics of everyday life in which there is a de-differentiation between signifier and signified so that spectacle predominates: where once meaningful cultural artefacts invited contemplation and interpretation, the postmodern cultural object is spectacular, that is, by virtue of its position in the flow of signifiers and its detachment from referents, the impact it has is at the level of sensation – it excites and it mesmerises. Secondly, there is the centrality of new class factions – the new petite bourgeoisie engaged in the 'cultural' professions, that is, what Bourdieu (1984) calls 'occupations involving presentation and representation (sales, marketing and advertising, PR, fashion, decoration . . .) and in all institutions providing symbolic goods and services . . . medical and social assistance (marriage guidance, sex therapy) and cultural production and organization (youth leaders, radio and television producers . . .)' (p. 359). Members of this faction have taken up styles of life entailing consumption that is eclectic, that pursues symbolic and cultural differentiation, and which is, in part, highly conspicuous. They practise a transgression of traditional consumption patterns and engage in an accelerated turnover of styles, fashions and goods. This class faction serves as a model group which fosters an ethos of transgression and accelerated turnover. Finally, there is the actual decentring of the subject. Whereas in the past subjects were historically furnished with the textual tools by which to socially construct more or less coherent identities, in the postmodern era, such texts, by virtue of their instability – they are subject to transgression (by other texts) and accelerated turnover (substitution by other texts) – can no longer sustain the integrity of the subject. According to Lash and Urry, this decentring has come about because of such factors as: the fragmentation of working-class communities and the occupationally structured experience of sections of the middle class; the influence of electronic mass media; and the disruption in our perception of space and time in everyday life. The role of television in the decentring of identity is highlighted: by exposing individuals of all groupings to a general information system, there is a negative effect on the solidification of collective identity.

In addition, a number of synthetic commentaries on the 'postmodern condition' have recently attempted to contextualize the phenomenology of the postmodern in the substantive social, cultural, political and economic changes of late capitalism. In the cases of David Harvey and Anthony Giddens changes are not held to be the epochal, dramatic break with the past that others such as writers Gergen, Lash and Urry in common with Lyotard and Baudrillard have suggested. Rather, they are conceptualized as accelerations or aggravations of the characteristic dynamics of capitalism and late modernity.

Harvey (1989) stresses the speeding up of production processes, exchange and consumption patterns with an attendant acceleration in information flows and communications. With respect to consumption, Harvey focuses on, for example, the mobilization of fashion in mass markets and the increased consumption of services whose relatively short life-span (in contrast to durables) facilitates accelerated consumption. All this interweaves with a heightening in the volatility and ephemerality of products, ideas, ideologies, images and values. As Harvey would have it, there is an increase in the values and virtues of instantaneity and disposability. This is further alloyed with what Harvey calls space-time compression by which he means that, with the advent of ultra-fast transport and communication systems, space shrinks to a 'global village' or a 'spaceship earth'. The upshot is that images tend to become interchangeable – 'spaces of very different worlds seem to collapse upon each other, much as the world's commodities are assembled in supermarkets and all manner of subcultures get juxtaposed in the contemporary city' (pp. 301–2). In consequence, a strong sense of the 'Other' is overtaken by a weak sense of plural 'others'. To summarize the phenomenological counterpart to postmodern structural change, we can recount Harvey's list of characteristic postmodern experiences: fragmentation, ephemerality, dispersal in philosophical and social thought, radical discontinuity, decentring.

In passing, we can note the relation between Harvey's account of the diminution in our (hostile) sense of the 'Other' and Sampson's prescription that we celebrate the other. Harvey detects that under contemporary conditions we are perhaps less likely to constitute ourselves through the process of differentiation and denigration of the other – there are too many such others. This, of course, is not a genuine dialogism in Sampson's sense, but it does suggest a partial actualization of necessary, if not, sufficient conditions (though, contact theorists – cf. Brown and Hewstone, 1986 – might argue otherwise).

Now there are obvious substantive similarities between the accounts of the rise of the postmodern self provided by Gergen, Lash and Urry and Harvey. However, I want to concentrate on just one: the rise of the postmodern self, while it is mediated through all manner of interpersonal, technological, institutional and ideological dynamics ends up being related to a patterned, global change – it folds into a broader historical developmental narrative. Despite these micro- and meso-dimensions of the process of social construction, identity is being hitched in some causal way to the march of what I have called big history. Broad social dynamics – changes in communication technologies, in cultural artefacts, in class constitutions – impact upon the local, interactional, micro-sites to shape the production of selves. What is missing in such accounts is how these local sites – these everyday loci of intersubjectivity – are the sites which must 'receive' these impositions or, rather, mediate them. How does 'one' come to take on the changes in one's patterns of air travel, consumption of telecommunicational goods or perceptions of cultural artefacts? How do we come to be sensitized to these changes? How do Westerners 'yield' under the weight of 'empirical experience'? Do these ordinary people also not, like their social theorist brethren, interpret and critique and reflect? How do these social, economic and cultural trends get 'realized' at the multiple sites of everyday interaction and exchange? Or, rather, how does the infinity of intersubjective encounters come to yield something like Western culture and allow us to construe something like a Western identity and its discrete, periodized development?

Another point needs to be made. The big histories I have been considering are correlated with big identities. We are not concerning ourselves with such 'little identities' as a shopkeeper, a supporter of the British monarchy, a patient or a worker. Rather, we have focused upon those historically huge selves that have cast a mighty shadow across time-space – epochal selves like the self-contained, responsible Westerner or the fragmented, decentred spectacle-consuming postmodern. Yet, these big identities are mediated by the little identities – it is in the doing of these little identities in little situations that the huge identities are manifested and the big histories realized.

Snug Institutions: Tracing the Changes

If the above section has focused upon the epochal construction of identity, the present section will consider the 'intermediate' domain of institutions. How do particular institutions with their local procedures, dynamics, discourses and practices go about constituting specific sorts of individuals? What are the technologies of the social and the self (Martin et al., 1988; Henriques et al., 1984) that are developed and disseminated in and by such institutions? And what exactly are the contents and forms of identities that they produce?

The obvious theorist of this process is Michel Foucault (1965, 1979b, 1981).

His work has brilliantly explored the processes by which the individual is constituted in and through the procedures of measurement, surveillance and correction that characterize such institutions as prisons, hospitals and psychiatric units. Foucault, and those who have followed in his wake, have been fundamentally concerned to ground such processes in an account of how particular human sciences simultaneously yielded and were substantiated in concrete, institutional techniques – means of demarcation – which inscribed the limits and contents of the human being. In the field of psychology, perhaps the best-known exponent of the Foucauldian tradition is Nikolas Rose (1985, 1989a, b).

However, before going on to interrogate some of this work as it concerns the production of identity, I want to distinguish it from other treatments of the role of psychology in the social construction of identity. Authors such as Shotter (1975), Sampson (1981, 1983), Parker and Shotter (1990), Parker (1989) and Gergen (e.g. 1982, 1985) have considered the way that orthodox psychological models of the individual (and their attendant vocabularies, metaphors, discourses) have served in the entrenchment of particular identities. The media by which psychology has so acted remain a little obscure – basically, a version of Giddens' (e.g. 1984) double hermeneutic in which the products of an academic discipline diffuse into the lay world. As Giddens puts it:

> The concepts that sociological observers invent are 'second order' concepts in so far as they presume certain conceptual capabilities on the part of actors to whose conduct they refer. But it is in the nature of social science that these can become 'first order' concepts by being appropriated within social life itself . . . . (p. 284)

Now, to the extent that psychology contributes to this 'trickle down' (of course, there is also trickle up), it does so through a multiplicity of channels. What I am interested in in this section is, however, how these 'second order' concepts come to be realized through the practices of particular institutions and complexes of institutions, and the relation of such mediations to microsocial forms.

Rose (1989b) documents the ways in which developments in technique and conceptualization in psychology, and in the constellation of specialisms around it, were intimately bound up with the 'government of the human subject'. For example, by tracing such innovations in relation to the problems of morale, selection, rehabilitation and so on associated with World War II, Rose shows how, on the one hand, psychological science emerged as 'vital for the maximization of the use of human resources in institutional life' (p. x), and, on the other, individual pathology came to be conceived as a 'group phenomenon' and cure became 'a matter of rehabilitation of asocialized individuals' (p. 50). The upshot of this was that, in the post-war period, the process of adjusting individuals to their institutional roles would gather pace, and the techniques would become applicable across more and more organizational and social domains. In all this, Rose is not concerned to mount an attack on the psychological sciences for dominating and controlling the individual. Rather, these initial post-war developments, and their interconnected innovations in the areas of work and family, have led to a focus upon the free subject, most clearly evidenced in what Rose calls the obligation to be free. The corollary expertises and technologies of subjectivity contain within them criteria and standards of 'happiness, wisdom, health and fulfilment'. It is against the backdrop of these 'ideal selves' that we self-inspect, self-problematize, self-monitor and confess. Crucially, according to Rose, such self-scrutiny and self-regulation must be willingly conducted: indeed, ironically, it is only through exercising freedom in the practice of these technologies of the self that we attain the ideal selves that we seek.

Rose's historical investigation shares some of the characteristics, some might say malaises, of Foucault's histories (e.g. Fairclough, 1992; Law, 1994). While Rose to some extent avoids the charge of an over-synchronic histori-ography, he nevertheless is interested primarily in tracing the 'government of the soul' as a series of movements and coincidences of technique (in the most encompassing sense). Or rather, as with Foucault's writings, what we are pre-sented with is a series of freeze-frames or snapshots of the pattern of discourse and practice in a given domain such as the family. While Rose's periodization is less sweeping than Foucault's, the fact that the snapshots are historically closer together and refer to relatively subtle shifts in the configu-rations of the government of the soul, there is still a deliberate and informed inattention to narrative coherence. Now, there are good reasons why one should be sceptical about such narratively coherent or linear histories. For example, Poster (1984) in his commentary on Foucault's method, remarks that he is a historian of discontinuity: if orthodox histories trace continuity and assign causes, for Foucault this is 'a means of controlling and domesti-cating the past in the form of knowing it' (p. 75). The purpose of such a perspective is to undermine the possibility of totalization – rather 'Foucault proposes a multiplicity of forces in any social formation, a multiplicity which is dispersed, discontinuous, and unsynchronized' (p. 88). But as Poster goes on to point out, such a historiography should not be rendered unproblematic. When Foucault first addressed these issues, it was important to argue for the constructed nature of historical accounts. Nowadays, this observation is commonplace (White, 1987; Danto, 1985). It is now possible to be strategic about the sorts of histories one writes without making claims to 'truth' – acknowledging their constructed character is no longer a big epistemological deal. Genealogical, Marxist or Whig histories, Poster remarks, will all be 'able to illuminate certain aspects of the historical field and the merits of each position *vis-à-vis* the others are relative not absolute' (1984, p. 91; see also Law, 1994, pp. 104–10).

So, the type of history one writes reflects the sorts of purpose one wants that history to serve. Rose's aim is to 'use history . . . to think through the meaning and consequences of the new devices that have been invented for the govern-ment of the self, and to unsettle some of our comfortable illusions about their truthfulness and humanity' (p. ix). In contrast, my immediate aim is to high-light how such government 'penetrates' the person, how the pre-existing identities of persons have come to be supplanted, in the more or less local encounters between the expert and the non-expert. For all Rose's documentary brilliance, for all Foucault's virtuoso descriptions of surveillance, for all Donzelot's (1979) vivid depictions of the juvenile court at the heart of the tutelary complex, the ways in which the discourses are inscribed upon the body, diffuse into it to generate a new identity, remain hazy. How do the traces of these techniques, architectures, discourses become durable? At essence here is the issue of local process. For Fairclough (1992), in relation to the analysis of discourse, Foucault's work is marked by a neglect of 'practice' – instances of people doing, saying or writing things – which effectively reduces it to structures. What is missed out in Foucault's work is an account of change that follows 'practice' – a history that moves through local instanciation and struggle (although, as we shall see in Chapter 4, Foucault's work provides one lineage for the approach introduced and tentatively advocated in the rest of the book, actor-network theory).

What I want to point to now is the way that it is possible to relate empirical examples of process and practice in local situations within institutions to the construction of identities. In doing this, we can begin to trace how the institution is reproduced, challenged or changed. However, in order to do this we need to turn to other traditions, such as those of ethnomethodology (Mehan, 1987), textually oriented discourse analysis (Fairclough, 1992) and symbolic interactionism (Law, 1994). (See below.)

Before going on to look at these middle-range treatments of the construction of identity in the, albeit problematic, context of institutions, I want to consider those analyses which attend to the social construction of identity in what one might call 'acontextual situations' – situations whose character is essentially that of an 'encounter' unburdened by any explicit link to broader historical contexts such as that of an institution (however tentatively formulated). Here, what is at stake, or, rather, what is analytically emphasized, is some sort of legitimation of self. In other words, it is self-presentation (Goffman, 1959) that is uppermost in structuring the way that identity comes to be realized. The reason I do this is that, while these latter treatments obviously address broader social patterns – if not always institutions, then something like ideologies, for example – they nevertheless analytically emphasize some form of self-presentation as the driving force behind the local construction of identity. In other words, the concern to appear 'good, accountable persons whose actions are warrantable' is undoubtedly instrumental in such ostensible processes of identity constitution. The point is that it is also important to see how such a concern relates to institutional dynamics in the construction of the person.

'Acontextual Situations': Warranting and Rehearsing Identity

In this section I will consider social constructionist approaches to the study of identity that focus on its mediation in local situations, but that do not, by and large, feature accounts of the 'wider contexts' of big history and snug institutions. Here, identity is accessed through interview technique which, though often directly reflected upon, nevertheless serves as the warrant for the interpretations of the interview transcripts. What these transcripts of (bits of) interview sessions yield under analysis are patterns of representations which by virtue of their internal patterning aim to generate or impart a particular self-image. Now, such analyses might focus upon these patterns in terms of contradiction (e.g. Potter and Wetherell, 1987) or the mutual implicature of representations of the self and of society (Edwards and Potter, 1992; Wetherell and Potter, 1992). What they have in common is that the same *generalized* moral self is being constituted; what is missing is an attention to the ways that such representations serve in the mutual and durable (re)construction of the self and the interlocutor, and the ways that such representations, on the one hand, carry with them the trace of wider networks and, on the other, project the possibility of certain networks – in John Law's terms they are 'modes of ordering' and as such necessarily contribute to the contingent production of identities.

In other words, what many of these discourse-oriented analyses focus upon is the efforts and putative impression management goals of the main speaker – on the processes of 'accomplishment'. I will look at two examples of this approach chosen simply on the basis that they can serve to illustrate some of the points I want to raise. The third illustration, Billig's (1992) rhetorical analysis of identity in relation to the British royal family, has a different function – that of challenging some of the generalizations I all too glibly make.

In social psychology, the *locus classicus* of the discourse analytic approach remains Potter and Wetherell's (1987) *Discourse and Social Psychology*. However, I will begin with John Bowers' (1988) review essay of that text – primarily because he raises important questions about the 'functionality' of discourse which Potter and Wetherell are so keen to stress. Bowers develops a critique of what he sees as their overly constricted linking of discourse to function. Bowers notes that Potter and Wetherell's argument that discourse is deployed in order to accomplish particular things according to the exigencies of the immediate situation can be recast in cognitivist terms. For example, it might be argued that discourse is guided by individual goals. Bowers suggests that discourse can be related to the functioning of wider, 'sociological' phenomena rather than cognitive or immediate situational conditions. To quote: 'Rather than relate discourse functions "down" to the cognitions of individuals, we might attempt to forge links with grander social theory' (p. 187). That is to say, it might be that discourse functions to reproduce, or otherwise, higher order structures such as ideologies or institutions. The point is that there are multiple contexts that pertain to any single piece of discourse, and that how one construes discursive function is a reflection of the context, or configuration of contexts, that one analytically (and politically) presupposes.

The central observation, then, is that in attaching a function to a discourse, discourse fragment or discursive pattern, one is implicitly contextualizing that text. In the case of Potter and Wetherell's work, the need to explicate context is underplayed because the analytic focus is upon the way that discursive fragments are structured with respect to one another, that is, their contradictory inter-relations. Out of this emerges context in the form of situational exigencies to which the speaker is responding. Potter and Wetherell argue that individuals in so structuring their discourse, in deploying their repertoires as they do, accomplish a particular end, that specified by the exigencies of the immediate situation. However, 'accomplishing' is a problematic category – especially for the discourse analyst whose techniques do not simply reveal the mechanism of that accomplishment, but in the process debunk it. If we follow Heider's (1958) example and posit a contemporary version of his lay psychologist, namely a lay discourse analyst, we can expect that people's discursive efforts will be open to constant critical scrutiny. The simple point which follows is that such accomplishment is a social exercise in which the listener plays an equal part: it is her or his acquiescence that makes for 'accomplishment'. However, for Potter and Wetherell, 'accomplishment' does not refer to the 'actual' convincing of the listener – rather, it is attached to the sense of 'satisfaction' or 'ease' that the speaker derives from her utterances: there is a social logic to her talk that allows her to sense that she has accomplished something.

However, such a functional model raises other issues. At a metatheoretical level, 'accomplishment' implies a complex judgemental procedure on the part of the analyst. It is arguable that in the above judgement of 'accomplishment', the analyst identifies 'accomplishment' because she or he implicitly accesses the cognitions/interiority of participants who 'feel' or have a sense of closure in the social exchange. Alternatively, it might be the case that the analyst uses certain behavioural or social parameters such as the signals of closure (e.g. the ending of a social encounter). However, this is premised on some 'ending' and such endings are always analytically negotiable and open to a review which questions the parameters which allow us to adjudicate over an ending. Questions that spring to mind might run as follows: what if one of the speakers leaves the interaction still mulling over the exchange? (Who has not left a conversation thinking about what she or he would have liked to have said or will say when she or he next encounters his or her interlocuter(s)?) What if the encounter continues later on; or if the conversation is resumed by the original speaker with some other more or less innocent party? Under such circumstances can we say that there has been an 'accomplishment'? Further, it might be that 'accomplishment' is situationally managed (no doubt tacitly) on the part of the interviewer: his or her silence or lack of challenge or passivity can serve to facilitate a reading of the statements of the speaker as 'accomplishing', whereas under duress, when such statements are explicitly countered, then they might be interpreted as, for example, 'desperate efforts to assuage', 'tentative formulations' or 'invitations to negotiation'.

So, 'accomplishment' even at the micro-level is a matter of analytic judgement – it is not an empirical given. The episodic nature of social interaction is a matter of analysis in its own right as ethogenists have long noted (Harré and Secord, 1972; Harré, 1979). In discourse analysis the danger is that the analytic completion of episodes is used to ground the understanding of discourse uncritically. In essence, there is an implicit parcelling of time (and space) by the analyst, and, as we have noted, that parcelling can occur at all sorts of levels – behavioural (leaving the site of interaction), phenomenological (internal monologues), social (end of interaction) and so on.

In sum, the notion of accomplishment points to the role of the analyst in deriving discourses and tracing their integrity, seemingly exclusively, from the discourse data/material itself. Of course, the point is that the perception of accomplishment by the analyst works because she or he has already brought to bear a mixture of discourses, episodic understandings and political commitments. But in order to achieve such closure, that is, in order to tell an analytic story, it is also possible to mobilize macrosocial contexts. Accomplishment, as Bowers points out, can be tied to macrosocial 'entities' such as ideologies and social institutions and structures. Treating discourse analysis as a textual form, there is a multiplicity of ways of 'closing' the analysis, and, indeed, of showing how discourse is located in a contradictory complex of stories/narratives which might or might not attain closure (see also Davies and Harré, 1990).

In relation to the social construction of identity, the accomplishment of this or that impression is mediated by the 'successful portrayal' of certain identities. For example, Wetherell and Potter (1989) consider the discursive use of narrative characters to mitigate culpability for police violence in the context of protests during the 1981 Sprinkbok rugby tour of New Zealand. They detect different characters such as the flawed person provoked into violence or the rational or role-related self which uses violence instrumentally to prevent greater violence in the form of, say, a riot. As Wetherell and Potter note, they are not concerned 'with the effectiveness of these different styles of mitigation' (p. 218), and they suspect that a very different pattern might have emerged had the interviewees been confronted with more antagonistic interviewers. (However, it is important to note that Wetherell and Potter, 1992 expand the contextual horizons of their discourse analytic approach in order to address the relation of discourse to ideology and social reproduction.) Nevertheless, the characters have been articulated in a context which the authors are happy to characterize unproblematically as, more or less, congenial. Assumptions are made about the speakers' reading of the interaction which is grounded in their responses, yet their responses can only be understood by a particular reading of the interactive situation. There is here a sort of bootstrapping – a hermeneutic.

Now, this perhaps is all we are ever able to do, but as the above argument suggests, it is also important to question our readings of the situation, to bring to bear different hermeneutics – as it were, to admit polysemy into the situation and the speaker's reading of the interviewer, not only as a more or less pleasant or antagonistic generalized 'other', but also as a representative or embodiment of a particular macrosocial entity such as the legal system or the retributive and coercive state (Atkinson and Drew, 1979) or as an interested but sceptical public (Michael and Birke, 1994a). The sense of 'accomplishment' – the interviewee's view that his or her own responses were sufficient – likewise is predicated on a phenomenology of the speaker and an episodization of the situation. What is of interest in this dual process of impression management of self and the use of mitigating narrative characters is just this process of self-reproduction which is mediated, in part by the use of these characters. For this to be followed through, to be traced in its actual (not hoped-for) durability, we do indeed need to attend to the 'effectiveness'. Functionality comes not merely to be tied to the person and their impression management concerns, but to social ordering. As such we need to meditate upon what sorts of durability are accomplished, upon the idea that discourse does indeed impact upon others, and upon how those others adopt and reproduce the discourses deployed by accomplished speakers.

Sue Widdicombe (1993), in her analysis of the autobiographical talk of two 'goths' as they account for the way that they came to adopt their unconventional appearance, shows how change is represented as taking place independently of the influence of significant others. Moreover, these others remain unnamed and of limited similarity. Finally, speakers claim that 'change is motivated by a true self which is independent of appearance, but which is expressed through appearance' (p. 108). These 'descriptive sequences' are, Widdicombe suggests, 'solutions to a problem of authenticity' such that 'they are designed to address potential and negative inferences that change is motivated by a desire to conform to a particular image, or merely to copy others, and is hence insincere' (p. 108).

While Widdicombe's chapter is fundamentally interested in the portrayal of authenticity, its prime focus is upon language, that is, the discursive resources that allow for such portrayals. She is careful to reflect upon the contingency of her interpretation and acknowledges that the encounter with the goths may be read in any number of ways. However, there is an acontextual situation being constituted in all this: the conversation-as-exemplar-of-the-language is all, it is the locus at which discourse or language shyly manifests itself. Yet, what the conversation is, how it is to be read reflects on the assumptions made by the analysts about how the interviewer has been interpreted as an audience by the interviewee. In other words, within the interview, the addressee is an audience of a particular or multifarious sort. As remarked in the foregoing, interviewers are not simply some sort of 'generalized other' – they are a 'polysemic other'. The interviewer can represent, signify or embody multiple audiences and many constituencies that stretch, so to speak, beyond their surface comportment as 'interviewer'. How we as analysts 'carve up' this polysemy is a matter of complex judgement – one that is often implicit. At this point, Potter and Wetherell's (1987) injunction not selectively to ironize the talk of speakers (see also Woolgar, 1983 on instrumental irony) is effectively irrelevant. It is not a question of not ironizing (to ironize would be to fail to treat people's talk 'seriously' in its own right, reading it simply as a way of illustrating some theoretical or political precommitment). Rather, it is a question of ironizing justly (where justly may refer to a complex of contingencies that might encompass, for example, respect for the speaker, narrative coherence, political purpose).

However, there is a further dimension here: such talk is not simply about accomplishing a self in the presence of polite social scientific company. Its performative effects are also vitally important. Such talk is about engendering effects in listeners – making them particular sorts of persons liable, in the future, to do particular sorts of things. After all, and this is a crucial issue, let us not forget that our speakers were once listeners – they had to somehow absorb the discourses that they now ply. As such 'accomplishments' are not simply a sort of unconscious self-satisfaction, they are mediations, impacts, shapings and orderings. But these are all multifarious – they can span (or attempt to span) the polysemy of the other, to reduce its multiplicity and bring it down to a few manageable others. In other words, the speaker is 'generating an other' as well as 'responding to an other'. He or she is embroiled, then, in a process of ordering – of self and other – that might or might not 'work'. (Of course, it is a matter of great interest whether it does work, and something that is sorely neglected in such variants of social constructionist social psychology.) There are questions one can begin to formulate in the light of all this: What identities were represented by the interviewer? Were interviewers liable to be read as members of, or sympathetic towards, the perceived subculture? Do we as interviewers end up being the intermediaries of our own interviewees, enrolled into their projects, and proceeding to carry out those projects in the interviewees' absence? Or are we resistant, already willing and able to represent them for the purpose of our own 'accomplishments' in our own social academic world?

So far there has been a rather unalloyed humanism creeping into this discussion. Let me try and undermine this a little. Who is having, or attempting to have, the impact: the speaker qua human individual actor or the subculture as macrosocial actor? At this point we come to a second layer of interpretation: the way that the analyst warrants his or her accounts in relation to his or her favoured audiences, and in the process responds to and shapes those lay and expert constituencies.

The final, and perhaps most elaborated, approach to the construction of identities in local situations concerns Michael Billig's pioneering work on rhetoric, argumentation and ideological dilemmas. This ranks as one of the major contributions to recent social psychology (e.g. Billig, 1987, 1991; Billig et al., 1988) and I will give a very brief overview of his approach in order to contextualize the later discussion.

In developing a rhetorical social psychology, Billig (1991) proposes a dual movement: on the one hand, social psychology must come to analytic terms with rhetoric; on the other, it must 'recognize that the processes of everyday thinking can be processes of "ideology". . . . this means that common sense not only has a wider history, but that it also possesses present functions, which relate to patterns of domination and power' (p. 1). For Billig, ideology is necessarily paradoxical, at once structuring human thought and providing the terrain upon which individuals invent or create discourse. This is a paradox that needs to be encompassed by social psychology, not resolved. The importance of rhetoric derives, in part, from its capacity to render accessible the argumentativeness, sociality and contradictoriness of human thought and common sense. Billig's (1987) *Arguing and Thinking* is concerned with the role of rhetoric, specifically in the context of argumentation, in social inter-action and human thought. He argues that the metaphors of the theatre and the game that inform much of social psychology are too one-sided; not only do they neglect the rhetorical aspects of social behaviour, they can only be sus-tained by the editing out of the wider context of literal role-playing and rule-following. Billig does not want to dispense with these models; rather, he wants to supplement them with metaphors that directly encompass argumen-tation and rhetoric. To this end, he turns to the ancient rhetorical tradition. Protagoras emerges as the hero of this. From his maxim that 'in every question there are two sides to the argument exactly opposite to one another' (p. 41) follows the point that contradiction is part of argumentation and that every argument is potentially controversial. The psychological implication that Billig elaborates is that human thought is characterized by variety and by con-trary views. Further, 'One-sided psychological theories seem to invite a Protagorean response, which points out a contrary, and neglected, aspect' (p. 50). In the present instance that aspect is made up of rhetoric and argumen-tation. Billig has gone on to apply his rhetorical framework to such social psychological givens as opinion, prejudice, cognition and categorization.

As noted, this rhetorical form of thought is contextualized within the domain of ideology. But ideology is not uniform, it is dilemmatic – it contains contrary themes and people's thinking reflects this. Thus in order to under-stand the meanings and functions of people's utterances and writings, it is necessary to reflect upon what it is they are arguing against. Billig phrases this point in the following way: 'The context of opinion-giving is a context of argumentation. Opinions are offered where there are counter-opinions. The argument "for" a position is always an argument "against" a counter-posi-tion. Thus the meaning of an opinion is dependent upon the opinions which it is countering . . .' (1991, p. 17). This applies to the analysis of texts as well: 'Unless readers of propaganda understand the counter-position, against which the message is directed, they may be misled by the message' (p. 19). Billig et al. (1988) elaborate on the ways in which the analyst may apprehend such counter-themes in ideology. They argue that there are two levels of ide-ology: lived and intellectual. 'Lived' refers to society's way of life, to common sense: ideas and beliefs are not formalized in the way that they are in intellec-tual ideology. The latter is constructed by professionals and can be found in systems of religion, philosophy and political thought, for instance. Dilemmas or conflicts operate at various levels within ideology. For example, one can find contradictions between lived and intellectual ideologies, where ideologues or social theorists embrace a grand theory which greatly contrasts with their everyday lives. Marx and Engels are paradigmatic examplars of this. However, we also find dilemmas within lived or intellectual ideologies. Billig et al. cite the example of individualist theories and philosophies. Individualism is often equated with capitalism and while it is often highly regarded, it is also opposed. The counter-theme to individualism might concern traditional communality. Billig et al. show how in the UK there exists a thoroughgoing individualism whose focus is upon the freedom of individuals to pursue their own ends. In contrast, in Germany, individual rights were always discussed in relation to the state. This implies that in the UK there was an anti-statist stance. In fact, the UK was blessed with a relatively secure political authority which individualist thought could barely problematize. The secure state and society thus functioned as the necessary conceptual and social backdrop against which individual freedom could be discussed. In Germany, a weak state existed, so the individual was discussed in terms of its relation to the state. In sum, Billig et al. suggest that it is possible to unveil the counter-themes by philosophical exegesis, that is, unpicking the contradictions in a given text. Alternatively, they can also be detected sociologically by mapping how discourse, by virtue of being argumentative and involved in arguing against some more or less implicit assumption or position, takes various counter-themes for granted which *prima facie* appear to be attacked.

Billig (1992) has applied this complex and variegated perspective to an analysis of the ways in which people come to talk about the British royal family. In the present context, I will concentrate on just a few themes in his book. Billig traces how his participants hold to a muted nationalism by laying stress on the uniqueness of the British monarchy and the history and authenticity that this signifies. This serves in a rhetorical economy in which 'we' become the envy of the world, with others, especially the Americans, gazing longingly at 'us'. But Billig also documents the ways in which people identify with and differentiate themselves from the royal family. Thus 'we' are similar to 'them' (they are only human like us, after all), yet as a backdrop it is assumed that they 'are marked by an element of "royalness"', which distinguishes 'them' from 'us' and which uniquely qualifies 'them' for 'their job of image-making'. Billig regards this latter as a 'premise of the common-sense talk of royalty' (p. 114) against which equalizing talk is played out. Here, identity turns on a series of tensions or dilemmas – a 'double-declaiming' in which 'as people make claims about the royal family, justifying its position of privilege, so they will be heard making claims about the desirability of their own unprivi-leged lives' (p. 23). All this, of course, occurs within the context of argumentation: Billig is keen to promote what he calls the 'repopulation' of social psychology wherein analytic accounts should resound with human chatter – in argumentation. Such argumentation processes reflect, according to Billig, the thinking-in-process, but also, in that appeals to common sense are routine, they draw upon accepted 'common places' – those broad themes of common sense.

This sort of approach requires not only an attention to the detail of argu-mentation, but also a broad scholarly consideration of the ideological, historical, sociological etc. context (cf. Billig, 1988a). Arguments are embed-ded in history – there is no acontextual situation as such, but a folding of the overt nuggets of discourse into their rich ideological and historical amalgam. Billig does not resort to an acontextual situation, as I have facetiously called it above; for Billig these discourses, their turnover and mutation all occur within the cut and thrust of familial discussion. But if Billig locates these commonplaces in the general reading of common sense – one based on the fully recognized vicissitudes of 'scholarship', he is not obviously interested in tracing how, if not singular discourses, then dilemmas, come to be absorbed by the speakers he wants to populate social psychology (cf. Billig, 1994). He is not overtly interested in how these repetitions of dilemmas and instanciations of ideology come to constitute and order self and others in durable ways. Moreover, for Billig, as for the other authors we have considered, the issue of the extradiscursive – the nonhuman context and its contributions to this durability – remains unattended. The further point I wish to raise, or rather reiterate, is that the individuals out of whose mouths come instanciations of commonplaces are not the sole actors present: we see here macrosocial actors working. The identities of pre-existing (techno)social orders, as well as human actors, are being played out here.

All this will be elaborated below, when I consider actor-network theory. Suffice it to say for the moment that Billig's concern to populate social psychology raises important issues about the craft of the discourse analyst. We as analysts are no less prone to, at once, warranting ourselves to various audiences and constructing our readers as particular sorts of beings. Sometimes these constituencies are the people whom we have 'studied', sometimes they are our peers. The point of all this is that this process and patterning of warranting and formulating reflect allegiances to and associations with individuals, subcultures, ideas, standards of living, social positioning and ethics. What these associations are can only be worked out after the event. We should not prioritize persons, for what is to count as a person is something that is subject to negotiation, struggle and construction (see Chapter 7). To return to the questions I posed at the beginning of the chapter: the 'who' of our analysis is a highly variable entity, but by problematizing this 'who' we can at the very least begin to narrate, no doubt crudely, the production and reproduction of identity.

Conclusion: Pulling It All Together?

In the preceding sections I have dealt, albeit superficially, with several different treatments of the appropriate context (micro, meso or macro) of the social construction of identity and its analysis. While there has been a degree of crossover between these different domains, none have systematically and self-consciously attempted to theorize the inter-relations of these different levels as they impact upon, and are mediated by, identity. This has been the concern of this chapter – namely, to point to the (sub)disciplinary disaggregation of these dynamics.

However, this is not to say that there are no such attempts: the micro/macro-debate and efforts at its 'resolution' or 'dissolution' clearly suggest otherwise (see Chapters 3 and 4 for some instances), though there are few empirical efforts at such 'syntheses'. Hugh Mehan (1987), for example, has considered the local construction of learning disability students as this is affected by institutional constraints and facilitations, and John Law (1994) has provided brilliant accounts of the situated deployment of particular 'characters' in a physics research laboratory which carry with them an implicit model of institutional functioning and, in the process of their articulation, serve to 'perform' that institution (see also Bowers and Iwi, 1993).

In this section I want to address one particular treatment of these various levels, namely, Norman Fairclough's (1992) multidimensional discourse analytic perspective: text-oriented discourse analysis. I choose this particularly because it serves as an appropriate counterpoint to the approach I will advocate in subsequent chapters. For example, it focuses our attention on the status of the agency and effectivity of participants in interactions. Furthermore, it serves to distinguish between, on the one hand, a more or less traditional view of micro-situations 'embedded' in institutions and histories and, on the other, a conception of 'macro-structures' as products of micro-situations (products which, nevertheless, if they can be successfully locally represented can have an identity, and agency, all of their own). Finally, Fairclough's approach helps us raise the spectre of the non-social or the nonhuman – it can act as a backdrop against which the profile of the non-social's micro-situational contribution to the construction of identity can be delineated.

Fairclough's 1992 volume extends the approach he first developed in his *Language and Power* (1989). In the earlier work, he outlined a way of looking at discourse which incorporated treatments of the formal characteristics of the text (e.g. grammar), the local interactional context of discourse production and interpretation, and the broader institutional and social context (e.g. institutions and society as a whole). These three levels have since been refined. Firstly there is text analysis in which there is attention to the formal properties of the text organized under four main headings: vocabulary, grammar, cohesion and text-structure (including conversational turn-taking) (cf. 1992, p. 75). The next level is that of 'discursive practice' wherein are considered the processes of text production, distribution and consumption. Here, the focus is upon where and how texts are socially produced, how they are consumed in different ways in different social contexts – that is how interpreters come to 'reduce the potential ambivalence of texts' (1992, p. 81). For Fairclough, context plays a major part in this process of ambiguity reduction, but, as he points out, people must first interpret the context in order for it to reduce ambiguity. As in the interpretation of texts, this 'involves an interplay between cues and members' resources, but members' resources in this case is in effect a mental map of the social order' (p. 82). Such situation-readings entail the selective foregrounding of aspects of the social identity of participants. The final dimension of Fairclough's schema is that appertaining to social practice. Here, he relates discourse to ideology, power and hegemony, and suggests that 'discursive practices are ideologically invested insofar as they incorporate significations which contribute to sustaining or restructuring power relations' (p. 91).

Fairclough illustrates these three dimensions with a contrast between two sorts of medical interview. In the standard interview we find that the doctor controls the interaction by, for example, opening and closing each cycle of the interaction, accepting/acknowledging the patient's responses – it is the doctor who offers and the patient who accepts turns. This is paralleled by 'topic control': it is the doctor who defines the problem in terms of a narrowly medical content, ignoring in the process the patient's efforts to introduce moral and personal content. As Fairclough notes: 'One has the sense of a doctor shifting and constraining the topic in accordance with a pre-set agenda, which the patient is not being allowed to disturb' (1992, p. 141). Fairclough goes on to link this up to broader structures such as the mode of medical professionalism, but also to the way that such routinized interactions allow for more efficient and speedy processing of patients which is a partial response to the 'huge pressures on doctors and other professionals to increase their efficiency' (p. 149).

The foregoing contrasts with the 'alternative medical interview' between a patient and a doctor who belongs to a 'minority group within the British National Health Service which is open to "alternative" (such as homeopathic) medicine, and the treatment of the "whole person"' (p. 145). What we find in this encounter is a conversational structure in which the interactional control features of the standard medical interview are largely absent. Turn-taking is collaborative and the introduction and changeover of topics is managed by the patient. In sum, there is a more informal, 'natural' feel to the interaction which bears marked similarities to counselling.

Fairclough suggests that these two forms of interview entail different values attached to differing representations of the patient – from something like 'broken-down machine' to 'whole person', but also from 'medical patient' to 'consumer' or 'client'. Further, these shifts (or tensions, for these models are in contest) relate contradictorily to broader social practical dynamics. While the alternative interview is in accord with general cultural changes in which professional texts and discourse increasingly address themselves to a 'self-steering self' – 'a consumer characterized by the capacity to choose' (p. 220), such techniques in the context of medicine will be prohibitively costly in a climate of increasing economic constraint. If standard medical interviews fit more comfortably with prevailing economic contradictions, they run against counter-trends towards increasing informality.

In terms of identity, what we have here are two models of identities for both the 'patient' (machine/consumer) and the doctor (mechanic-expert/listener-counsellor). Moreover, these are linked to social practice – those changes in the surrounding ideological context. In what follows, I will use this all too scanty outline of Fairclough's three-dimensional approach to discourse analysis to begin clarifying some of the characteristics of actor-network theory.

There are three points of contact between Fairclough's pathbreaking work and actor-network theory that I will consider. The first concerns the question of levels – epochal, institutional, interactional. Fairclough's concern to address the characteristics of textual, interactional and broader social contexts suggests that these can be unproblematically 'read off' and used to anchor analytically the processes of social construction. However, we as analysts do nothing more or less than the participants about whom we write: they too use these various representations of different levels in their exchanges and in their production of identities and the social order. Each of these levels can be attributed properties of contextuality, agency and effectivity in ways which serve in current interactions. What do these representations represent exactly? Actor-network theory would emphasize that these discursively represented levels (micro, meso and macro) serve in the (re)production of a range of nestled networks and associations. In relation to Fairclough's example of the medical interview, there might be such networks as the doctor–patient relationship, the state of the British National Health Service, the condition of the British economy, and the typically individualistic agent of Western society. It then becomes an analytical task of unpicking the ways that given discursive exchanges, and their associated manifested identities, feed into each of these networks. But further, these levels can themselves be actors, or can be represented by we actor-network theorists as such. In our own academic narrations, we can ascribe agency to these levels (they purposefully pursue goals and interests) or effectivity (they enable certain possibilities). The point is that our access to these differently sized actors needs careful attention: we might unproblematically assume them under certain circumstances; we might decompose them under others. As we shall see in Chapter 4, whatever the size of actor, actor-network theory is fundamentally interested in looking at how size – macro-ness – comes to be achieved.

The second issue concerns change. Fairclough's work tends to focus on the reproduction of certain discursive practices and their contexts. But what of the process of innovation wherein we find new discourses, texts and artefacts developed, disseminated and stabilized? For example, if the consumer/counsellor model of the medical consultation is an example of wider cultural changes, what are its origins? How has it been sold and incorporated as viable? To put it another way, how has the disparate range of local developments in the representation of identity come to cohere as a more or less identifiable, discrete cultural shift towards something like 'the Western individual as enhanced consumer/agent'? Actor-network theory addresses the more general question of the way that new practices and representations are adopted and advocated, and how people come to be enrolled to promote these new practices and representations, thus acting as intermediaries and extending the network. Once again, we can refer to Fairclough's example: the contrasting medical consultation formats he identifies are the sites at which different networks are performed and potentially extended. But they can also be sites of struggle, where different forms have clashed in the past and where the 'black box' of the bedside manner has been opened up, such that the 'right' model of the consultation has become controversial. What Fairclough's work neglects to do is address how these controversies arise, and are resolved (where one form of the medical consultation triumphs and becomes predominant) or are managed (where the two forms separate into divergent networks, say those of orthodox and alternative medicine).

The final issue relates to extending the spectrum of participants that can be active in local exchanges to accommodate nonhumans. Fairclough's work, for all its reservation about radical social constructionism, particularly on political grounds, nevertheless shares with that broad school in the privileging of the social. This is not an altogether fair accusation to level at Fairclough – his prime interest is in discourse, after all. Nevertheless, to the extent that he is interested in social reproduction and change, we could begin to identify what is missing from his purview. At the point of local interactions there are not only individual persons and macrosocial entities present – there are also architectures, furnitures, technologies, bodies, other organisms. To what extent should these be given voice in the analytic account of such interactions? Do these not too embody morality, furnish resources of acquiescence and resistance (cf. Michael and Still, 1992) and impact upon the situated constitution of persons, identities and worlds? In what measure should we attribute agency to nonhumans, how might we articulate their 'purposes', and how might we go about disentangling the autonomy of their impact from the discourses in which they are at once buoyed and constructed? These are horrible questions – but taking a different tack, we might say that these very questions are what should be addressed in relation to human actors. For the sake of narrative tension, for the moment I will merely say that in Chapters 4 and 7, I will begin to address the roles of nonhuman actors, both 'technological' and 'natural'.

This chapter, neither systematically nor comprehensively, has considered several approaches to the social construction of identity. I have attempted to show that there are different levels of analysis and different contexts (that serve as analytic anchors) in operation, and that these can be brought together at the site of interaction. We find a model for such ambitions in Fairclough's analytic schema. But we also find several absences. For example, there is no (outline of a) theory of the relation between micro and macro – that is, an account of the mediations between these levels and of how they variously impact upon identity. Attention to the mechanics of change is likewise attenuated. Further (and this is no doubt an annoyingly familiar refrain by now), we find that the social is all too readily prioritized.

In the next chapter I will consider some of the criticisms of social constructionism in order to open up an analytic space – a theoretical haven – into which the non-social and the nonhuman can be introduced, there to nest quietly and unostentatiously under the wing of actor-network theory, making its gentle, ambiguous, but nevertheless valued contributions to the construction of identity.

3

Constructing a Critique of Social Constructionism

In the previous chapter we saw how various social constructionist approaches to identity were, with relatively few exceptions, focused on specific domains, and incorporated differing frames of history and units of analysis. The purpose was to show how such disparity militated against a detailed consideration of the multiple and sometimes contradictory dimensions (or levels) of identity, and of the historical rise of new constructions and their entrenchment. Towards the end of the chapter I suggested that the non-social also needed to be introduced into the equation that described these regularities. However, in order to sustain such an argument, it is necessary to provide a critique of social constructionism that generates a feasible space for the non-social. In Chapter 1, I provided a minimal definition of social constructionism: social practices constitute givens which have consequences. Here, I am concerned to outline some of the limitations that can be placed around the phrase 'social practices constitute givens'. Thus, in the rest of this chapter, I consider some critiques of social constructionism that, while sympathetic, nevertheless attempt to find a conceptual space for the non-social. These critiques can be listed as follows: Critique from Reflexivity; Critique from Postmodernity; Critique from a Possible History of Disciplines; Critique from a (Speculative) Version of Contemporary Politics. All these critiques can engage with social constructionism on its own terms – each provides a way of simultaneously problematizing and accepting social constructionism, of holding these in creative tension. The dilemma or contradiction is one which is not resolvable (Billig et al., 1988); rather, it is a basis for the breaking down of some of the strictures imposed by social constructionism on doing 'good' research. As such, the critiques I consider are somewhat different from (critical) realist critiques or positions, which advocate, in one way or another, an invariant real (however problematic it might be to access) which escapes construction. These differences will be addressed in the final section of the chapter.

Critique from Reflexivity

As we have seen, Sociology of Scientific Knowledge (SSK) is a prime intellectual resource for social constructionist social psychology. Recently however, Woolgar (1988a) has directly problematized the 'ethos' of representation that

infuses SSK. In other words, the practitioners of SSK and social constructionism have tended to reify the social in order to explain certain phenomena.
Thus, for example, 'interests' have been unproblematically used as resources
to explain the positions and strategies of scientists engaged in particular controversies. Such 'interests' should be regarded as topics of investigation: as
rhetorical tools used by scientists in the process of argumentation, accounts
about one's own and others' interests should take analytic priority over a sociological approach that regards interests primarily as explanans (cf. Woolgar,
1981, 1983; Barnes, 1981; Mackenzie, 1981; Callon and Law, 1982). In
Woolgar's view, SSK needs to reflect upon its own status as a research programme that represents and socially constructs the processes of
representation and the social construction of scientific facts and artefacts. To
this end, effort is directed at developing modes of writing that can reflect
upon themselves and that admit of their own status as representations by
effectively de-constructing the textual means by which representation is
achieved. The consequent relativism is not seen as a reason for lamentation,
but as the cause of celebration – SSK texts should playfully explore their own
constructed constitution. Examples of this reflexive strategy have included the
development of various novel textual forms such as multiple voices intervening in the text, plays, strange loops and encyclopaedias. (Woolgar, 1988a, b,
1989, 1992; Ashmore, 1989; Mulkay, 1985. However, see also: Furhman and
Oehler, 1986; Doran, 1989; Collins and Yearley, 1992a, b).

  This is allied to a more general critique of 'representation' as ideology.
Accordingly, Woolgar (1988a, 1989) is concerned with the way that the representational activities of science and social science tend to 'objectify' – to
occlude the operation of agency in the construction of representations and
thereby to obscure their constructed and contingent nature. In other words,
representations have the quality of suggesting that they directly access the
'real'; there is thus in operation what he calls the 'ideology of representation' –
'the set of beliefs and practices stemming from the notion that objects (meanings, motives, things) underlie or pre-exist the surface sign (documents,
appearances) which give rise to them' (Woolgar, 1988a, p. 98).

  In contrast, we can draw out some of the functions that social representations (e.g. Moscovici, 1981, 1984) supposedly fulfil, in order to problematize
Woolgar's problematization. According to Moscovici, social representations
are concepts, statements, images and explanations that arise in the course of
inter-individual communication. These function in the process of 'objectification' (through say figuration or personification) which 'saturates the idea of
unfamiliarity with reality, turns it into the very essence of reality' (Moscovici,
1984, p. 38). For Woolgar this is in and of itself ideological. Billig (1988b) has
criticized this process, pointing to the counter-process of de-objectification in
which the non-material and transcendental are emphasized. However, for
Woolgar, what is at issue is the implicit claim of representation, and that
includes representation of the transcendental, to access the 'real'. This claim
is grounded in the exclusion of agency in the production of the representations so that when a representation is problematized it is by 'spotlighting the

involvement of agency, by emphasising the possibility of arbitrariness, or distortion, of motivated, actively constructed representations' (Woolgar, 1988a, p. 99).

Woolgar's purpose is to loosen up this representation–real connection or correlation. To this end, he recommends that we practise a reflexivity in our writing through new literary forms that reintroduce agency into the text and thereby make the reader aware of its constructed status. However, if the aim is to show how one's own analytic text is dependent upon a range of social factors, as soon as one begins to identify those factors, that process of identification too is subject to a parallel array of social factors – and so on. For reflexivists such as Woolgar, Ashmore and Mulkay, this seems to point to an inescapable paradox that construction and representation, the word and the world are dependent upon one another – in sum, that each reflexive deconstruction posits a real. The point of reflexive writing is to render these interdependencies and paradoxes transparent.

Such textual strategies have, however, been criticized on various counts. For instance, there is the obvious point that someone will always come to reflect upon that text – to question the very usefulness of this sort of reflexivity. That is to say, reflexivity is a collective endeavour. Further, now that reflexivity is more or less firmly situated upon the academic agenda, and according to some theorists of postmodernity, is part of the lay condition, however unreflexive some texts are, they will always self-deconstruct under the weight of history, so to speak. In other words, any academic reader is now culturally predisposed to deconstruct willy-nilly. We can further embed this problematic of reflexivity historically by drawing upon Mary Douglas' (1986) useful analysis of radical scepticism – the questioning of the very possibility of an independent reality. I take some forms of reflexivity to be radically sceptical insofar as they problematize the reality of all things by always reflexively applying the tools of social construction to one's own analysis. Douglas' point is that radical scepticism is allied to political and practical marginalization – it is a reflection of powerlessness or the acceptance of powerlessness (her comparison is between the Brahmans, Russian intellectuals of the 1830s and 1840s, Foucault and Feyerabend versus Western Christianity, Bolsheviks, realist/orthodox Marxists).

Though it should be noted that the two do not exactly equate, what is it that makes us stop short of radical scepticism and profound reflexivity? Douglas' point contains one answer: that people want to engage in the world – to control, to have material impact. As such they must construct as much as deconstruct if they want to engage with those collectives, groups or communities whose texts they have deconstructed. To put it another way, we might almost regard the point at which reflexivity halts or seizes up as a marker of particular political or social commitment.

Latour (1988b) makes a rather different point, but one which also explicitly reintroduces power into the equation. He distinguishes between two forms of reflexivity. The first he calls metareflexivity. This is characterized by the underpinning assumption that readers too readily believe texts and it is a problem of note if they fail to comprehend the constructed nature of these texts. In contrast, infrareflexivity attempts to avoid, as opposed to encourage, not being believed. Of course, this also applies to metareflexivity: after all, while the above-mentioned textual strategies attempt to force the reader to problematize sociological accounts of science, it nevertheless encourages us to believe in the soundness of reflexivity. In other words, as scientific and social scientific objects are de-reified, reflexivity becomes reified. In contrast, for Latour, the more reflexive we are, then the more realist we become: for to make realist claims and to go on to the side of the 'known' is exactly what is needed to play the game of enrolment, of persuasion, of, in sum, politics.

To return to social representations and the 'ideology of representation', Woolgar's concern with representational objectification as ideological con-trasts with the positive status ascribed to objectifying social representations. For Moscovici, this process is a means of coming to grips with the unfamil-iar, but also a means through which the world is settled into a domain in which communication, community and identity can be played out. As with Douglas and Latour, representation serves as a means of mediating relations of power and hence it is an intrinsic part of both science and everyday life. However, on the epistemological level, Woolgar's concern to problematize the objectifying role of social science texts does need to be taken into account in relation to the theory of social representations. However, this can be dealt with by acknowledging Latour's argument, namely, that reflexivity is a col-lective process and that the more reflexive one is, the more one recognizes that one is engaged in relations of power, that one is inevitably involved in the enrolment of readers, and that one's purpose is to convince or persuade one's audience. In this respect, social representation theory is itself a form of social representation, objectifying the everyday. It furnishes a means of conceptually mastering the social processes of objectification and constitutes for itself a communal identity. Moreover, in relation to the theory of social representa-tion's ideological status, we can say that, if anything, it is, at least in part, concerned with critically teasing out the operation of negative ideology – negative in the sense of being instrumental in domination (Thompson, 1984) – by examining the constitution and social embedding of social repre-sentations. As such, its focus is upon the content of social representations and their ideological functioning as opposed to their formal properties of objec-tification. Here, ideology is concerned with content and specific groups; thus, their objectifying function per se cannot be what renders them ideological. In other words, objectification, under some circumstances, is a politically nec-essary and good thing. Objectifying the working classes, particular forms of domination and their institutional bases is valuable insofar as it facilitates struggle and critique.

This returns us to Latour's advocacy of a strategic realism (infrareflexivity). If what we aim to do is convince others via our polished representations, and if part of this process entails the attempted inoculation of our texts against the outrages of the deconstructionists who everywhere lie in wait, one option is to evoke and invoke the real as energetically and cannily as possible. This 'real' could be the typically 'social' (e.g. interests, values, institutional positioning and the like), or it could be the typically 'non-social' and 'nonhuman'. It all depends on the contexts and exigencies – both social and non-social. Thus to 'reify' the environmental crisis, animal suffering or human disease and despair is perfectly acceptable when one's purpose is to enable and encourage political action and to enrol others as political activists.

In sum, if the 'social' of social constructionism and SSK rests on the real, why not incorporate the real explicitly into accounts – we know that these reals are constructed, as we know that our constructions embody the real. Either we can attempt to reflexively and textually interrogate and celebrate these narrative mutualities (or dialectics or strange loops), or we can occlude such mutualities through the stories we tell in the sure and certain knowledge that there are bound to be packs of readers out there waiting with baited breath to refuse the subject positions we have so carefully fashioned for them.

Critique from Postmodernity

The preceding section turned reflexivity upon itself to reveal the inescapability of politics, and the dependence upon the 'real' in the conduct of political struggles. In contrast, the present section suggests that insofar as the social constructionist movement can be brought under the rubric of postmodernism, then the reintroduction of a 'real' is allowable as an aesthetic (as well as political) option.

K. Gergen (1992) has outlined the parameters of a postmodern (social) psychology. If modernist psychology adheres to a commitment to a knowable world of mind or behaviour, the investigation of universal properties, the empirical method and a notion of research as progressive and knowledge as cumulative, with the postmodern turn, we find the focus shifts to linguistic resources and conventions, context, method as rhetoric and value-laden change. The immediate payoffs for social psychology include, according to Gergen, 'a professional investment in which the scholar attempts to de-objectify the existing realities, to demonstrate their social and historical embeddedness, and to explore their implications for social life' (p. 27). As a corollary, 'the psychologist is invited to conjoin the personal, the professional and the political' (p. 27). Examples of this are found in feminist psychology, social constructionist psychology, discourse analysis and rhetoric studies, social representations.

So, within its own social constructionist terms of reference, we can interpret Gergen's programmatic outline as the forging of an, albeit decentred, identity for the discipline. Now, if one of the defining parameters of the postmodern turn in social psychology is the importance assigned to language as the medium by which typically 'social psychological' phenomena are realized (e.g. Parker and Shotter, 1990; Shotter and Gergen, 1989; Potter and Wetherell, 1987; Parker, 1989), this has been aligned with the overt political purpose of changing prevailing conceptions of the human being and the social world. The constructive potency of language and this explicit generative intent (Gergen, 1982) suggest an important tension within postmodern social psychology. Postmodern social psychology, as with all 'sciences', produces texts (e.g. Latour and Woolgar, 1979) which have particular performative impact and constructive ramifications. More specifically, such texts can be said to project particular subject positions (e.g. Fairclough, 1989; Henriques et al., 1984) for the reader. If this is the case, what exactly is the subject position so projected, and how appropriate is it to the social, cultural and political aspirations of postmodern social psychology?

It is the stated aim of some theorists in social psychology to promote some alternative 'self' to the prevailing Western, modernist, self-contained individualized identity (e.g. Shotter and Gergen, 1989; Sampson, 1993). If the exact social route by which this strategic intervention by social psychologists might remain somewhat opaque, there nevertheless remains the use of the texts of postmodern social psychology. Despite their select audience, these writings can attempt to project a subject position that lies at some remove from the 'centrality and sovereignty of the individual' (Shotter and Gergen, 1989, p. ix).

One candidate for this contra-individualist alternative self can be derived from the analyses of several writers who, though they span a variety of disciplines and epochs, share a perception of the 'self' as altogether more dispersed and decentred. The following list of dichotomies reflects not only the range of terms and metaphors deployed to 'capture', or, more properly, construct, this dichotomy, it also suggests a narrative resource by which a postmodern alternative might be realized. As such, the array of oppositions can be seen as both descriptive, in that it maps out individualist/anti-individualist dichotomies, and prescriptive, in that it begins to promote the move from the modernist to postmodernist self. The terms on the left are individualist and modernist; the terms on the right are anti-individualist and postmodern: Apollonian/Dionysian (Nietzsche, 1956; Benedict, 1935); Discursive/Figural (Lyotard, 1971; Lash, 1988); Contemplative/Ecstatic (Baudrillard, 1983; Lash and Urry, 1987); Terminus/Communitas (Liminality) (Turner, 1969; Martin, 1981); molar (sedentary, root-ish)/ molecular (nomadic, rhizomic) (Deleuze and Guattari, 1984, 1988).

Though it is no doubt intellectually suspect to gather all these writers together within the space of half a paragraph, such close proximity nonetheless facilitates the derivation, with all due caution, of an aggregated contrast. The 'modernist' individual is 'self-controlled', unitary, discrete, orderly, oriented towards thought, language and representation. The postmodern is 'un-controlled', decentred, multiplicitous, transgressive, oriented towards affect, image and simulation.

In light of the political intent of postmodern social psychological texts, the question that arises is: to what extent do these writings not so much clarify the divide as actively project a postmodern subject position? In the present context, we compare the chapters by K. Gergen (1992) and M. Gergen (1992) in the volume, *Psychology and Postmodernism* (Kvale, 1992). In the former, the modernist subject position is retained: the chapter is eminently rational-ist in its form. In contrast, M. Gergen's chapter deploys just the sort of techniques which 'disorient' the modernist reader – indeed, they project a postmodern subject position (while simultaneously raising major reserva-tions about the political efficacy of the postmodern turn, especially for women).

However, the above comparison is too facile: the projected postmodern audience of M. Gergen's text does not preclude a modernist reading. Indeed, if the postmodern penchant for irony and parody are being 'inculcated' in some way, then an ironic reading can be made of a postmodern text which renders it modernist. Thus, the 'real meaning' behind the overt textual and formal pyrotechnics is that parody, irony and transgression are 'good' things, or that 'anti-representation' can be profoundly addressed, not to say repre-sented (Latour, 1988b). The point of this is that, within the postmodern, modernist positions are perfectly feasible. It is a question of what is priori-tized amongst the array of characteristics that delimits the postmodern. If the emphasis falls primarily upon the linguistic turn, then the suggested inter-penetration of the modern and the postmodern is highly problematic: the modern is bracketed by virtue of its neglect of the linguistic turn and its abid-ing foundationalism. If, however, transgression (irony, parody, heterogeneity, etc.) is highlighted, the interweaving of postmodern and modern seems a legitimate, and perhaps, inevitable development. It is an interweaving that corrupts the boundaries of the 'real' and the constructed, the human and the nonhuman, and the social and the non-social.

So, to continue to engage critically with the postmodern project as articu-lated above, what is needed is a transgression of disciplinary boundaries that is generalized beyond the humanities, arts and social sciences; there should be a venturing into the natural sciences. In other words, the 'natural' can be inte-grated into the postmodern project. The next chapter outlining actor-network theory suggests one route towards this. In the present instance, we can point to the work of Donna Haraway (e.g. 1989, 1991) as an example of an attempt to interweave the multiplicity of levels, narratives, characters and discourses into a single text that seeks neither resolution nor hierarchy. In her 1989 book *Primate Visions*, Haraway attempts to unravel the way that primatology – in both its academic and its popularized incarnations – mediates and reflects the major themes in Western thought and practice: gender and family, race and colour, human and nonhuman, culture and nature, Western and non-Western. In doing this, she does not subordinate the personal (e.g. individuals' biogra-phies or career trajectories) to the structural (ideology, discourse, social position); she does not relegate the natural (e.g. the primates themselves) beneath the socially constructed. Stories, descriptions, accounts of both the natural and the construction of the natural are juxtaposed in a narrative mosaic that at once attempts to incorporate the natural as an autonomous, 'other-worldly' actor (cf. Haraway, 1992; Noske, 1989) while acknowledging its status as a social construction. But here we find a problem: Haraway's textual strategy is, as hinted, primarily one of juxtaposition. Now, this juxtaposition and the narrative leaps between registers are not simply matters of style: this is all an intellectually and politically proactive strategy. The purpose is overtly to problematize the divisions (between the natural and the social, for instance) that one finds loitering at the heart of (Western, white, middle-class, masculinist) social science.

If such a textual activity places into sharp contrast these various modes of social scientific explication, description and explanation, it nevertheless does not fully problematize their integrity – Haraway does not consider as fully as she might do the transformation of actors, from the social to the non-social, the human to the nonhuman, the micro to macro, and back again. In contrast, as we shall see, actor-network theory's stories also accommodate actors or actants that range from the subatomic to the macrosocial. However, in contrast to Haraway's work, actor-network theory, not always convincingly, attempts to help us understand how these differently sized, differently constituted actors relate to one another – how, indeed, small actors become big ones, how small actors are kept small, how non-social actors are rendered non-social, how all actors are heterogeneous networks incorporating both the human and the nonhuman. Indeed, according to Latour (1993), such hybrids (or what Haraway calls cyborgs) have always been around in modernity. Modernity has been fundamentally concerned to purify these monsters, to disaggregate them into their ostensibly component, neatly categorized parts. Thus, we moderns have routinely indulged in dualism; for example, we have represented nature as transcendent, while society is seen to be our free construction. Yet, beneath all this activity of purification, the hybrids – the quasi-objects – have been multiplying at alarming rates. Postmodernism has, Latour assures us, partially sensitized us to this process: it has fundamentally problematized the structuring role of nature, but has ended up rejecting science as a result. However, by acknowledging that 'Nature itself is no longer natural' (p. 134) we can move closer to science in action – that is, we can begin to show how scientific activity is integral to the production of these heterogeneous networks and hybrids. As a result, our stories about identity and social ordering, in order to accommodate postmodern plurality, need also to be (re)populated with nonhuman actors.

Critique from a Possible History of Disciplines

As I have mentioned in the introduction, the histories (or perhaps more accurately, the lineages) of social constructionism tend to be intellectualist. Despite avowals to the contrary, social constructionism is regularly represented as an improvement on cognitivist or realist accounts – it does more ontological and epistemological justice to persons and social processes. In essence, it is as if the social contexts that conditioned the rises and falls in those sciences and human sciences – social contexts which social constructionism has extensively laid bare – did not apply to social constructionism itself. We might then ask: What are the conditions that have led to the emergence of social constructionism?

What are the specific ideological, moral, political etc. contexts which have enabled social constructionism to be manifested in so many different fields, in so many different versions?

Fortunately, there are emerging attempts to explore the disciplinarity of social psychology from a constructionist perspective. For example, the work of Jim Good (1993) shows how efforts to forge social psychology as an inter-disciplinary project were hampered by pre-existing disciplinary commitments (to psychology or sociology). However, in the present case, it is more impor-tant to reflect on how the nonhuman has been marginalized in social constructionist accounts. Here we can draw on Horigan's analysis which addresses how it was that the 'natural' was variously differentiated from the 'social' in an attempt by social anthropologists to separate anthropology from its parent disciplines of biology and natural philosophy. The long-term result, according to Horigan, is that there has been a privileging of social fac-tors to the extent that the influence of natural factors upon human social behaviour and structures, by and large, has been bracketed (cf. also Ingold, 1989; Noske, 1992, argues a similar point in relation to 'anthropocentrism' of the social sciences). Horigan's point is that we cannot assume that the prior-itization of the social is not historically contingent – that it has intrinsic to it some emancipatory potential. (There are, of course, various attempts to ground liberatory or radical accounts of human conduct and potentiality in biology (for example, Kropotkin, 1939; also, for a more recent attempt see Dickens, 1992).) However, the tendency here is to objectify nature – to attribute to it a more or less unproblematic reality. In other words, we can show how social constructionism is socially constructed, this time not only in an abstract reflexive turn that suggests such scrutiny for *a priori* reasons of consistency, but also in relation to a more or less detailed study of the growth of the roots of contemporary social constructionism.

Horigan (1988) traces how culture has become 'the object of the human sci-ences . . . [which] . . . stress and defend the autonomy of culture as a uniquely human realm resting essentially on the ability of humans to impose meaning on the world through the use of symbols' (p. 4). This (continuing) prioritiza-tion, originally a concern of the anthropologist Franz Boas, was linked to an effort to separate the categories of culture and race, to defend a view of cul-tural phenomena as things that 'could only be understood in terms of culture' (p. 5). The strategic aim was to undercut the premise of eugenics and racial anthropology and to attack the associated perception that the 'cultural and historical achievements of a people were a product of their racial composi-tion' (p. 5). In the process, anthropology was to establish itself as a 'theoretically independent institution'. Horigan goes on to examine how this initial groundwork facilitated later efforts by such anthropologists as Kroeber, White, Lévi-Strauss and Sahlins to 'proclaim culture as an independent level of reality, championing the cause of anthropology as an academic discipline' (p. 19). In sum, Horigan identifies how these advocates of the autonomy of culture deploy a metaphysical distinction between nature and culture in order to ground and demarcate their discipline. The general point, and it is one that is well illustrated on a much less grandiose scale in SSK, is that these divisions and rifts are not purely epistemological – rather, they are also matters of more or less parochial political (institutional) struggles.

The point is that the sort of story Horigan has told about anthropology can potentially be paralleled in social constructionist social psychology. The prioritization of the social – its 'autonomization' – is equally a matter of parochial struggles (as well as moves in the broader political terrain). The implication here is that such parochial struggles, insofar as they take hold, can end up closing off certain avenues of scholarship and thought, specifically those that take the 'nonhuman' seriously as something other than 'mere' social construction, while taking social constructionism very seriously indeed.

It is beyond the scope of the present volume to attempt to excavate the ways in which social constructionist social psychology has emerged. However, a brief consideration of the roots of the separation of the human and nonhuman (and the subsequent prioritization of the social in some arenas) is to be found in Latour's (1993) review of the work of Shapin and Schaffer (1985). Latour's basic insight is that Shapin and Schaffer, in their account of the struggle between Hobbes and Boyle to define science and its appropriate context, ultimately explain Boyle's triumph in terms of his efforts at doing politics. However, ironically, in so doing, they ultimately accept Hobbes' prioritization of the political sphere and the terms he has fashioned to inhabit that sphere – politics, interests, power. Here, then, we have a root of the categories that inform social constructionism that, when turned upon Boyle's constructionism, reproduce themselves. To this extent, Horigan's account suffers from the same malady – an un-reflexive prioritization of the social. Nevertheless, this does not mean that, even without avoiding the dangers that Latour identifies, it is infeasible to call for a critical history of the rise of subdisciplines that would scrutinize the social and institutional (and ultimately, following Latour, perhaps, the non-social and nonhuman) contexts in which the ideas of such figures as Wittgenstein, Austin, Barthes, Derrida, Foucault and Schutz could take so firm a hold. Nevertheless, such a programme of research by virtue of being, albeit so inadequately, sketched here problematizes the intellectualist, epistemologized, progressive form of the narrative that we find undergirds the culture of social constructionism, and raises the issue of the role of the non-social and nonhuman in the constitution of the social.

Critique from a (Speculative) Version of Contemporary Politics

The corollary of such a (realist and unreflexive) historical approach which addresses the contexts of emergence of social constructionism is an analysis of the contemporary pressures that have eroded or are in the process of eroding the priority of the social. Just as certain social conditions and parochial political exigencies have facilitated the prioritization of the social and the cultural, so we might expect the emergence of mirror conditions to produce a realignment, if not rapprochement, between the social, human and natural sciences with their various 'objects' of study.

For example, recently, Benton (1991) has concerned himself with the historicity of what he perceives as the re-emergence of 'nature' on the social science agenda. In other words, he has attempted to identify some of the pressures placed upon the social/biological divide and the dichotomies that characterize it (mind/body, culture/nature, society/biology, meaning/cause, human/animal) by contemporary social movements such as feminism and environmentalism. These political interests, fundamentally concerned as they are with the role that 'nature' has to play in constituting and delimiting present-day social dynamics, are not satisfied with purely sociological explanations and characterizations. The limits of the 'body' and of the 'environment' also need to be taken into some sort of account. Benton is very circumspect in his recommendations, but his case nevertheless rests on the assumption that social scientific researchers are sensitive to such political trends. This is not unwarranted – many such researchers have long been committed to justice in one form or another, and as more or less active members in new social movements, one might expect that they will respond to the environmental concerns of their lay peers (cf. Eyerman and Jamison, 1991).

However, there are also other, less altruistic dimensions to these developments that mirror the parochial politics mentioned above. One story of the contemporary political/economic context of British academia with which we might conjure tells us of funds made available for research in Global Environmental Change. It tells us of the 1988 speeches by the then Prime Minister, Margaret Thatcher, to the Royal Society and to the Conservative Party conference which sought to align Conservative 'traditionalism with conservation' (Yearley, 1991, p. 1). It tells of the responses by numerous agencies, including the research councils responsible for funding research in universities, in forming, in 1990, the UK Inter-Agency Committee on Global Environmental Change. As its most recent overview and projection of the UK national programme of research into global environmental change (UK Global Environmental Research Office, 1993) notes, there is a need 'to foster interdisciplinary collaboration. . . . it is vital that mechanisms are found to remove barriers and provide incentives for collaboration if advances are to be made' (p. 42). To the extent that this will lead to funds being made available for such interdisciplinary collaboration, we might expect social scientists, constructionists among them, to be inevitably, especially under the competitive circumstances prevailing in the UK university sector, drawn into formulating inter-disciplinary research projects. I am not suggesting that such workers will abandon their epistemological commitments at the drop of a research grant cheque. However, it is possible to imagine that such commitments will be questioned as constructionists, say, are exposed to traditional positivist approaches turned to ostensibly good ends (saving the planet), or as they are persuaded and enrolled by traditionally more 'powerful' or better resourced natural scientists. For example, Steven Yearley's 1991 volume, *The Green Case*, is caught on the horns of this dilemma, on the one hand arguing that environmental problems are social constructs, and on the other unproblematically accepting the reality of these problems when, for example, addressing the predicaments of developing countries faced with the choice between economic modernization and environmental integrity.

In contrast to this concatenation of different epistemologies, it is, of course, also possible to imagine a polarization between disciplines, and a retrenchment of epistemologies as differing 'standards of evidence' clash and as the very character of the problem cannot be agreed upon (cf. Robbins and Johnson, 1976; Gillespie et al., 1979). Nevertheless, the point is that such commitments can be 'compromised', or 're-oriented' as other interests, such as the need to secure research funds or the desire to contribute to environmental movements or policy formulation, become more prominent.

It should be stressed that such interdisciplinarity is not epistemologically motivated, it is opportunistic. Moreover, it is ad hoc. The document mentioned above suggests that research into Global Environmental Change will, in the light of limited resources, need to be focused. Such focusing does not necessarily facilitate coherence across the area. By way of analogy, we can turn to Turner's (1992) remarks in relation to interdisciplinarity in the medical sciences which are likewise constrained by resources. Here, alliances between disciplines are rather 'the unintended consequences of economic necessities than a consciously selected epistemological goal' (p. 139). The resulting ad hocery constitutes a 'fragmented and decentralized scientific landscape' (p. 139). Turner likens this to the type of scientific world implied by postmodernism. Each pocket of research operates with locally negotiated standards, compromises and intellectual innovation.

The point to the above discussion is that national (and international) political and economic networks can foster interdisciplinary alliances. The sorts of association that social scientists generally, and social constructionists in particular, enter into – both as politically responsible actors and as practising academics faced with an increasing entrepreneurial research culture – will set up conditions for pragmatically breaking down disciplinary divisions. If such is the case, we might expect the 'natural', the 'nonhuman' and the 'non-social' to become increasingly something other than mere targets for deconstruction.

Now, the present volume could be seen as a version of this process. However, the way I have narrated this remains oriented towards the social. It is still social constructionist insofar as I have stressed the constitutive role of the social. In advocating the rehabilitation of the 'non-social' and the 'non-human', I should have supplemented my version of contemporary (academic) politics with a version of the emergent environmental conditions. In other words, I should have ascribed some role to the 'non-social' and 'nonhuman' in the breakdown of the disciplinary boundaries: an account in which the 'non-social' and 'nonhuman' have been instrumental in deprioritizing the social. However, I do not want to end up reifying the 'non-social' – attributing to it the status of 'real'. Rather, as will become clearer in the next chapter and in Chapter 7, the 'non-social' can be a narrative character in our accounts – this, as with social characters, does not render it fictitious. Such a character might be mysterious and it might be 'other worldly', but it is nonetheless an intervening actor. However, this might smack of something like critical realism. In the next section, I want to clarify some of the differences between the current actor-network perspective and that of the broad school of (critical) realism.

Real Differences and Different 'Reals'

In the preceding sections I have argued that there are good aesthetic, historical and political reasons why the 'nonhuman' and 'non-social' should not be excluded from our accounts of the construction of identity. At the same time, I have stressed that such an incorporation needs to be reflexive and circumspect. This concern with the 'non-social' has been expressed by other commentators as well, especially those drawn to critical realism. In this section, I simply want to consider some of the points of difference – conceptual and political – between actor-network theory and the array of endeavours that fall under the general rubric of realism.

Realism (e.g. Bhaskar, 1989; Greenwood, 1992; Parker, 1992) has been concerned to posit the existence of a transcendental (or intransitive) ontological realm of causal generative mechanisms. This stands in contrast to the transitive realm, the epistemological domain in which the world is 'observed' or 'described' – but not in any simple empiricist or positivist sense. Rather, critical realists are generally willing to acknowledge that such 'data' is constituted through social practices. This separation rests on an acknowledgement of an epistemic fallacy that pervades much philosophy of science – that is, it is not legitimate to define something solely in terms of our knowledge of it. The aim is to allow for the possibility of understanding the world in order to change it – the critical realist project is fundamentally concerned to contribute to the process of emancipation.

There are two points I wish to make in relation to the criticisms that are mobilized against social constructionism and its supposed relativism from the perspective of critical realism. I choose these two because they serve to illuminate further actor-network theory. Greenwood (1992) argues that 'the undoubted fact that psychological discourse can be employed to serve all kinds of social functions, such as excusing, does not constitute any argument in support of the denial of the descriptive role of psychological ascriptions' (p. 139). Greenwood's rhetorical moves can be comprehensively deconstructed (Potter, 1992) to show how it is possible to ensure that 'realism remains one good story' (p. 172). Such a move shows that the discursive work of critical realists remains necessarily entrenched in the messy transitive world. This is in keeping with other social constructionist responses which contest the 'analytic usefulness' of an intransitive dimension, preferring to retain a focus upon the transitive as this is, to put it crudely, where the (only) action is (Shotter, 1992, 1993; Fay, 1990; Stenner and Eccleston, 1994). However, this does not necessarily render such constructionists averse to positing some sort of real. Thus, for example, Stenner and Eccleston endorse a (reflexive) metaphysics of textuality; and Shotter (1993) and Harré (1992) base their versions of social constructionism on the ontological privileging of the conversation.

Here, I want to briefly interrogate Harré's (1992) transcendental conditions for the possibility of discursive practice. If discourse must create and sustain persons, do these necessarily have to take human form? If discourse is person-produced in joint action, what happens if we impute to 'natural entities' the status of persons? If the 'real for social constructionism, properly formulated [*sic*] . . . must be whatever is intransigent to individual desires (and that is) the human conversation' (Harré, 1992, p. 157), what happens when we suggest, following Latour (1988a, pp. 158, 166), that non-human actors offer their own gradients of resistance in the process of interaction with others (whether humans or not)? The point is that such transcendental conditions do not preclude other 'reals', properly formulated. Moreover, insofar as 'persons' are created and sustained in discourse, we might expect that in the process of conversation there are certain exclusions – those who remain constitutionally uninvited to participate – non-persons. Sometimes these non-persons are humans and sometimes they are nonhumans. The point here is that this conversation–discourse–person nexus is a subset of broader processes of construction which involve interaction through media other than the linguistic and which nonetheless yield the regularities of identity. Whether these come to be constituted as something like the conversation–discourse–person nexus is a matter of further negotiation and/or struggle (see Chapter 7).

Knorr-Cetina (1988) likewise gives analytic priority to the interactional situation, but this time in the context of the macro–micro controversy in sociology. Methodological situationism is seen by Knorr-Cetina as the appropriate way to theorize the way in which the macro is rooted in the micro, specifically through the way negotiating, that is to say, broadly political, actors situationally accomplish representations of the macro. Obviously, the macro refers to the macrosociological – the state, classes, epistemes and the like. However, what happens if we broaden the interactants in the micro-situation to include nonhumans who contribute not only to the generation of representations of macrosocial entities, but also to the representation of macro-natural entities? Again, here we prioritize the micro-situation but one that can be construed as incorporating numerous, so far neglected nonhuman 'characters'.

The other supposed advantage of critical realism is that it feeds into a broadly socialist emancipatory project. This assumes that such a real serves to anchor critique, and that the relativism of social constructionism disables critique (Parker, 1992). However, there are various responses to this. Firstly, as Stenner and Eccleston (1994) note, much social constructionism has directly engaged in political critique of one form or another on the level of content (e.g. racism, sexism, heterosexism, etc.). Secondly, social constructionism (e.g. Collins and Yearley, 1992a) can claim that it is directly concerned to expose the contingency of powerful, accredited knowledges. In yet other instances, critique is grounded in the form of the approach. For example, Billig's (1991) rhetorical psychology deploys an explicitly utopian model of communication (not unlike the Habermasian ideal speech situation) as a site from which to engage in critique. To the extent that this could be interpreted as a symptom of relativism, it should be remembered that utopianism is not alien to other modes of critique, for instance, Marxist critical theory (Held, 1980) and Foucault's work (Anderson, 1983). Thus, Billig, in deflecting the accusation of relativism, points to the existence of a utopian vision at the heart of his rhetorical social psychology when he writes:

> The rhetorical turn . . . is neither a flight from argument, nor an abandonment of ideological critique. . . . a moral vision can be placed at the centre of the rhetorical perspective to enable such critique. The turn to rhetoric can be formulated as a celebration of argument. At its core can be placed the utopian vision of everyday philosophers arguing in conditions of enjoyment and freedom, with their arguments soured neither by stupidity nor by the social conditions of distortion. (Billig, 1991, p. 26).

Actor-network theory certainly is concerned to disentangle the ways that the 'powerful' become so, but it does this by attempting to reveal the heterogeneous materials and processes which are mobilized by certain actors to persuade others, to shape them as particular sorts of beings with particular sorts of interests, properties and knowledges. However, what these 'powerful' (and 'powerless') are – what their make-up is, their distributed-ness across networks, the extent to which they straddle the boundaries of the human and the nonhuman, the degree to which they can be afforded 'rights' or 'worth' and so on (and 'who' does the affording) – is seen as a matter of historical contingency and argument and struggle. In the process, actor-network theory reveals how things might have been otherwise; it is from this exposition of contingency that critique derives. As we will see in the next chapter, actor-network theory attempts to develop an explicit theory of power, even if its analysis of domination remains underdeveloped. For the moment, it will suffice to note that, in common with social constructionist defences against the charge of relativism, we as actor-network analysts are not immune to the moral currency of our own networks – it is not a case of anything goes. However, what we come to see as the 'dominated', how and why, are issues that we have to address very carefully.

Conclusion

This chapter has presented a series of sympathetic critiques of social constructionism. The aim has not been to set up some absolute divide between social constructionism and actor-network theory, or to claim that the latter marks a substantive intellectual advance over the former. Rather, in the spirit of John Law's (1994) modest sociology, Bruno Latour's (1993) refusal of denunciation, and following the precedent nicely articulated by Hilary Rose (1993), I have attempted to exercise a both/and (as opposed to either/or), or a 'well, why not?', narrative structure. That is to say, I have tried to argue the case that social constructionism turned upon itself opens up some further avenues of exploration, specifically, a consideration of the constitutive role of the 'nonhuman' and 'non-social'.

4

Constructing Actor-Network Theory

In the previous chapter, I provided a number of critiques of social constructionism. Particular emphasis was placed on the following. Firstly, I argued
that social constructionism did not adequately address its own roots, and, in
particular, the rationale behind the prioritization of the social and the exclusion of the non-social. I implied that actor-network theory was better
equipped to deal with the non-social and the nonhuman – to integrate them
into an analytical framework that attends to the mutual construction of the
social and the non-social, the human and the nonhuman. Secondly, I suggested that while social constructionism was keenly sensitive to the uses of
linguistic resources in the production of identity, these tended to be situated
in such diffuse locations as 'culture', 'ideology' and language. In contrast,
ANT, partly in keeping with its Foucauldian roots, attempts to trace these to
their institutional and social, albeit contingent, origins in particular actors
(like scientists or scientific organizations). Moreover, ANT, by situating the
adoption (and rejection) of identities in the context of relations of power, to
some extent resolves the tensions between the different components and units
(micro, meso and macro) that make up the linguistic context that resources
the construction of identity (see Chapter 2). This is because ANT looks at the
ways that the adoption of particular identities or roles serves the goals of others (the enroller) – others who might be macro, meso or micro actors – which
require regularities in behaviour/action for the continuation of the network.
However, as we shall also see, such a process cannot adequately deal with
'betrayal' – when once accepted identities are rejected – or with the implicit
tensions and contradictions in the discourses of identity that such betrayal
might point to.

   In this chapter, I introduce ANT, pointing along the way to some of the
continuities and differences between ANT, its precursors and its others. Thus,
for example, at one point I will suggest that ANT is part of a longstanding,
though fragmented tradition of the theorization of power, perhaps best
embodied by Foucault. My main aim, however, is to detail some of the prime
theoretical components of ANT and illustrate these with examples from the
ANT literature. Inevitably, given the fact that ANT has been a rapidly developing perspective, and given the sometimes disparate emphases of its
proponents, the overview I give is necessarily simplified – which is another
way of saying that this is, inevitably, a constructed portrayal. This will set the
context against which, in the next two chapters, I show how ANT may aid in
the analysis of identity. The structure of the chapter is as follows: initially, I

will spell out some of the key tenets and analytic tools that have characterized ANT. Then I will trace some of the implications, weaknesses and modifications of ANT in relation to three inter-related issues (or sets of issues). These are: firstly, power, agency and marginality; secondly, network durability, ordering and the relation of ANT to micro–macro debates; thirdly, the status of the nonhumans ('technological' and 'natural') in the (re)production of networks. I will finally consider some of the ramifications of the foregoing discussions for the study of identity.

ANT: Tenets, Principles and Terms

Some of ANT's roots lie in the Sociology of Scientific Knowledge (SSK) and yet it departs markedly from the latter's immediate concerns. If some of the practitioners of SSK have been primarily concerned to consider the ways that the constitution of scientific knowledge is through and through pervaded by human interests ('cognitive', professional, institutional, cultural, social and so on), it has also tended to focus upon the ways that these find expression in the practice of science, at the laboratory bench and amongst scientific communities engaged in disputation. Consequently, there has been a profound excavation of the range of resources that scientists bring to bear in their negotiations: discourses, rhetorics, representations. Mainly, these resources have concerned the science itself (e.g. what is to count as a 'real replication') and other scientists (e.g. who is to count as a 'trustworthy, reputable scientist'). Less prominent has been a concern with the way that such disputes also entail the mobilization of other sorts of materials and actors, the organization and arrangement of key allies (although see Latour and Woolgar, 1979; Knorr-Cetina, 1981). These allies might belong to what we would normally count as 'the world of science' – for example, experimental materials and equipment. Alternatively (or complementarily), they might reside beyond its borders – for example, consumers, funders, public supporters and the like. It is one of the key strengths of ANT that it has been able to map how the position of scientists (and their ability to generate 'truth') rests upon their capacity to align a whole range of disparate or heterogeneous elements – as such, science is to be viewed as spanning both the putative 'scientific' and the putative 'non-scientific'.

As a corollary to this, it becomes important for sociologists to recognize that they themselves are no less subject to these processes. They do not stand outside looking in on science, pointing, in some disinterested way, to the interests that animate scientists. They too are harnessing resources to make their own social scientific explanations stand up to scrutiny (Latour, 1981). Scientists are engaged in an 'autosociology' whereby they use social and personal factors to go about their work; for sociologists, rather than prejudging what these might be, the aim would be to follow scientists as they go about their everyday business of simultaneously imputing ideological corruption to colleagues and laypersons and conducting experiments, and as they set up boundaries through which the former is hidden and only the latter appears. The point is to treat scientists in their entirety and to ensure that, in the process, the sociologist does not, by default or design, end up occupying the epistemological high ground.

How then are actor-network theorists to go about this? One strategy is to articulate principles which guarantee that scientists are not analytically over-simplified. Thus, the actor-network perspective rests on three tenets (Callon, 1986a): generalized agnosticism – analytic impartiality as to whatever actors are involved in controversy; generalized symmetry – the use of an abstract and neutral vocabulary to understand the conflicting viewpoints of actors, entities or actants (these terms will be used interchangeably); free association – the repudiation of *a priori* distinctions between the social and the natural or the technological. Within this metatheoretical framework, scientists are treated not simply as scientists but as multifaceted entrepreneurs who with skill and aplomb engage in activities that might otherwise be deigned political, sociological or economic, as well as those practices tradi-tionally assigned the label 'scientific'. Thus, they harness a multiplicity of humans and nonhumans, materials and techniques to extend their influence beyond the laboratory. They must engage in what Law (1987) calls 'heteroge-neous engineering'. To do this they must enrol others. ANT has evolved a variety of terms with which to conceptualize this process.

At a general level is interressement – 'actions by which an entity attempts to impose and stabilize the identity of other actors it defines through its problematization' (Callon, 1986a, pp. 207–8). In other words, one actor raises issues about the identities of other actors. A statement which captures this process might have the following form: 'You have identity X (you are fisher-men or farmers), yet you are hampered from fully realizing that identity (ensuring fish stocks, protecting your flocks).' Furthermore, interressement encompasses a variety of strategies and mechanisms by which one entity – whether that be an individual like Pasteur (Latour, 1988a), a small group like the three biological researchers of St Brieuc Bay (Callon, 1986a) or an insti-tution like the Electricité de France (Callon, 1986b) – attempts to 'corner' and enrol other entities such as scientists, publics, institutions, scallops and elec-trons. This is achieved by interposing oneself between the target entity and its pre-existing associations with other entities that contribute to its identity. Only with the successful disconnection from these other associations can enrolment be said to have, albeit temporarily, succeeded.

However, enrolment is not a unilateral process of imposition: it entails both the 'capturing' of the other and the other's 'yielding'. It is a multilateral process. For Latour (1986) power is not a possession, but an arrangement of assent: '"Power" is always the illusion people get when they are obeyed. . . . [they] discover what their power is really made of when they start to lose it. . . . it was "made of" the wills of all the others. . . . power [is] a consequence and not a cause of collective action' (pp. 268–9). I will return to the issue of power below.

Enrolment has been fleshed out through a consideration of a variety of other concepts which examine how it is that some entities are in the thrall of others. Translation is the means by which one entity gives a role to others, from the macrosociological to the subatomic. In other words, through these moments of translation, actor A defines actor B; as analysts, in investigating such a process 'we have to define the medium' by which such translations occur (Callon, 1991, p. 141). To put it another way, the translator sets itself up as their spokesperson.

Following Michael (1994), this can be summarized, albeit simplistically, in the following quasi-syllogism:

> This is what you really want to be. (Interressement)
> We are the ones who can help you become that. (Translation)
> Grant your obedience by your own consent. (Enrolment)

If these identities are to take hold, then also necessary is the invention of a geography of 'obligatory points of passage': for those elements and entities that wish to continue to exist and develop, and which the enrolling entity wishes to enrol, then such points constitute unavoidable conduits – what we might call narrative bottlenecks – through which they must pass in order to articulate both their identity and their *raison d'être*. Another mode of translation is displacement: this refers to the ways in which entities organize and structure the movement of materials, resources and information. By the organization of meetings, the making and maintaining of contacts, and the carrying out of experiments, an actor can accumulate just those materials that render its actor-network more durable. But these accumulations need to be rendered invisible, made natural and unproblematic. In other words, their internal workings – the ways in which different materials have had to be calibrated, organized, aligned, coordinated – are made invisible. They are constituted as 'black boxes' whereby 'no matter how controversial their history, how complex their inner workings, how large the commercial or academic networks that hold them in place, only their input and output count' (Latour, 1987, p. 3; Callon and Latour, 1981). The prime sites where such invisibilities take shape are what Latour calls 'centres of calculation' where the heterogeneous elements are brought together. Such bringing together is textual – representations in the forms of 'specimens, maps, diagrams, logs, questionnaires and paper forms of all sorts' (Latour, 1987, p. 232) are gathered and combined. It is the visibility – the two-dimensionality – of these inscriptions that is, according to Latour (1987, 1990), their key property. It enables the merging of figures, numbers, graphs – essentially, more and more events can be condensed into simpler and simpler representations. The aim of the actor-network analyst is then to disassemble this 'cascade' of ever-simplified inscriptions that lead to harder and harder facts, and greater and greater costs for anyone aiming to dissect them (see also Latour, 1983; Scott, 1991).

These inscriptions also have another property – they are resilient. Now, the processes of enrolment are particularly problematic when they are conducted across longer distances. One of the prime modes by which the disruptive potential of distance is combated is that of the immutable mobile (Latour, 1987). The immutable mobile is a text – writing, graphs, figures, formulae – which can be moved, remains stable, and is combinable with other such texts. It facilitates the capacity of particular actors (mainly scientists) to centralize and monopolize such meanings at centres of calculation, such as laboratories, where these materials, traces and so on can be tied together. But it is also important to note that the immutability of such mobiles is still contingent on the network. It is 'relational' as Law (1994) puts it. In other words, their undisputed potency is nevertheless an effect of the state of the network.

By the state of the network, I mean the extent to which it is unproblematic and where identities, roles, black boxes and so on proceed without hiccup – that is to say, where the durability of the network is relatively assured. Callon (1991) has directly addressed the issue of durability by elaborating such notions as intermediaries, actors and convergence. Thus, an intermediary is 'anything passing between actors which defines the relationship between them' (p. 134) and this can include 'scientific articles, computer software, disciplined human bodies, technical artefacts, instruments, contracts and money' (p. 134). Such intermediaries compose, order and form the medium of the network they describe – 'they define and distribute roles to humans and nonhumans' (p. 137). But such intermediaries are usually hybrids in the sense that they are mixtures of texts, artefacts, human bodies and money. For example, we can describe a typical household item – the washing machine – as a text of instructions, an economic status (having the funds to service the debt and cover the costs), a disciplined body (living in a relatively small social unit) and so on. The articulation of these facets echoes the multilayered meaning of the washing machine: it can be decomposed so that it 'points back' to the network beyond the machine itself, the network which renders it functional (banks, technologists, marketing executives, contemporary living arrangements). Thus, a washing machine at once reflects and mediates these other arrangements and associations. In such mediations, in setting up and reinforcing particular identities for 'washing-machine users', such an intermediary becomes an actor – what Callon defines as 'any entity able to associate texts, humans, nonhumans and money' (p. 140).

But as Callon goes on to ask, what, then, is the difference between 'actor' and 'intermediary'? What differentiates the idea of an 'actor' is that it is also an author – it is a point of action which brings together intermediaries to create a new generation of intermediaries. Actors are 'those who conceive, elaborate, circulate, emit or pension off intermediaries, and the division between actors and intermediaries is a purely practical matter' (p. 141). Accordingly, it is a matter of empirical investigation if we are to identify who/what is the entity by virtue of whose activities new intermediaries have arisen (or to which, at least, we can convincingly attribute authorship). Such actors can be humans, groups, institutions, nonhuman and so on; it is essentially a question of who/what can 'persuade' us that they comprise such a locus of agency (Law, 1994).

Through the authorship of actors, the movement of intermediaries and the processes of translation networks come to be durable. Such durability rests, Callon tells us, on 'convergence', where agreement is generated between elements in a network which work together despite their heterogeneity. Thus, where technicians, scientists, salespeople, computers, buildings and so on have complementary identities that are aligned and coordinated, the network that is their institution becomes more stable – indeed, it can begin to work as an actor in its own right. Callon further ventures that 'the more numerous and heterogeneous the interrelationships the greater the degree of network co-ordination and the greater the probability of resistance to alternative translation' (1991, p. 150). This is because such networks, as bundles of inter-relationships, have associations that are likely to be more tightly coupled: attempting to redefine any one element will lead to a major process of general retranslation with all the upheaval that that entails. (To introduce a markedly larger washing machine suggests redefining the user across family units, implies alternative finance arrangements, a redistribution of skills and so on.)

At this point, it is worth waylaying a suspicion that has no doubt arisen in the reader's mind: isn't what Callon et al. are doing simply redescription? Where there is the same old institution, Callon talks about durability. Where there are people working in and across groups, Callon muses about conver-gence. Where are the explanations that reveal to us those factors that yielded such institutions and underpinned their longevity? Redescription? Well, pos-sibly. But this is, after all, an attempt at developing a neutral vocabulary as a means of accessing the role played by heterogeneous entities (nonhumans as well as humans) in stabilizing the relationships that make up institutions and groups, and of being agnostic about the generic locus of agency/authorship that structures these associations. But, more importantly, such (re)descrip-tions aim to enter the interstices of a network, to show the work being done in order to generate associations. The point is not to appeal to some overar-ching, general analytic construct that will do all the necessary explaining (e.g. class, interests, pathology). Rather, the explanations that Callon, Law and Latour aim to provide are local, contingent, practical and reflect the character of the specific network under study. Thus, interests, rather than being mobilized as explanations that stand outside, animating the action so to speak (Bloor, 1976; Barnes, 1977; Shapin, 1988), are treated as relational; for Callon and Law (1982) they are what are locally 'induced' by certain actors in other actors with the aid of intermediaries. They may be used to explain a given event, or the network under scrutiny, but they do so contingently, for they themselves can be unravelled to reveal a whole set of enabling conditions (other actors, intermediaries and so on). As Latour (1988b) puts it: 'I am all for throw-away causes and one-off explanations' (p. 174). Such local expla-nations can only emerge in the description of the networks, but it has to be a description (or more accurately, a narration) that does not *a priori* disqualify certain actors and intermediaries from the list of *dramatis personae*.

While Callon addresses durability, he is of course aware that networks are always potentially unreliable. That is to say, particular traces, immutable mobiles, materials, technologies can suddenly become problematized (un-black-boxed). The roles and identities assigned by one entity to another may suddenly be challenged, undermined or shattered. Where once the 'enrolling' actor had organized the obligatory points of passage for others, it finds itself forced to traverse the obligatory points of passages that are now 'dictated' by others. And it is not only social others who intervene; the heterogeneity of the networks means that any entity can begin to step out of semiotic character within the network – electrons, microbes, scallops, the Atlantic.

The preceding discussion has been somewhat abstract, not to say abstruse. For the rest of this section, therefore, I will illustrate ANT with some case studies. As a first example, we can draw upon Callon's classic (1986a) study of the scallops, researchers and fishing community of St Brieuc Bay. The researchers attempted to construct an actor-network in which they narrated the roles of the component actors. Thus, the local fishermen were represented as fundamentally interested in restocking and sustainably farming the local scallop beds; the scallops were represented, through various scientific techniques, as potentially cultivable; and the relevant scientific community was represented as an assenting constituency which underscored the researchers' expertise and competence. So, as regards the fishermen, the scientists 'translated' them into persons who wanted to ensure sustainable harvests of scallops. In the process, the scientists set themselves and their experiments as obligatory points of passage – for the fishermen to realize the goal of sustainable scallop yields, they had to give of their consent and invest their trust in, and demonstrate their support for, the plans and expertise of the researchers. However, this subsequent 'power' of the scientists could only endure as long as each of the actors in the researchers' network played their allotted parts, and as long as their techniques of larval cultivation remained black-boxed. For instance, when the fishermen betrayed the scientists by, contrary to their supposed long-term aims and corollary identity, fishing to the point of decimating the scallop beds, then it was no longer feasible for the three scientists to claim to represent the interests of the fishermen. Their 'power' (or rather their relation of power to the fishermen) was dissipated. Likewise, when the scallop larvae levels became hopelessly low, the stories the researchers could tell about themselves as competent scientists and cultivators became subverted. In sum, the relations of power they had so assiduously cultivated, dispersed and decentred across the network as they were, became catastrophically undermined.

Another classic example of ANT is Callon's (1986b) analysis of the efforts at network building by the Electricité de France. In 1973, the Electricité de France produced a plan documenting the need for an electric vehicle. In order to make this a viable proposition, in other words, in order to enrol the necessary actors, the Electricité de France had to define both those actors and the context of which the electric vehicle itself and those other actors were a part. Thus, it represented recent social history in terms of the urban post-industrial consumers and new social movements that attacked the internal combustion engine-driven car on the basis of associated pollution and noise levels, and its pivotal position in a discredited consumer society. Electric propulsion would overcome all these concerns, the Electricité de France argued. In the process, the Electricité de France defined the roles of a range of actors: consumers; Renault who would build the chassis; the Government which would institute favourable regulations and subsidies; the public transport companies. But these are all social actors: the Electricité de France also demarcated the roles to be played by nonhumans such as electrolytes, accumulators and batteries. If these technological actors did not also play their roles, the whole network would disintegrate. Each of these elements was necessary to the Electricité de France's actor-network and, for each one, the Electricité de France acted as their spokesperson. As a result, to realize their new-found identities these entities had to pass through what was effectively a geography of obligatory points of passage: the Electricité de France's proposed network constituted a series of loops through which target actors needed to pass. To get rid of pollution, it was necessary to develop the electric vehicle; to produce the electric vehicle, it was necessary to invent new fuel cells; to invent these cells, it was necessary to conduct experiments at the Electricité de France's laboratories. In the end, the Electricité de France would become the central obligatory point of passage for those other actors that, in its network, have been represented as committed to reducing pollution. But in order for the Electricité de France to achieve the pivotal status of spokesperson and obligatory point of passage, it had to translate and displace the surrounding actors. By putting into circulation a variety of texts (such as memos, reports, surveys and scientific papers), by orchestrating meetings and symposia, and by controlling the movement of moneys and relevant materials, it aimed to render itself central and its network more stable.

Callon shows that essential to the Electricité de France's efforts is the black-boxing of the constituents of its network. Entities were simplified in the Electricité de France's representations: no longer in complex flux, they were reduced by means of translation into a simpler set of characteristics. Moreover, by judiciously juxtaposing the various entities, their roles became more clearly defined. Renault, fuel cells, electric vehicle – each was demarcated in the context of the other. So, Renault came to be simplified from a major car manufacturer into a chassis builder, and fuel cells were reduced into perfectly functioning power units. Yet behind these lay complex networks. Renault wanted to remain a major car manufacturer, it disputed Electricité de France's representation of consumers' need for electric vehicles – perhaps they would prefer better public, petrol-engined transport? In the process, Renault resisted its identification with a particular social future in which the internal combustion engine had but the tiniest role. Thus, the simplification of 'fuel cells' served to occlude the struggles of the scientists and technologists, the behaviour of electrons and the longevity of platinum. It was when these actors' resistance was tested that their composition revealed itself as complex and multiple. In the laboratory, the fuel cells turned out to be less effective than in the Electricité de France's attempted actor-network – the struggling scientists and the sometimes unpredictable electrons that constituted the 'fuel cells' were suddenly exposed when the fuel cells proved to be recalcitrant. Further, Renault contested the Electricité de France's social history and cultural projections; in the process, Renault announced itself to be comprised of politically astute technologists, as well as car manufacturers and chassis builders. In the end, the Electricité de France's network fell apart.

As mentioned above, as a development of SSK, ANT is interested in looking at the social and political resources that allow scientists to become so powerful in order to show that this power is not the inexorable outcome of science's technical and intellectual monopoly of the 'truth'. However, clearly, the ANT perspective can be applied to associations between actors who are not so directly concerned with overt science: parents and children, state and civil society, church and worshippers, doctor and patient, and so on. In particular, it aims at addressing the links between identity and power and the techniques by which these links are mediated to produce sociotechnical change. However, there are various underdeveloped aspects within ANT. The following section deals with a number of these.

Power, Agency and Marginality

Power

There are certain continuities between ANT's and Foucauldian understandings of power and, beyond that, the work of Etienne de La Boétie. As the above quote from Latour (1986) shows, power is an outcome, not a cause. As he later notes:

> No matter how much power one appears to accumulate, it is always necessary to obtain it from others who are doing the action . . . . Thus it is always necessary to redefine who is acting, why it is necessary to act together, what are the boundaries of the collective, how responsibility should be allocated . . . . (p. 276)

This issue of the two-way-ness of power finds an elementary expression in that proto-anarchist tract, *The Discourse of Voluntary Servitude* (1975) written by La Boétie probably in 1552 or 1553. As Rothbard notes in his introduction:

> . . . every tyranny must necessarily be grounded upon general popular acceptance. In short, the people themselves, for whatever reason, acquiesce in their own subjection. If this were not the case, no tyranny, indeed, no government, could long endure . . . . The tyrant is but one person, and could scarcely command the obedience of another person, much less of an entire country, if most of the subjects did not grant their obedience by their own consent. (p. 13)

Now, Foucault treats power as 'positive'. By this, he aims to point to the way that power, through knowledge-producing discourses and practices such as those that operate in the context of medicine, psychiatry and psychoanalysis, the law, education, prisons and so on, constructs individuals with particular capacities and interests. As Foucault (1986; see also 1979a) puts it:

> The individual is not to be conceived as a sort of elementary nucleus, a primitive atom, a multiple and inert material on which power comes to fasten or against

which it happens to strike, and in so doing subdues or crushes individuals. In fact, it is already one of the prime effects of power that certain bodies, certain gestures, certain discourses, certain desires come to be identified and constituted as individuals. (p. 234)

As such, power pursues true knowledge – the truth about society, our bodies, our morality. This pursuit pervades society, seeping through the multiplicity of relations amongst people. To study such relations of power, it is necessary to interrogate the institutional sites at which power/knowledge relations function and develop: the hospital, the mental institution, the prison, the classroom, the courtroom. It is at these loci that we find the constitution of persons into what we recognize as 'modern individuals'. Starting from these local, detailed operations of power/knowledge, it is possible, Foucault argues, to 'ascend' to discover the 'centres' – how these local mechanisms are colonized, transformed and extended by more general mechanisms like the state or the bourgeoisie.

I will now try and draw out some of the differences and similarities between ANT and the following three perhaps more familiar perspectives on power: Gramsci's Marxism and specifically his notion of hegemony (1971); Lukes' (1974) three-dimensional formulation of power; and Gene Sharp's (1973) theory of power and criticisms of this by Martin (1989) and McGuinness (1993). The aim is to clarify ANT's conception of power.

Gramsci's (1971) notion of hegemony essentially holds that domination and order is always partial and contingent, primarily because these rest on the generation of alliances. These alliances, in turn, are not based on brute force, but on the integration of the other (the target group or subordinate class): there is a winning of consent through a dual process of concession and ideological indoctrination. This seems to be in keeping with the general perspective of ANT. The difference with Gramsci's view and that of ANT is that the former tends to focus upon the role of those large-scale ideological, political and economic media by which alliances are struck between classes or social blocs. In contrast, ANT stresses the microsociological site at which such struggles and alliances take place. In other words, it looks at the local interactions between individuals in order to uncover the ways that particular actors – say scientists or politicians – end up extending their influence and their networks. Accordingly, the great political macro-actors of Marxism – the classes – must daily maintain themselves as coherent, more or less integrated, actors. The conflicts that we find between the bourgeoisie and the working classes are never empirically between classes per se: no one has ever directly witnessed a class (or a state or an institution – cf. Knorr-Cetina, 1988) – only other people (or representations) in local situations. The aim of ANT is to uncover how it is that these local situations serve to so construct the identities of actors that they will tend to act in accord with this or that actor's wishes and with uniformity across space and time.

There is a similar point of contact between ANT and Lukes' (1974; see also Clegg, 1993) three-dimensional conceptualization of power. Lukes' view focuses upon the most effective form of power – to control the political agenda, in part by instilling in a target collectivity the thoughts and desires you want them to have and thus to guarantee their compliance. As Clegg points out, Lukes is committed to a discourse of 'real interests' – the 'power-holder' effectively changes the interests of their target constituency somewhat like tinkering with the internal workings of a machine so that it acts in a different way. In contrast, Clegg, partly drawing on ANT, suggests that it is more important to follow the operation of power by identifying what strategies and practices are deployed by given actors to persuade or recruit others to particular views of their interests – views that accord with the goals of the enrolling actors. At stake here is the difference between 'controlling thoughts and desires' (Lukes) and 'recruiting views of one's interests' (Clegg, ANT), with the corollary contrast between, on the one hand, the 'corruption of one's real interests' and a 'constraint on one's real identity' and, on the other, 'the contingent constitution of interests' and the 'on-going construction of identity'. Where the former stresses oppression and denial, the latter emphasizes construction and production. These two trends need not be completely opposed: as Fairclough (1992) notes, the production of identity at once entails construction and constraint, the construction processes (in the present case, those of enrolment, translation, displacement) have to work on pre-existing identities and, as such, can end up being constraints. However, in the case of ANT, I would argue that it is potentially particularly good at excavating the ways that pre-existing identities (say that of citizen, farmer, fisherman or doctor) are drawn upon piecemeal – certain aspects of them are highlighted and stressed in accordance with the aims of the enroller (or main protagonist), while others are suppressed or occluded. For example, of all the aspects of 'member of society' that could be drawn upon (e.g. everyday decision-maker and local policy-formulator), it is that of 'citizen-as-voter' that is emphasized in parliamentary democracies. As we shall see in Chapter 6, in the case of 'official science's' efforts to enrol the public, it is the aspect of 'willing but scientifically illiterate citizen' that needs to be 'sold' to the public. A version of this identity might already pre-exist in the public, but it needs to be drawn out and reinforced in order to ensure the compliance of the public.

Finally, I will look at how criticisms of Gene Sharp's theory of power (1973) fare when extended to ANT. On the surface, ANT and Sharp's theory share a view of power that is voluntaristic. A neat summary of Sharp's views can be found in Brian Martin's paper (1989; see also McGuinness, 1993), who writes: 'The essence of Sharp's theory of power is quite simple: people in society may be divided into rulers and subjects; the power of the rulers derives from consent by the subjects . . .' (p. 213). The parallel with ANT is that there is an emphasis on the giving up of consent as the key to power. However, as McGuinness points out in relation to feminist critiques, such giving up of consent must rely on pre-formed agents of equal status, something which many feminists are unwilling to accept for the case of women who are seen as structurally disqualified from such status. Certainly, there is a tendency for ANT to assume a sort of uniform agential status across all actors. However, I would argue that this practice has more to do with the norms of story-telling than with some deep theoretical commitment to the pre-existing equal agency of all relevant actors. These norms generate dramatic stories of enrolment and betrayal. As such, they generate narratives with considerable rhetorical resonance. However, this practice need not be central to ANT. This becomes clear when we note ANT's analytic focus on the way that the agency of others is constituted through various means (such as scientific papers, media coverage, architectural space and technological design) which serve to 'draw out and sell' certain versions of relevant selves which come to characterize target actors. In other words, the vision of agency (subject-ness) and non-agency (object-ness) that operates in ANT is one in which these statuses are much more up for grabs than in Sharp's theory. It is not possible to tell who (or what) is a subject or an object until after the event – after the association has been made and the network built. At the point at which that association is being forged, despite the quote from Latour (1986) above, and more in keeping with Foucault's view of the subject as an emergent entity from the operation of power/knowledge, the agential status of both enroller and enrolee is highly ambiguous. It also points to ANT's superior reflexivity: ANT practitioners routinely reflect on their own embroilment in networks, on their status as network-builders and enrolees, and on the way that their story-telling constitutes others in particular ways.

Perhaps a more serious criticism of Sharp's theory concerns his neglect of structural inequalities and the impact of macrosocial dynamics upon the relations between ruler and subjects. Martin is particularly trenchant on this point. He remarks that the consent theory of power works best where there is an obvious oppressor; where the oppressor is less obvious, as in Western democracies, the ruler–subject dichotomy and the role of consent are less analytically appropriate. Under such circumstances, there are all sorts of other influences – upbringing, division of labour, craft and ethnic allegiances – which shape that relationship and predispose actors to act in ways that do not map easily on to the 'giving of consent'. ANT is not completely exempt from this criticism – it has tended to avoid use of such macro terms as institutions, the state, class, race, patriarchy and so on. However, it does not neglect these 'large actors'; rather, it aims to examine how these entities come to be constituted as such – coherent, consistent, uniform across time and space. The purpose of ANT is to unravel what keeps these large actors together, to show how they are networks which need to be repaired and reproduced moment by moment by their constituent actors. Thus, while one might readily point to the role of the police or the army in coercing subordinate groups, ANT would expose those processes by which such arms of the state are made possible. The questions it would ask are: How are the constituent actors of the police and army produced? What are the mechanisms by which certain sorts of individual are created in these institutions? How are functionaries recruited, persuaded, shaped and formed in such a way that they 'cohere' as those more or less unitary entities, the police and the army? In sum, ANT moves towards uncovering the conditions by which such networks came to be stabilized: it reveals their history and their inner workings with the express aim of showing how things could have been different.

Agency and Heroism

The above discussion has slipped, not altogether innocently, from a consideration of power into a concern with agency. This is because the issues of power and agency are inextricable: the traditional view of power, as something that can be accumulated, rests on a notion of a power-holder who can do the accumulating and consequently exercise, as Law (1991b) puts its, discretion. But as we have seen above, agency is like power – a product and an effect. Law (1991b) notes the following in suggesting a definition of agency:

> I want to say that an actor may be pictured as a set of relations which in some measure has the effect of (a) characterising, (b) storing and (at least in some instances) offering a degree of discretion with respect to 'power to' and 'power over' . . . . In this way of thinking, agents are both sets of relations, and nodes in sets of relations. (pp. 172–3)

However, despite this thoroughly Foucauldian concern with the constructed nature of agency, a number of the case studies that have been conducted in the actor-network tradition have tended to start out from highly calculative agents – heroes and managers.

This practical and analytic emphasis on heroes and managers has been instanced in Callon's case studies of the three biologists' efforts to convince the scallop fishermen of St Brieuc Bay of the viability of scallop farming and of the Electricité de France's attempt to promote the electric vehicle, and in Latour's account of Pasteur's successful endeavours to persuade a range of other actors of the efficacy of his theories and methods. In all three cases, particular actors are followed, their 'goals', methods and translations are enumerated. We are presented with a narrative in which actors rise to, and, in Callon's two case studies presented above, fall from, a position of 'power'. In sum, the networks of Callon and Latour have tended to be clean and clear. What we have seen to be multiplicitous actors often emerge as a unitary entity (though this is always a provisional state); this is not simply a product of the state and configuration of the network being studied, but is rendered singular by the flow of the narrative of the particular case study. In other words, and at the risk of 'metareflexivity' (see Chapter 3), it is through the crafting and storying of a network that the actor-network theorist conjures out of the empirical materials and data the particularity and identity of the target entities. This is, of course, part of the job of the analyst: to detect patterns, narratives, ordering. However, problems arise when the singularity of the entities within the analytic narrative threatens to occlude the indeterminacy and the ambivalence of entities and the associations into which they are tied. Perhaps this is linked to the recurrent metaphor of war that runs through ANT: certainly, it often seems as if these accounts are structured by magnificent victories and disastrous defeats. We are transported into a dramatic world of meteoric rises and tragic failures.

Marginality and Ambivalence

But how are we to conceive otherwise of such networks? An alternative to the world of heroes and betrayers, triumph and disaster might be that of permanent reform; the world we wish to examine is one of inherent instability and incessant skirmishes. Thus, the multiplicity of given actors is reflected in the shifts and changes in the associations amongst them; that is to say, they are endowed with an intrinsic uncertainty. Following Singleton and Michael (1993; Singleton, 1993), I elaborate a metaphor that can help us grasp these facets better.

Around a film camera – let us call this our analyst(s) – there is a dense scaffolding that extends in all directions, in three dimensions (let us call this the network). Its components are strands, more or less solid (let us call these associations), and nodes, more or less opaque (let us call these actors or entities or actants). The camera is also connected to the scaffold: what it can do is constrained by its connections. As it rolls, focuses, zooms and swivels on its tripod, the camera detects more or less dramatic changes in the scaffolding, in the quality of the connections and the opacity of the nodes (let us call this history). Through this camera we see another camera (let us call this Callon and Latour) and we see some of its mechanisms. We notice that it is particularly good at time-lapse photography: initially, it sees a node make new connections, grow and become more opaque (sometimes this node is called Pasteur, the Electricité de France or the three biologists); then it sees another connected node struggle and free itself (sometimes this node is a microbe, an electron or some fishermen); then it sees the original node become more opaque, more dense and dark, or it sees it become less opaque as it begins to unravel in a mess of more or less damaged connections.

We see that this other camera favours a particular focus and aperture setting: what it sees in the dense scaffold of connections is, to us, a rather thin slice through the matrix – it picks up only those connections to a node that fall within its somewhat shallow depth of field. Despite this, it has an excellent zoom facility and will home in on nodes to reveal the most intricate patterns of connections that constitute them. In contrast, our analysts flatter themselves that their camera is a little better connected: the deep depth of field reveals many connections that remain out of focus to other cameras. We see a node – it is multiplicitous, its connections are multifarious, and as our analysts manipulate their lens these connections come in and out of focus. Indeed, even when they leave the lens on a single setting, we find that the scaffold is in constant motion and that connections come in and out of focus of their own accord. Some of these connections seem to pull at the node in different directions – while a node is embedded in one concerted sub-matrix of the scaffold, it is simultaneously being pulled outwards. It is at once central and peripheral, inside and outside, at the core and at the margins. Yet, we notice that this opposing pull does not simply create tensions within the sub-matrix. As we follow the connection, we see that it connects to other nodes and other connections and some of these can be traced back to the sub-matrix. This very dynamism and vibration, we find, contributes to and sustains what in another depth of field, time-period and field of view it seems to undermine.

Before going on to illustrate how this metaphor might allow us to approach ambivalence and uncertainty, marginality and multiple network membership in more detail, it is important to consider John Law's and Leigh Star's recent reflections on the central, mobilizing actor of the network. Law (1991a) argues against the above managerialist or heroic reading of ANT. The slogan 'follow the actor' – who ends up being the hero of the piece – does not necessarily entail reification of that actor. Thus he notes that:

> Bruno Latour may have chosen to study Louis Pasteur. But the object of the study is not so much to celebrate as to deconstruct the subject. Thus for Latour, Pasteur is an effect, a product of a set of alliances, of heterogeneous materials. To the extent that Pasteur 'is' a 'great man', we need to see this as an outcome rather than something inhering in Pasteur. (p. 12)

While the detailed examination of such big and powerful actors is motivated by the desire to debunk them, as well as to show how 'everything else being equal, their modes of organizing and ordering shape much more about the heterogeneous networks of the social than do the strategies of the unsuccessful' (p. 13), Law suggests that it becomes dangerous to focus too exclusively on the workings of such 'heroes'. For, as both Law and Star point out, if there are other actors who are excluded from, or who are marginal to, the great networks, how is ANT to give these actors voice? How do we take into account the idea that 'every enrolment entails both a failure to enrol and a destruction of the world of the non-enrolled' (Star, 1991, p. 45)? How does ANT serve, not only in reconstructing the means to triumph of the big and the powerful, but also in the recovering of alternative 'failed' or marginal networks and actors? As Star notes, these other, marginal networks are rarely completely destroyed. They lurk in the background and they inform, perhaps more loosely, actors who are enrolled into larger networks. For example, in tandem with enrolment to the networks of orthodox medicine are enrolments to alternative medicine. Multiple memberships and multiple marginalities need to be incorporated into ANT. In Star's words:

> People inhabit many different domains at once . . . and the negotiation of identities, within and across groups, is an extraordinarily complex and delicate task. It's important not to presume either unity or single membership, either in the mingling of humans and nonhumans or amongst humans. We are all marginal in some regard, as members of more than one community of practice (social world). (p. 52)

Moreover, where the network is multidimensional and contains within it relatively obscure associations and roles – that is, where there is a network-within-a-network – actants have many resources to draw upon which, while problematizing certain components of the original network, can ultimately contribute to its durability.

So, if networks are multiplicitous and multidimensional, as Star argues, it might be the case, as Singleton and Michael (1993) suggest, that they are rendered durable by the way that actors at once occupy the margins and the core, are the most outspoken critics and the most ardent stalwarts, are simultaneously insiders and outsiders – in sum, are ambivalent. Thus, Singleton and Michael illustrate the central role of ambivalence with an analysis of general practitioners' (GPs') discourses around the Cervical Screening Programme.

They show how, within the Cervical Screening Programme, the GP actor exposes itself as an association of heterogeneous elements each of which associates its own elements. Within the British Government's Cervical Screening Programme network (set up through a range of official documents and institutional arrangements – see Singleton, 1993 for details), GPs are simplified and represented as ambassadors of medical science, as skilful providers of the cervical smear test, and as publicists engaged in persuading women of the value of the test and of the necessity to participate. GPs are enrolled into this network; yet the GP also exposes its own network-ness. Elements that did not exist in the governmental Cervical Screening Programme actor-network are introduced such as speculums, practice nurses, cervical secretions and cellular fixatives. Other actors with which the GP is associated within the Cervical Screening Programme are exposed as adopting a multiplicity of identities – as networks in their own right. Further, the simplified representation of GP identity constructed through the governmental Cervical Screening Programme actor-network is re-represented in contrary ways. The GP 'complexifies' and problematizes itself in order to redefine and transform itself into an important skilled actor and an obligatory point of passage in other co-existing networks that also feed into the Cervical Screening Programme network.

Hence GP interaction within the black-boxed governmental Cervical Screening Programme actor-network is characterized by ambiguous associations, multiple identities and ambivalent discourse. Here lies the paradox: the resultant uncertainty and indeterminacy exist within, and are dependent upon, the stability and structure of the governmental black-boxed Cervical Screening Programme. GP identity is historically and textually bound to it. The GP partly exists through it: GP identity is simultaneously dependent upon and negotiated through the identities and associations of an array of heterogeneous entities that constitute the governmental Cervical Screening Programme actor-network . Within the discourse of GPs, what has been simplified and unified reveals its complexity and multiplicity – GPs problematize their own, and other entities' identities and associations in order to renegotiate their own identity. For example, in circumstances where they need to stress their centrality to the network, GPs point to their autonomous role in interpreting the smear test results that come back from the laboratories (e.g. the GP's naked-eye view of the cervix is an invaluable adjunct to laboratory results). Where GPs want to emphasize the efficacy of the programme as a whole, they black-box the laboratory as the source of true knowledge about cervical cells. In other words, GPs simultaneously play out and problematize their assigned role as they go about mediating the black-boxed Cervical Screening Programme. GPs emerge as at once simplified identifiable actors with distinct unitary identities and as networks in their own right with a complex multiple identity.

Taking the above one step further, Singleton and Michael conceptualize GPs as internal network builders who construct their own GP Cervical Screening Programme actor-network from within the governmental Cervical

Screening Programme. In terms of the cinematic metaphor, they alter the depth of field to record a whole range of other connections and associations that were previously out of focus. That is, like the Government, the GPs construct an actor-network that defines their own identity and associations. However, this network building is going on within the black-boxed Cervical Screening Programme and paradoxically it is dependent upon it. One might say, along with Singleton (1993), that the Cervical Screening Programme has become a benevolent adversary to the GP. To overly stress uncertainty and multiplicity would be to endanger the governmental Cervical Screening Programme and undermine the GP role; yet, to follow unflinchingly the Government's model of the GP role would be to render that role unworkable. Complexity and diversity, expressed in the GPs' ambivalence, make the Cervical Screening Programme at once stable and unstable.

So, GPs are engaged in translating heterogeneous entities in order to redefine their own identity. The GP ambivalently destabilizes and stabilizes elements, on the one hand adhering to their assigned, black-boxed role, and on the other problematizing that role and demonstrating their own multiformity. The GP is working from both within and outside the black-boxed Cervical Screening Programme.

It is the necessary ambivalence of the GP that allows the black-boxed Cervical Screening Programme actor-network to be maintained in the very dynamism and complexity of its functioning. The GP can be seen as an ambivalent analyst committed both to questioning and to validating his/her subject matter. The GP and the Cervical Screening Programme are simultaneously stable and yet perpetually evolving. In uncovering this ambivalence, the time frame usually found in actor-network studies has been concertinaed. By going into the discursive interstices of the GP actor, we find an ambivalence that draws upon many associations, and we discover some of the ostensibly latent resources – those associations that otherwise would remain out of focus – that can be mobilized by GPs if and when they finally and unequivocally betray the Government's Cervical Screening Programme actor-network .

This 'otherness' of actors (like GPs) who are internal to the relevant network is only one possible version of marginality. Thus, Star (1991) treats 'others' as essentially excluded from, marginalized from, the target networks analysed by actor-network theorists. However, within a network, external 'others' can play a major role in sustaining a network. For example, Michael and Birke (1994a), though not using ANT, draw attention to the way that pro-animal experimentation scientists represent a series of 'others' (e.g. foreign scientists, the cosmetics industry, pet owners, etc.) as a way of rendering themselves in a more positive light. While such 'others' might be rendered explicit in interview, we might tentatively expect that they normally serve as a rarely articulated representational backdrop against which the identities of scientists within the 'network' of animal experimentation are played out. Another example comes from Mort (1994; personal communication). Mort points out that sociological analyses of missile guidance systems (MacKenzie,

1990; Spinardi, 1994), while they show up the contingency of the technology (and the networks of which that technology is a part), neglect to consider that central to the complex networks of military, government, research laboratories and industry are those who actually produce the technology: namely, skilled artisans. These workers need to be enrolled too; without their contribution none of these technologies could be produced in suitable numbers or even at all (after all these workers embody specialist skills few others possess). In the process of enrolment, it is often necessary to 'pacify' workers who could otherwise be resistant to the use of their skills to produce military technology. One way of doing this is to claim that, without military technology, there would be wide-scale unemployment. The 'others' here are the 'unemployed' – marginals who, so to speak, signify from the sidelines, disciplining the remaining workers. One could say that these marginals serve as 'absent intermediaries' – certainly they are not physically present in the immediate network of military technology development, yet their representation is pervasive within it. In sum, 'others', marginals, absent intermediaries can play a major role in networks – their very exclusion, and the representation of their exclusion, serves as a further medium by which a network is rendered durable.

The foregoing paragraphs have illustrated how ANT can help to excavate the links between identity, otherness, marginality and durability. In the next section, I look at this in more detail, and link it up to some recent thoughts on the macro–micro debate.

Network Durability, Ordering and the Relation of ANT to Macro–Micro Debates

ANT is not only a means of studying the way in which knowledge comes to be accredited – it also provides a series of analytic tools with which to rethink the production of society and social order. In brief, ANT takes a microsociological stance, emphasizing the local (re)production of the social in the intersubjective practices that make up situated interactions. However, to this basic social picture, ANT adds a further dimension: namely, a consideration of the role of other stabilizing influences or resources of ordering are imported into that local situation. As ever, the potency of these influences and resources are contingent, but, nevertheless, within a given historical frame, some will be seen as routinely more durably influential. These additional resources are the nonhumans – architectures, texts, technological artefacts – that within a given frame (that is to say, network) have a greater durability. I shall return to these dimensions below. Here, I will consider the basic models of social ordering entailed in ANT.

For Callon and Latour (1981), one cannot *a priori* distinguish between macro-actors such as institutions and states and micro-actors such as groups and individuals. Their difference in size is a matter of negotiation. The question that follows is: how does a micro-actor become a macro-actor? This stands in marked contrast to the macrosociological assumption that macro-actors exist unproblematically – according to Callon and Latour, such a presupposition obscures the fact that these macro-entities are achievements and, in the process, affirms the power relations entailed by them. Rather, it is important to 'flatten' macro-actors into a series of micro-situations and thus to map out the multiple negotiations that necessarily contribute to the (re)production of the relations of power entailed in macro-actors. For Callon and Latour, an actor who makes other actors dependent upon itself, translates their wills into its own language, and renders these translations more durable has grown in size. As we have seen, Knorr-Cetina (1988) notes that there are no macro-actors that are separate from local contexts – we only operate within such local situations in interaction with other people. It is in these contexts that macro-actors come to be represented – and this is what macro-actors are, namely, representations. However, Knorr-Cetina focuses solely on the social – she does not take into account the fact that present in all these interactions are nonhumans of various sorts that likewise represent the macro, but do so (contingently) in a number of ways (not always through language or signs). Moreover, Callon and Latour would question the status of the macro as simply local representation: for them, the macro suggests a series of regularities of comportment on the part of other actors (after all, that is what the 'durability of translations' means). How, then, are these regularities achieved?

Callon and Latour (1981; see also Latour and Strum, 1986; Strum and Latour, 1988) explore this through a comparison between baboon and human societies. For baboons there are no long-lasting interactions, society is never reified – hierarchies constantly shift, relations have to be ongoingly repaired, socially skilful practices must be continuously deployed in order keep local conspecifics in line. In contrast, human societies incorporate associations that last longer than the interaction that formed them. Through contracts (texts), walls (architectures) and technologies (nonhumans) one can enlist (human) bodies and durable materials that can go on to act upon others and that yield durable associations. Such enrolments effectively black-box relationships – they become unyielding, automatic, unproblematic. What the 'heroic' actor is effectively doing here is aligning a series of intermediaries – chains of black boxes – texts, machines, humans who automatically do as he/she wills. But they never function on some larger scale – in each instance their effectivity operates at the local level.

One can illustrate this in relation to Mouzelis' (1993) recent treatment of the macro–micro debate. Mouzelis bemoans the contemporary emphasis on the micro and the neglect of the macro (p. 678). He chides 'interpretative sociologists' for their reluctance to deal with macro-actors – a reluctance fuelled by a 'predilection for "lay persons", "ordinary members of society", "mundane" encounters' (p. 677). As a result they ignore collective actors and what Mouzelis calls 'mega-actors' – that is, 'individual actors in control of considerable resources, whose decisions stretch widely in space and time' (p. 679). A corollary of this is that the 'identification of interaction with micro, and of institutions with macro, leads to an underemphasis of social hierarchies' (p. 679). Mouzelis' point here is that, contrary to Knorr-Cetina's representational view of the macro, 'face-to-face encounters are not necessarily micro, they can constitute macro events in their own right' (p. 681). This is because such face-to-face encounters have impact that stretches across space and time and that this is by virtue of existing hierarchies (that mediate their influence). Thus, 'the face-to-face encounter between Churchill, Roosevelt and Stalin at Yalta in 1945 led to crucial decisions which, among other things, shaped the postwar map of Europe and profoundly affected the lives of millions of people' (p. 679).

Now ANT has little problem with Mouzelis' argument because it directly engages with 'hierarchies', but rather than presuppose that they are simply 'there', it can be used to excavate the multiple interactions and associations that comprise them. How is it that these three human actors, Churchill, Roosevelt and Stalin, have extending from them chains of intermediaries – humans, texts and technologies – that stay in place? What makes the relations between the various intermediaries durable? How is each text, technology and role rendered as a black box? How has the 'automaticity' of the various components that make up the networks which come to be known as 'Yalta' been accomplished? These are the sorts of questions ANT would deal with.

In sum, ANT does not neglect these 'macro' micro-situations but attempts to dissect them – to trace the sources of their potency and resonance, to articulate how they are achievements in their own right. I will now consider two examples of ANT analysis of the production of social order – or rather ordering, including hierarchies. These two studies differ from the usual ANT case studies in that they pay close attention to the discourse of participants.

The first example comes from John Law's (1994) book *Organizing Modernity* which starts out with a nice, simple question: 'what on earth is the social order?' Yet for Law, this whole question becomes subverted. Thus, there is no singular social order – orders are always plural. Thus, there is no completed order, only ordering – it is central to Law's project to challenge the modernist delusion of order and 'hideous purity'. Thus, the social is but one element in the ordering process, for such a process is heterogeneous – the 'non-social' and the 'nonhuman' also play their part.

In essence, Law situates his enterprise at the intersection of three traditions: symbolic interactionism, post-structuralism and actor-network theory – each of these supplements the other. So, for example, post-structuralism in the form of Foucault's genealogy, while it orients us to a view of agency as an effect and highlights the material nature of the social, nevertheless suffers from a tendency to view the production of social order in terms of reiteration and reinstanciation. In contrast, symbolic interactionism allows Law to scrutinize the situated performances of discourse, and furnishes him with the tools to follow the meetings, confrontations and fusions of different discourses (or modes of ordering) that yield and reflect fluidity and change. On the other hand, ANT forces us to take very seriously indeed the role of the non-social in such orderings, to regard them as always contingent and uncertain, and to recognize that they are effortful – mediated through 'translations' where heterogeneous materials are used to 'foresee and forestall the resistance put up by the bits and pieces that make up the networks of the social' (p. 102). From this theoretical interweaving emerges the idea of 'Relational Materialism' which aims to capture the way that those entities (both human and nonhuman) that have durability and material impact, that are instrumental in the process of social ordering, that can be identified as loci of agency are themselves emergent within a network, are themselves heterogeneously constituted, are, in sum, effects as well.

Empirically, Law explores these issues in relation to an ethnography of Daresbury Laboratory. Law does not try to give a global characterization of this institution because, as he notes, his narrations rest on only a partial engagement with Daresbury: 'I had a terrible anxiety about being in the right place at the right time. Where I happened to be, the action was not' (p. 45). Daresbury is, of course, many places (the machine area, the office area, the experimental area). It has many histories, tales and characters. For example, there are discourses used by the participants at Daresbury that Law calls evolutionary which represent the history of Daresbury Laboratory as 'a reasonable and unfolding evolution of scientific and technical concerns moderated more or less by financial constraints and the need to maintain the Laboratory on an even keel in a difficult world' (p. 55). These accounts tended, according to Law, to sound measured and bureaucratic. In comparison, another ordering discourse which Law calls 'heroic' implies discontinuity and deploys a *leitmotiv* of struggle. 'Heroism told of the way the Laboratory had gone through good periods and bad. And, most of all, it talked of revolutionary change and the role in such revolutionary change of crucial individuals' (p. 56). These multiple, co-existing discourses (and others – charismatic, visionary) serve as 'ordering resources for working on and making sense of the networks of the social . . . . They shape (and are embodied in) action . . .' (p. 71). But these orderings are not simply regularities – they are also hierarchies or rankings. Moreover, these rankings are performed: performed by both superiors and subordinates; performed with the aid of different practices and materials of representation (talk, paperwork, images); performed within the ranking (institution) and to its audiences.

For instance, Law interprets a moment of tension in which the hierarchy becomes exposed. This incident (or rather, this perception on Law's part) involved the commissioning of an additional linear accelerator in the process of which the scientists monopolized the work to the exclusion of the technical crew who, by virtue of being denied knowledge of what was going on, became frustrated by the whole exercise. This moment, for Law, captured the performance of hierarchy. 'Together the physicists, the crew members, the equipment and the topography of the control room, embodied and were constantly performing asymmetries in the distribution of agency' (p. 123). Yet, as Law asks, how was this done? How were these interdiscursive arrangements played out? The 'physicists perform a version of vocational stories of hierarchy . . . between creative puzzle-solvers on the one hand, and those who are passive, uncreative and unskilled on the other . . .' (p. 123). The crew were being performed by the physicists into a set of restricted roles. But, Law

reflects, these are not completely passive roles, though certainly they leave little space for initiative on the part of the crew. The crew themselves resent
these performances; yet they go along with them. One reason for this which
Law suggests concerns the crew's supplementary stories that distance them
from the work of Daresbury. For the physicists, the stories of desire and work
are relatively tightly coupled: 'they tell of wanting to excel in their science and
engineering' (p. 125). In contrast, the leader of the technical crew relates
'desire stories' wherein aspirations to achievement and agency are connected
to activities outside Daresbury (skippering a boat). To do this he needs 'work,
at least for a time, to sustain this project. So he sits at the controls (at
Daresbury) . . . and performs a kind of hierarchy' (p. 126).

In sum, Law is pointing to the performative dimension of social ordering
and ranking. But he is also indicating the multiple networks in which actors
operate and the ways that different identities 'cross-over' and serve as
resources in the reproduction of ranking in other networks. This performative
aspect is also addressed by Bowers and Iwi (1993) in their study of discourses
which define and perform the wider social. These researchers, drawing on
data from a corpus of semi-structured interview material, derive a range of
models of the social that are used rhetorically to 'either legitimate the respondent's argument or undercut an opponent's' (p. 368). From their data, they
derive eight models of society. Here are some examples: 'Society as uniform
and total' in which society is represented as uniform (internal differentiations
are not emphasized) and in which we are all commonly implicated; 'society as
an instance of a category' in which society 'is formulated in relation to a particular category which it is alleged to exemplify' (p. 380) – for instance, late
corporate capitalist society; 'society as opposing the speaker' – here, society
'is attributed with alien values, beliefs and dispositions to action' that con-
tradict the speakers' own (p. 383). These discourses have certain functions: the
first permits the speaker to render a given valuation of an issue like pornog-
raphy as unproblematic by equating it with society as whole; the second
facilitates related arguments so that characterizing society as an exemplar of
late corporate capitalism allows arguments 'about the nature of the economy
and the legitimacy of interventions in it' (p. 380); the third does not undermine the speaker's warrant – rather society comes to be seen as deficient in
relation to the speaker's positions (it is immoral, domineering or oppressive).

The performative dimension of these discourses is 'the rhetorical one of
convincing others' (p. 387) and such a process 'depends upon the associations
that an argument manufactures or can fall back on' (p. 388). The corollary is
that such discourses should also disassociate, that is, demolish alternative
representations of society. In sum, Bowers and Iwi's respondents are 'offering
us a network of associations in their arguments, a set of alliances between
actors intermingled with associations between actors and states of affairs, values and beliefs . . . which if found convincing and acted in accordance with
could be(come) society' (p. 389).

It is interesting to contrast the work of Law and that of Bowers and Iwi. For
Law, multiplicity of discourses and orderings is paramount. In comparison,

for Bowers and Iwi with their catalogue of representations of society, the emphasis remains on singular representations and their performative impact. Yet, of course, such discursive practices are typically characterized by contradiction, as Potter and Wetherell (1987) have argued. How, in the light of these sometimes contradictory, multiple representations and discourses, is it possible to trace out ordering? For Law, this is not a problem because multiplicity is a key constituent of the institution he examines; indeed, for Singleton and Michael, multiplicity, and its attendant ambivalence, is functional for the maintenance of their target network (the network as seen from their analytic perspective, that is). The point is that the efficacy of these orderings rests on a whole array of other actors and representations (as Bowers and Iwi acknowledge, many practical resources are required in order to extend associations), including the ongoing (re)casting of the roles of self and others. But, beyond this, the multiplicity of ordering discourses and the multiple roles prescribed by these lend institutions durability and serve to structure regularities of action within those networks. Where these regularities are dissonant, this simply reflects the fact that the network is comprised of disparate actors all of whom have to be accommodated, that is, translated, by ordering discourses.

The Status of Nonhumans in the Production of Networks

In the preceding section, I have remarked at several points on the role of nonhumans in the processes of social ordering. By nonhumans I have in mind, in this context, technological artefacts that impact upon humans, thereby ordering, albeit contingently, their actions. This section will focus exclusively on such technological artefacts to the exclusion of other sorts of intermediaries, such as texts and nonhuman 'nature', including animals and the 'natural' environment.

The structure of this section is as follows. Firstly, I will consider the relative durability of technological artefacts and their role in social ordering. Secondly, I will briefly note a recent exchange in which the role imputed to such artefacts is challenged as analytically mistaken and politically retrograde.

We can begin with a quotation from Law (1991b) who writes in relation to agency:

> On the one hand we live in and are constituted by a set of relations which are organized in a range of different ways and have a series of effects; and on the other hand, we are embodied in a range of materials . . . . one of the best ways of stabilizing relations . . . is precisely to embody them in durable materials: relations that tend, everything else being equal, to generate effects that last. (p. 174)

What, then, are these materials, how do they work, and how do they come to embody and mediate social relations? Latour (1991, 1992; Latour/Johnson, 1988) has provided the prime account of this. As with Law, Latour stresses that nonhumans are present in all human encounters:

We are never faced with objects or social relations, we are faced with chains which are associations of humans (H) and nonhumans (NH). No-one has ever seen a social relation by itself . . . nor a technical relation . . . . Instead we are always faced with chains which look like this H-NH-H-NH-H-NH . . . . (1991, p. 110)

However, nonhumans are no different from humans in one respect – they are themselves effects; they are networks in their own right and as such carry with them certain properties and functions. Given their networks, certain nonhumans come to be highly resistant to un-black-boxing; their roles, functions, properties and impacts come to have an automacity and an invisibility that allows them to be unproblematically instrumental in day-to-day social ordering.

Latour particularly emphazises how nonhumans can replace (potentially unreliable) humans who would normally need to be disciplined into performing their tasks. Such disciplinarity requires the expenditure of much energy. A more efficient way of ensuring that certain things get done is to delegate to nonhumans. In those interactions, which, if managed by human intermediaries would require those intermediaries to be controlled, observed, normalized and so on, one could 'substitute for unreliable humans a delegated nonhuman character' (1992, p. 231).

So, for example, Latour illustrates this point with an analysis of the function of a door-closer (or groom – the mechanism which slowly closes the door without slamming). As an alternative to a human concierge, porter, gatekeeper or bellboy, such a mechanism needs somewhat less disciplining. However, it also begins to shape the behaviour of the humans who use it. Thus, a mechanical groom with a very strong spring which slams the door would, in order to function, require swift reflexes and movement on the part of human users. Even the more sedate grooms require certain skills and capacities on the part of humans. Thus, as Latour (1992) notes: '. . . neither my little nephews nor my grandmother could get in unaided because our groom needed the force of an able-bodied person to accumulate enough energy to close the door later . . . . these doors discriminate against very little and very old persons' (p. 234).

At issue here is the way in which the artefact acts upon the capacities of the body to shape and discipline the human actor – to give them a particular identity. Here, a physical constraint is imposed, which, while not overly inconveniencing some humans, forces others to enrol other humans and nonhumans to do their door-opening for them. Drawing on Akrich's work (cf. Akrich, 1992; Akrich and Latour, 1992), Latour calls this prescription (or proscription, affordance or allowance) – 'What a device allows or forbids from actors – humans and nonhuman – that it anticipates; it is the morality of a setting both negative (what it prescribes) and positive (what it permits)' (Akrich and Latour, 1992, p. 261). Thus, these nonhuman entities are moral – they embody a 'local cultural condition' (Latour/Johnson, 1988, p. 301) which, while it is normally invisible to human users, nevertheless structures human behaviour.

It is this contextual structuring through which humans partly demonstrate 'identity' – those routine, repetitive, regularized behaviours that can be said to constitute identity. However, these structurings or orderings are, as ever, contingent. They can be resisted or subverted under certain circumstances. Thus, Akrich and Latour coin a couplet of terms – subscription, and its opposite, de-inscription – to capture the way that actors take on or resist the prescriptions or proscriptions of ordering actants, especially technological artefacts. These 'target' actors have their own antiprogrammes according to which they 'either underwrite . . . or try to extract themselves out of . . . or adjust their behaviour or the setting through some negotiations' (1992, p. 261) in their dealings with the prescriptions of (technological) actors. But, according to the state of the network, de-inscription, subversion, resistance is more or less possible.

But is not to call such technological artefacts 'delegates' also to indulge in anthropomorphism – are we not unduly ascribing human characteristics to the nonhuman? Latour uses this charge to argue that to insist that certain (traditional) properties are monopolized by humans is to close off certain routes of exploration as to the distribution of competencies, properties and skills and the ways in which these are exchanged in networks. Here, Latour is in accord with Law: agency is an effect and an accomplishment. To site it in certain (human) entities is to impoverish our treatment of the influences and chains of influences (enrolments) which shape us and in which nonhumans are centrally implicated.

One argument against such an approach rests on the perception of the role of nonhumans as autonomous influences upon humans. The mutual construction of humans and nonhumans levels the status of each – no longer can one speak of 'social construction' as such. Collins and Yearley's (1992a, b) critique addresses just this radical symmetrism of ANT – the common actant status that technological artefacts and natural entities and humans have within ANT is seen as highly problematic. The de-prioritization of the social that gives an autonomous voice to 'things' disguises the fact that these voices in actuality depend upon the mediation of human actors. That is to say, technological artefacts (and nature) never speak directly – they must always be 'articulated' or rather constructed through human categories. What influences technologies wield are the result of human agency: social and cultural resources have to be mobilized in order to design, manufacture, situate and implement these technologies. This view thus reinstates the social as the real site of sociological (social constructionist) investigation. It also serves to resist what Collins and Yearley see as a dangerous precedent in ANT. Technological artefacts never speak directly to us – we must always 're-construct' their meaning. To say that they do, when in fact they do not, is to hand power back to scientists and technologists, the traditional representatives and spokespersons of nonhumans. It is these experts who will tell us the meanings of these nonhumans, whereas it has long been the task of SSK to show how these experts do not have unmediated access to nonhumans, that they are necessarily engaged in socially constructing these artefacts.

As we have already seen, Callon and Latour's (1992) response is, in part, that technological artefacts are implicated in the very fabric of the social – they are social relations viewed in their durability and cohesion: as such the techniques by which agency is drained out of artefacts become the objects of study. Moreover, as regards scientists, we need to make sure that we can see how their constructions are influenced by prior nonhumans which are in turn constituted partly by prior humans. In other words, for ANT it is the chains of humans and nonhumans that are important – there is no 'last instance' in which the social is determinate. It is a matter of empirical study and narrative construction on the part of the analyst rather than an epistemological investment in the social.

In this section I have concentrated on technological nonhumans, and indeed most of the work on nonhumans in ANT has been on technological artefacts. However, there also 'natural' nonhumans. As we will see, it is somewhat more difficult to unpack the networks that inhere in 'natural' nonhumans – their functionality and prescriptiveness in networks is often obscure, their agency slippery and their impact upon human identity problematic. This range of issues will be further explored in Chapter 7.

Conclusion

In this chapter, I have presented my own construction of ANT – I have drawn on much of the literature, but I have inevitably been selective and I have read it with a view to developing an ANT treatment of identity. It goes without saying, in these constructionist times, that there are many alternative ways of navigating one's way through this corpus. However, with this sobering thought interned in the back of our collective mind, I will now briefly go through the ways in which ANT inflects in relation to the issues raised in my previous account of social constructionist approaches to identity.

To recap some of the questions that emerged from Chapter 2: What historical frame are we dealing with in the construction of identity? What is the spectrum of selves that emerges (from the local to the institutional to the cultural to the global)? How do we identify, however contingently, the sources of the linguistic, cultural, etc. resources that are instrumental in the construction of identity and how do we document their successful or failed deployment? How, then, do we account for changes in identity? How do we deal with the contradictions and ambivalences between the various resources that contribute to the construction of identities? How might we go about expanding the spectrum of such resources (i.e. include nonhumans)?

The brief outline of ANT presented in this chapter allows us now to begin to address these questions. So, for example, ANT allows us to self-consciously trace the historical time frame. The intermediaries that impact upon human actors, as networks in their own right, have their own history. Sometimes, it is possible to narrate these histories, thereby showing how the intermediaries came to be black-boxed and thus have the sorts of potency that they do. For example, one can look at the way that the door-closer came to be designed – the sorts of assumptions and conditions which made it the sort of more or less standardized technological actor that it now is. Likewise, one can trace the way that the Cervical Screening Programme developed in the context of the British National Health Service and the way it came to define the roles of women, cervical cells, laboratories, nurses and hence the identities of GPs. The point is that while the focus is upon the microsociological encounter, ANT has the analytic tools to pursue the actors and networks that at once shape that encounter and are mediated by it. In the process, ANT can aim to situate these actors and networks specifically (though this is not always the case) and to work out what are the failed enrolments and associations as well as the successful ones – it is fundamentally interested in giving an account of how certain identities (and networks and actors and intermediaries) have arisen and how they have persisted.

Further, the fact that ANT regards agency as an achievement and macro-entities as large, extended networks means that it can accommodate the role of active macro-actors (such as institutions) in the production of identities, but always with the proviso that these only ever function at the micro-level. Thus, in looking at the sources of a given identity one seeks to demarcate the inter-mediating actor as specifically as possible: What/who are these intermediaries? How have they communicated with, or inscribed, the actor? To the extent that a particular institution structures a given identity, what are the specific conduits of this prescription and in what ways does such prescription come to reproduce (or not) that institution? And if people are members of multiple networks, how, specifically, do they use resources from one network to problematize another? In all this we must not forget the role of nonhumans.

Some of these issues have already been illustrated in the present chapter, and others will be addressed or elaborated below. However, there is one outstanding detail that needs some reflection. Is it actually possible to talk of human identities any more? In the above ANT account of social ordering and identity, the focus has been on chains: chains of events (order-ing rather than order in Law), chains of humans and nonhumans (Latour), chains of intermediaries and actors (Callon). Our capacity to demarcate where the discrete links in these chains are reflects our own prejudices – we are easily able to pick humans from nonhumans, ordering discourses from one another, particular intermediaries, etc. by virtue of a well-practised vocabulary (however that might be disguised by the supposedly neutral terminology of actors, actants, intermediaries, associations and so on). In contrast, it is possible to begin to blur these divisions (and the notion of chains comprises one meek attempt at this) – to speak of hybrids (Latour, 1993), cyborgs (Haraway, 1991) and monsters (Law, 1991a) that incorporate humans and nonhumans, texts and talk. It is even possible by virtue of redistributing agency across these chains to begin to think of a new political order in which these chains have their own duties and rights – a parliament of things (Latour, 1993); 'a pessimistic liberalism in a nonhumanist mode' (Law, 1994, p. 193); a manifesto for cyborgs (Haraway, 1991). In the present case, I will make no attempt to redraw the boundaries of actors (new links in old chains). Rather, my efforts in the following chapters are about setting out, very tentatively and, no doubt, haltingly, to trace the dispersion of identity across networks, or rather how networks come to be 'condensed' or 'congealed' at nodes that we specify as human identities.

But before embarking upon this task, I will sound a note of caution. For all my best efforts to the contrary, I have no doubt ended up reifying ANT. ANT is only a heuristic – it allows us to raise and address new and interesting questions. However, as with all analytic perspectives, we cannot expect ANT to be all-encompassing. It does not, for example, deal very satisfactorily with loose coalitions of actors whose activities are coordinated, but who do not necessarily enrol one another. Neither, as we shall see, does it comfortably accommodate 'natural' nonhumans. Nonetheless, it serves the useful purpose of moving the debate beyond the boundaries dictated by social constructionism.

5

Actor-Network Theory and Identity

In the previous chapter, I introduced (my construction of) actor-network theory. In the process, I focused on some of its broad concerns: the practice of social order(ing); the nature of power; the analytic equalization of human and nonhumans. I also pointed to some of the shortcomings that have been identified: the overemphasis on the actor's agency; the pervasive managerialism and the exclusion of marginal actors; the role of ambivalence; and so on. In this chapter, I will look at the way that ANT can serve in the theorization of identity. The main aim of this chapter is, then, to illustrate with the aid of examples the way that actors attempt to demarcate identities in order to tie them into desired networks – that is, my purpose is to explore the way that particular actors function in the formulation, dissemination and entrenchment of certain identities, and how these serve in the production of social ordering. In addition, I will show how, in the process, actors also delimit their own identities.

In what follows, I will consider the way that identities are generated within networks. In doing so, I will first present some examples where scientists have constituted identities for both themselves and others in order to fulfil certain local goals, and, indissolubly in the process, to project and to engender desired networks. Thus, for example, I will draw on the work of Singleton (1993) to consider the way that GPs in the Cervical Screening Programme network operate with two disparate identities for women who do not attend for cervical smears, each of which addresses different aspects of their own position in the Cervical Screening Programme network. I will also consider the way that scientists involved in animal experimentation, in order to render their own identity as morally positive, in terms both of their treatment of animals and their willingness to enter into dialogue with their critics, need discursively to trace a whole network within which to situate both themselves and their detractors. Finally, I will consider more concerted efforts to portray animal experimentation to public constituencies and the identities and networks implied by these.

Constructing Identities, Constructing Worlds and Rendering Change

In this section I will present some examples of the ways that scientists, in constituting themselves as particular sorts of actors, simultaneously construct others around them, in the process defining the associations between them. These representations are one of the means by which enrolment comes to be managed.

For example, we can return to Callon's (1986b) account of the efforts by the French electricity utility, Electricité de France, to promote the idea and feasibility of an electric vehicle. In order to make this appear a necessary and viable transport option, the Electricité de France had not only to construct a particular role for itself (as the main 'centre of calculation' for the project) but also to assign a range of roles. Thus, for example, electrons and new forms of electrical batteries had to be convincingly represented to the relevant actors as easily disciplined. The near-future French public were represented as veering away from an easy acceptance of the internal combustion engine, as becoming more concerned with environmental issues, and as, nevertheless, still being committed to the family car. Finally, the major French car manufacturer, Renault, was represented as redirecting its efforts from the design and building of whole cars to concentrating on the production of car chassis. For a while all the various actors played their part. Then the electrons began to subvert their role, refusing to play their allotted part in the new design of batteries. And Renault produced a counter-report which, in addition to a critique of the technical aspects of the Electricité de France's original proposal, recast the identity of the public. According to Renault's alternative scenario, the public was still becoming concerned with environmental issues, but it was not simply interested in electric vehicles – rather, it was concerned with more efficient public petrol-fuelled transport. Now, in the battle, it is not difficult to decipher the projected networks of the two leading social actors, Electricité de France and Renault, and how their respective representations of the French public fed into these. The point is that the (re)production of a self-identity for these organizations was interwoven with a corollary characterization of the French public. Moreover, in order to construct a technology – the electric vehicle – that 'worked', it was likewise necessary simultaneously to construct a social context (which includes the public with its conveniently resonant interests and desires) which could properly accommodate that technology on its terms. In other words, two opposing 'packages' are being constituted by Renault and Electricité de France, each of which places a given technology amongst a series of other humans and nonhumans, all of whom can 'work' functionally and harmoniously together. To show convincingly that the functionality of any one of these entities is suspect is to undermine the whole normative edifice (network), and to undermine catastrophically the identity of the authors of that edifice (in this case, the Electricité de France).

Indeed, this is what we found in Callon's study of the scallops, researchers and fishing community of St Brieuc Bay (1986a) that was mentioned in the previous chapter. This too can be reinterpreted in terms of the production of identity. The three scientists who were attempting to develop techniques for cultivating the scallop, *Pecten maximus*, in order to restock St Brieuc Bay, simultaneously constructed an actor-network in which they narrated the roles of the component actants. Thus, the local fishermen were represented as fundamentally interested in the restocking, the scallops were represented through the various techniques of science as potentially cultivable, and the relevant scientific community was represented as an assenting constituency accrediting the work of the three biologists. The influence of the three researchers derived from the fact that they headed these three heterogeneous populations. In effect, their constructed identity was constituted across these three domains, each of which apparently supported their self-narration as experts, representatives, scientists, advisers and so on. However, this complex of identities could only survive as long as each of the actors in the researchers' network played their allotted part. When the fishermen betrayed the scientists by, contrary to their supposed long-term aims, fishing to the point of decimating the scallop beds, then it was no longer feasible for the three scientists to claim to represent the interests of the fishermen. Likewise, when the scallop larvae levels became hopelessly low, the stories the researchers could tell about themselves as scientists and cultivators became subverted. In sum, their identity, dispersed and decentred across the network as it was, became suspect – their texts of identity were effectively exploded.

Here, identity has been formulated and disseminated, but then subverted. This is because, the fishermen are in a position to enter into the definitional process – their networks, which include families, boats, knowledge of the sea and so on, allow them to engage in this process of undermining and redrafting the network of the biologists. Others are not in a position to do so. Rather, their identities are locally formulated for more parochial struggles as in the case of the Electricité de France's representation of the French public as nascently environmentalist. However, the victory that flows from such battles (e.g. between Electricité de France and Renault) can have all manner of consequences for those who were at one moment merely representational pawns. Thus, had Electricité de France triumphed, there might well have been a major upheaval in the French transport network and in the transport options available to the French public.

At this point it is worth reflecting on the fact that this formulation of the identities of various others (e.g. the French public, the fishermen) does not have to be as explicit as in Callon's case studies. It can be a tacit feature of science (or any network-builder, for that matter). Brian Wynne (1989) has considered the way that various official risk-assessing bodies have informed relevant publics about the risks associated with possibly toxic substances. In particular, he has unpicked the sociological assumptions that inform their assessments of these risks. Indeed, he has shown that when experts assume certain substances to be safe, they do so because they operate with an implicit set of assumptions about the social and practical contexts into which those substances are introduced. Thus, for example, he has analysed the continued recommendation by the Pesticides Advisory Committee that the herbicide 2,4,5-T (better known as agent orange) was safe. Through the 1970s, the Pesticides Advisory Committee issued eight reassurances that the herbicide was safe and that there was no scientific evidence of harm. This was in direct contradiction to the numerous case studies of poisoning presented by the representatives of the National Union of Agricultural and Allied Workers. In 1979, the committee issued another reassurance but added that the herbicide was safe so long as the 'product was used as directed'. This additional statement was highly significant, according to Wynne.

The experts on the Pesticides Advisory Committee were all toxicologists, and the scientific sources they drew upon consisted of the literature on the use of exact quantities and concentrations of the pure chemical on specially bred animals. By generalizing from this literature, they were tacitly drawing upon an idealized picture of the social world – that is, they were engaged in, what Wynne calls, a 'naive sociology'. They did not take into account such factors as, for example, the fact that under conditions on a farm it might be impossible to follow instructions (to wear the appropriate protective clothing, to dilute to specification). Moreover, they ignored the fact that farmworkers do not come into contact with only 2,4,5-T; they have already been exposed to a veritable cocktail of potentially toxic substances. Here, the unreflexive generalization of laboratory-based toxicological data into the vastly different domain of the working farm was implicitly based on an unarticulated and inappropriate model of the working farmer. What Wynne goes on to suggest is that in certain cases a scientific elite's pronouncements can, by virtue of not mapping, in some way, onto pre-existing cultural self-understandings (of, say, farmers), lead to outright disaffection rather than enrolment.

Wynne's example illustrates the importance of not rendering key actors overly 'managerial' or 'agential', in the sense of representing them as consciously mobilizing representations of relevant others in order to build their network. No doubt there can be elements of this. It is interesting to note that the Pesticides Advisory Committee were on the 'defensive' (or were reactive in the sense of responding to the claims of the farmworkers while attempting to maintain their definitional monopoly). In contrast, the three biologists and the Electricité de France were on the 'offensive' (or were proactive in the sense of attempting to build new networks). Of course, 'defensive' and 'offensive' are not simply descriptive terms: they also refer to the analytic perspective – which actors' point of view was being adopted? In other words, the naive sociology of the Pesticides Advisory Committee, and the 'sophisticated sociology' of the biologists and the Electricité de France, is partly the product of the academic narrative. This should remind us to remain circumspect when going about ascribing agency and foresight: it is, as Law (1994) warns us, important to keep in mind that these characteristics are always effects. The naivety or sophistication of actors' 'sociology', and the identities that inhere in this, is not a measure of agency as such, but one of alignment – had the key protagonists (the Pesticides Advisory Committee) marshalled all the appropriate resources in the network, and had they managed successfully to manoeuvre their target actors into their new roles, their efforts would have appeared 'sophisticated'. Let us recall that the effects of both the three biologists and the Electricité de France eventually failed; this was not because they were naive, but because they could not keep their target actors properly aligned. Conversely, had the Pesticides Advisory Committee's numerous pronouncements and reassurances succeeded in representing themselves as the sole source of knowledge about herbicidal poisoning, and had they managed to convince the farmworkers, even temporarily, that their own knowledge was at best anecdotal, and at worst worthless, they might have appeared 'sophisticated'.

A more ambivalent case of the tactical formulation of identity comes from the work of Singleton (1993; Singleton and Michael, 1993) tracing the Cervical Screening Programme network (mentioned in Chapter 4). At the inception of the Cervical Screening Programme, the British Government constructed the identities of a variety of actors, including women, pathology laboratories, cervical cells and GPs. In what follows, I will focus on the identity formulated for women by the Government, and then show how this was modified by GPs in pursuit of other goals.

The part to be played by women according to the Government can be summarized as 'Consumers and Recipients'. In essence, and this continues up to the present day, 'woman' in the Cervical Screening Programme is defined as symptomless, aged between 20 and 64 years and at risk of death from cervical cancer. The part she plays is to attend her GP or local clinic and to have a cervical smear test taken. The GPs, as the Government's intermediaries, generally see no reason to problematize such a role: they stress the value of getting women to have the Cervical Smear Test, or make statements to the effect that it is important to encourage women to come. Those who do not come are 'pathologized': they are Class V; they never bother with anything; they smoke and live on chips. While this dismisses women who do not attend for screening – blaming them for their inability to see its importance – GPs are also likely to excuse non-attendance when it so 'suits' them. This is particularly the case in light of the new government targets.

Complicating the way in which GPs now deal with patients is the recent increase in government involvement in the Cervical Smear Test and the screening programme. The Government's new system of targets means that GPs must now achieve a take-up rate of 80 per cent of their eligible women patients in order to receive higher remuneration: reaching the target can mean a difference in the GP pay packet of £2000 per year. Unsurprisingly, these target payments have become an extremely controversial issue and they were referred to repeatedly in discussion with the GPs (Singleton, 1993). In that the targets effectively formalize eligibility, they have undermined GPs' authority to use informal knowledge in judging eligibility for the Cervical Smear Test. The GPs' response to this is to lay stress on the complexities of eligibility. However, the complexity is emphasized in a specific way, in relation to such concerns as 'not upsetting the ladies', 'not imposing on freedom to get on with life without doctors', and 'allowing freedom of choice'. This seems to be a form of strategic problematization – the GPs are demonstrating the inadequacy of the standardization on which government targets are based. Further, by doing this through an emphasis on the women, the GPs seem to be asserting that their own motivations are patient-centred. The woman and particular social situations are problematized but are simultaneously rendered unproblematic through GP knowledge and understanding of the woman and the situations. There is, then, a shift from a representation of non-attendance in which the woman was represented as recidivist, passive, ignorant or confused to an alternative in which women are portrayed as active participants in the Cervical Smear Test, decision-makers with rational and justifiable concerns. The role of the doctor is represented as one of listening to, and advising, these women.

The point I wish to draw from this ambivalence on the part of the GPs is that while the women are not directly being enrolled by this discourse, it does have performative impact within the network – in relation to nurses, managers, government and eventually women if the networks of the GPs are strong enough. Thus, if they mobilize themselves as a bigger actor they can begin to problematize the recent changes in the Cervical Screening Programme. Already they are doing this, albeit discursively, by stressing that the Cervical Screening Programme is but a very small part in their own network – a network which includes all manner of other functions, interests, roles. Here, they rephrase their own identity as larger than the Cervical Screening Programme – they must deal with carrying out childhood immunizations, prescribing and advising on contraception, performing breast examinations, encouraging participation in national breast screening programmes, and advising on the symptoms and treatment of the menopause. In this network, the Cervical Screening Programme was often represented as a relatively unimportant actor.

This commitment to, and problematization of, the Cervical Screening Programme reflects the dilemmas that the GPs face, revealing how women come to be differentially formulated in this network. Further, these formulations are connected with different GP identities – on the one hand, as steadfast intermediaries of the Cervical Screening Programme; on the other, as critically reflexive, multiply employed physicians. In terms of the social ordering of the network, it is this very multiplicity that renders it durable. Without the dual characterization of the women (as well as other actors in the network, such as the interpretability of laboratory results and the nature of the doctor–patient relationship), the workability of the Cervical Smear Test and the Cervical Screening Programme would be further jeopardized.

'Others' and Flexible Identities

In the above examples, we have seen how women and the French public were formulated in such a way as to serve as representational tools in the performation of networks. These have been direct and delineating constructions, attending to the defining characteristics of the actors in question. In the case of the Cervical Screening Programme, while non-attending women were ambivalently represented – as recalcitrant objects or rational subjects – these were nevertheless nuanced narrative characters. As we will see below, under some circumstances, these representations can have minimal characteristics that allow for limited flexibility and, consequently, a more fluid association. However, before examining this, I will first consider a more indirect route by which identity is constituted, not through a direct representation of self, but a series of contrasts wherein the network that takes shape is disparate and fragmented – where a series of marginalizations and 'others' is required in order to represent the public as deficient on a number of levels. These insights are drawn from Michael and Birke (1994a, b).

'Others' and the Socio-Ethical Domain of Animal Experimentation

Michael and Birke (1994a) consider the construction and deployment of 'others' in relation to the animal experimentation controversy. A perennial focus of controversy in the past (Rupke, 1990; Tester, 1991), animal experimentation has over the last 20 years once again become an activity whose moral and scientific status is hotly disputed. The debate raises questions of ethics, epistemology and identity while the various antagonists struggle for the moral high ground (Jasper and Nelkin, 1992). The participants include scientists and animal technicians, politicians and funding agencies as well as philosophers, lobbyists and the lay public.

Increasingly, then, scientists are having to enter into the public domain to explain, justify or defend animal experimentation. This section investigates how scientists' articulation of the issues entails a dual process of definition of self and other in the process of attempted network building. Scientists are engaged in representing their activities, particularly to the wider public; they do this in the context of competing views of animals, debates about their moral status and about the rights of humans to use them in various ways. In this context, scientists portray animals, biomedical science, the 'human good', society and the anti-vivisection movement not only to gain rhetorical advantage, but also to structure a desired social (and non-social) world. Because the animal experimentation debate raises questions about the relative moral and ontological status of animals, scientists who participate in it have to engage in moral argument. There are various ways in which they might do this.

Scientists might, for example, attempt to show how their treatment of animals lives up to certain standards of 'humanity'. For example, they might stress their feelings for animals. Lynch (1988), in an ethnographic study of neuroscientists, has analysed the social and technical rituals used in laboratories to transform animals from subjects to objects, from potential pets to biological exemplars. Scientists can use this process as a rhetorical resource as they attempt to show how they must overcome emotional reactions in order to do scientific work. More positively, they could stress their appreciation of animals by reclassifying at least some of them as subjects (as opposed to 'mere' objects and resources). As Arluke (e.g. 1990, 1991) has shown in a study of scientists and animal technicians in the US, laboratory workers often 'recover' or 're-ascribe' pet-like status to certain animals. Thus, a slight quirk in physical appearance or personality that differentiates one particular animal from a batch may be used as a reason for illicitly excluding that animal from the experimental population. Moreover, that animal will be looked after and cared for as a pet. Such examples could then be used rhetorically to 'human-ize' the face of science. Here, then, there is a construction of the generic identity of 'animal' (as quasi-interactive subject) that is instrumental in the construction of scientific self-identity. To the extent that an acceptable asso-ciation between scientist and animal is being represented it normalizes scientists as people who possess a 'natural attitude' toward animals (Lynch, 1988). As such, these representations serve to safeguard against exclusion from the broader network of humans and animals.

Another discursive option available to scientists is to criticize the public directly. Gluck and Kubacki (1991) have outlined some of the rhetorics used by biomedical researchers in undermining the public. Most relevant to this discussion is the discourse that directly denigrates the public by representing anti-vivisection concerns as essentially trivial (see also Arluke, 1991). Similarly, in the Michael and Birke interviews, there were various means by which the public is shown to be of dubious moral and intellectual standing. Scientists often directly derogate the public as 'unscientific', 'anti-scientific', 'anti-intellectual', 'illogical' or 'ethically compromised' (see next section for more details). However, such derogation can also occur implicitly when sci-entists contrast the civilized practices of British animal experimentation against a complex series of 'Others' who deal with animals and/or use inva-sive techniques. The implicit aim of such discourse is to put the sceptical public in its place. The performative dimension of these representations rests on a perception of the interviewers as representatives of a scientifically liter-ate audience. Given that the interviews were conducted for the science magazine, *New Scientist*, it is more than likely that the role associated with Michael and Birke as interviewers was not only simply that of academic researchers; they also represented a journal that popularizes science in Britain (see Michael and Birke, 1994a for methodological and sample details). Insofar as the interviewers could be viewed as conduits to a wider audience, then they served the function of prospective intermediaries, who could convey a particular range of identities to the publics beyond the confines of the immediate scientific network.

The use of 'others' to establish the discursive space for a particular identity is well known in social psychology's intergroup theory (e.g. Turner, 1987), feminist critique (e.g. Fee, 1983; Halpin, 1989), social constructionism (e.g. Shotter and Gergen, 1989) and the sociology of postmodernity (e.g. Lash and Urry, 1987; Harvey, 1989). The above forms of analysis posit a process of self-delineation through comparison and differentiation from a group of 'others'. In the present context, scientists' distinctions between themselves and a range of 'others' have the effect of placing their own practices of animal experi-mentation in a positive moral light. At the same time, these contrasts are used to criticize their lay critics for failing to recognize the differences that distin-guish valuable animal experimentation from more disreputable uses of animals, including those found amongst the general public.

Before considering these discourses it is important to describe briefly the legislative backdrop to animal experimentation in the UK. The 1986 Animals

(Scientific Procedures) Act was brought in to replace what was felt to be the obsolescent 1876 Cruelty to Animals Act. The main provision of the later Act was a system of licensing and inspection, mediated by the Home Office, in which each institution needs a licence and a named person responsible for the fulfilment of that licence (usually the head of the institution); each project needs to be licensed individually; each person working with animals needs to be given a personal licence (this includes technicians and junior scientists). There is also a named person responsible for the day-to-day care of the animals. In addition, there is a named veterinary surgeon who is in charge of evaluating the condition of the animals. As regards evaluation, each project application contains section 19B, which specifies the proposed number of animals to be used, the procedures to be conducted, and the scientific and medical rationale (e.g. the benefits accruing from the research) for the experimental programme. In addition, Home Office Inspectors can now inspect facilities without prior warning in order to make spot checks on the conditions, labelling, the adherence to the procedures stated in the project licence, and so on.

Change and No Change

One striking finding was that, despite the fact that the 1986 Act was initially seen as imposing a further administrative burden on already overworked scientists, nearly all the scientists that were interviewed claimed that its overall impact upon actual procedures was fairly limited. The Act was seen generally as a 'good thing', even though scientists felt that the wider public failed to recognize its benefits. In sum, as the following quotes reveal, the Act is good, but has actually altered very little: the creative potential of science has not been hampered, and the experimental procedures have not been substantially changed with the implementation of the Act. So, for example, a senior scientist noted:

> So it hasn't actually altered the way we do science at all, the way I do science . . .

This seems to be the general picture – the main effect of the Act has been seen to be an increase in bureaucracy, both in the filling out of forms and in the keeping of records. However, while there has been no change, practice prior to the Act was just as responsible:

> When I say we haven't changed our practice, I jolly well know we were doing things correctly before the new Act came in. But I think it has provided a degree of recognition that we are doing what we ought to be doing. That wasn't there before.

> . . . I think we always were sensitive with regard to the treatment to the animals . . . I think the law has made people now sit down and think . . . go and get involved in tissue culture . . .

Michael and Birke admit that, at the outset of this research, they expected to find that the Act would be represented as a historical threshold, a point of substantive transition. Yet, what they actually found was that scientists claimed that it had not qualitatively changed their practices. Indeed, scientists argued, the concern for the animals was just as strong prior to the Act. It seemed important to the scientists to convey a belief that British animal experimentation is part of a tradition that has directed much effort and many resources to the care of animals. Yet, the scientists also welcomed the Act – it signified progress and improvement. Given the claim that animals have always been well treated, what form does this progress and improvement take if not in direct relation to the welfare of the animals? The scientists' responses to being asked to qualify their claim that things have improved focused upon 'thinking harder'. If animal researchers do so, they will 'increase awareness', which will lead to 'better science' in the end:

> . . . By having to put together a very large project application is to focus your thoughts. I think that's extremely useful. It's a pain . . . as well.

> Irritation at having to do it [follow legislation]. But the positive thing might be that people do actually think about it more.

To summarize the above rhetorical scenario: scientists generally welcome the 1986 Act and simultaneously assert that it has not changed their actual procedures (and indeed, the welfare of the animals has always been of utmost concern). The only perceived change is that more thought and reflection are required. Michael and Birke paraphrase this in the following way: 'Before the Act we were good; after the Act we are no more or less good but we think about it more now.' What is important here is the continuity of an identity wherein the Act has not changed the substance or essence of that scientific identity, merely its formal (bureaucratic) characteristics.

Constructing a Socio-Ethical Domain

In tandem with the above discourse in which the animal welfare record of British animal experimentation is represented as both traditionally 'excellent' and improved by the Act, there are another set of discourses which demarcate what can be called a socio-ethical domain. In this, the practices of a variety of 'Others', who are represented as relatively less caring, less concerned and less knowledgeable in relation to the treatment of animals, can be contrasted with UK animal experimentation. There is, then, a dual dynamic in which the definition of inferior 'others' serves to construct a self-identity (both in the local sense of one's own institution and in the wider sense of British scientific experimentation in general) and vice versa. Moreover, this co-construction of self and 'others' is 'passed on' to the interviewers, who, it is hoped, will be persuaded by it and who, in due course, will disseminate it. In other words, the interviewees can be read as being engaged in an effort to enrol Michael and Birke as intermediaries who will forge their desired network beyond their laboratories. There are a number of key sites at which this boundary between the identities of the 'other' and self is patrolled.

'Foreigners'

This is perhaps the most frequently cited 'other', being used by more than half the interviewees. Here, the moral upstandingness of British medical science is contrasted favourably with the laxity of non-British animal experimentation. In some cases, this was illustrated by reference to individual foreign visitors to British research institutions. For example:

> Had a professor here from Japan and he did not have the greatest respect [for animals], because it is a different culture . . .

In other instances, the 'others' resided abroad, as scientists recalled the practices witnessed at non-British institutions. For example, a cell biologist, who was responding to a question about the impact of the 1986 Act upon his work, firstly expressed his satisfaction with the Home Office and the licensing system, then went on to add:

> I worked for a while at a university in France which I resigned from because of the treatment I thought the animals were getting . . .

Finally, the practitioners and institutions of British bioscience are not simply contrasted with their non-British counterparts; Britain's political and cultural traditions are referred to as being at the forefront of animal welfare. Occasionally, other countries are presented in a positive light (for example, Germany and the Netherlands). However, here, while concern of these 'others' for animals is acknowledged, it is represented as being caught up in an overbearing system in which the policing of animal experimentation has become too extreme or impracticable. Thus, the British system is presented as superior because ethical concerns are interwoven with a sensible political pragmatism that nurtures a workable system of moral regulation. For example, in talking about the value and problems with local ethical committees and the prospect of a European charter covering animal experimentation, one respondent made the following point:

> Britain was the first country to really get its act together and to produce rational legislation. One of our worries is that it will be overturned by the European Parliament which will take a less rational approach.

In a similar vein, a senior physiologist, describing his experience of working abroad, commented:

> By comparison with the rest of the world, we are light years ahead in the way we have addressed these problems.

Commercial Cosmetics Sector

Another frequently mentioned 'other' was the cosmetics industry; indeed, nearly all the interviewees referred to commercial testing. On the whole, commercial testing was seen as a fundamentally trivial exercise which made no contribution either to knowledge or to the betterment of humankind. For instance, one scientist identified the public's concern with cosmetics testing as partly responsible for the 1986 Act, adding the following:

> . . . we've got to safeguard against trivial experiments . . . the cosmetics industry for instance gets the experimentation a bad name . . .

Another scientist, commenting on the claims of the anti-vivisectionists, endorsed the public concern with the cosmetics industry:

> I am very against testing cosmetics and things on animals . . .

The 'other' of the commercial/cosmetics sector has a further resonance for scientists. In the context of recent anti-vivisection campaigns, numerous scientists lamented the 'fact' that many critics confused scientific animal experimentation and commercial animal testing. There are two things to note here. Firstly, the derogation of commercial testing was itself relatively undifferentiated in the scientists' discourse (as in 'I am against cosmetics testing'); in contrast, the ethical dilemmas involved in the use of animals in 'pure' research were presented more subtly. Thus, many of the scientists emphasized the nuanced character of their own position, specifying how they would draw the line at using particular species or techniques. Secondly, drawing the distinction between 'good science' and 'bad commerce' serves not only to elevate the moral standing of the former, but also implicitly to construct the sceptical public as, on the one hand, 'ignorant' of the genuine independence and ethical difference between these two enterprises and, on the other, 'morally compromised' in its politically motivated, 'fact-neglecting' over enthusiasm to view science and commerce in the same light.

Pets

Occasionally, the inhumane treatment of pets was contrasted with the stringently policed ways in which animals are cared for in laboratories. Such comparisons have a dual rhetorical effect: they imply that the public is 'ignorant' since its members do not know what goes on in laboratories, and suggest that it is also hypocritical since many people's treatment of their own animals leaves a lot to be desired. One scientist, in suggesting that Britain has very effective systems to stop cruelty to animals, reflected as follows:

> I don't think cruelty in experimentation is any near as big a problem as is in situations, for example, of where people will use dogs to kill badgers in an arena . . .

In a similar way – contrasting one's own work to the behaviour of the public – a technician, in the process of describing his work on intact animals, commented:

> I have seen what the general public subject their pets to and things . . . which is unbelievable

Agriculture and Abattoirs

The view of scientists that public perceptions are spurious is reinforced in their comments on the 'others' of agriculture and abattoirs. While superficially it appears that it is the 'institutions' of meat production that are being criticized by the scientists, there is also a problematization of the public's perception and evaluation of these institutions. Again, there is an implicit charge of hypocrisy: if the public can reap the benefits of the 'meat-production industry' without being overly bothered about the conditions under which the animals are reared and slaughtered, then they should treat the medical use of animals with like forbearance, especially since biomedicine has always maintained a tradition of caring for animals. Moreover, the public again reveals its 'ignorance' and its politically motivated neglect of the facts by conflating the conditions and uses of animals in science with those in agriculture. The following quote comes from a scientist who has just suggested that the popularity of anti-vivisectionism is partly rooted in the public's lack of scientific understanding and in its sentimentality as regards animals:

> I think it's just a very emotive subject that we're supposed to be a nation of animal lovers and yet farmers' animals starve, pets are thrown out after Christmas . . .

Another scientist remarks:

> As someone who's been to abattoirs, I feel the way we look after our animals is infinitely better . . .

Clinicians

Finally, and most surprisingly, scientists occasionally compare their treatment of animals with clinical practice. Here, scientists claim that the legal and moral strictures upon animal experimentalists ensure that they are painstakingly careful and humane when using surgical techniques. In contrast, surgeons operating on human patients are somewhat less meticulous. Rhetorically, this observation invites the critical layperson to put themselves in the position of the experimental animal. The implicit promise is that, as an experimental animal, they would receive treatment that was more caring than the treatment they would be given had they been so unfortunate as to be human beings in need of surgery at a hospital. This view was most forcefully expressed in the following quote, which was made in the context of arguing that there are other activities more damaging to animals than animal experimentation:

> The attitude of the surgeon was totally cavalier by comparison. You begin to wonder whether you're far too careful with animals . . . . the attitude towards animals is infinitely more caring and exacting. The surgery on humans would take, I reckon, one tenth of the time that it took us on a ram . . . just because of the care taken.

Each of the above 'others' serves to demarcate a moral haven. My argument is that within this socio-ethical domain, British animal experimentation can be represented as relatively unproblematic. The recent change in legislation has moreover led to 'thinking harder'. Scientists agree that thinking harder is a result of the necessary discussions between themselves and Home Office Inspectors, as they debate particular licence applications or experimental protocols.

Differentiating oneself from 'others', thereby creating a moral haven, is perhaps unsurprising given the high public profile of animal experimentation.

Thus, various others can be represented as models of poor practice, serving to highlight 'humanitarianism' within British animal experimentation. Here, an identity of 'having a concern for animals' is discursively mobilized. However, these 'others' also serve another performative function, insofar as they underline the value of the Act in promoting reflection. The 'others' are inferior in terms of their capacity or opportunity for such intellectual clarification. Thus, clinicians or foreign experimenters may be represented as being culturally disabled from the painstaking ethical reflection that British animal experimentation epitomizes. At the same time, by defining the 'others', the scientists also construct a representation of their audiences – primarily, the educated lay public interested in science. Each of the 'others' that emerged in scientists' discourse implicitly appeals to, or criticizes, some characteristic of the public. Thus, the invocation of 'foreigners', whether they are individuals, institutions or national politics and culture, inevitably appeals to nationalistic propensities in the would-be audience. However, the audience of the *New Scientist*, while friendly towards science, is not necessarily pro-animal experimentation. What the talk of the scientists does is generate a space – an implicitly delineated socio-ethical domain – an identity. The perceived audience is implicitly invited to enter, or, at the very least, to recognize the existence of this domain. But to do so, it must adopt certain characteristics and eschew others; that is, incorporate certain new elements into their identity. These can be listed as follows.

References to the practices of the cosmetics industry constitute the sceptical public in terms of its willingness to sacrifice animals in pursuit of trivial consumables; biomedicine's utility is assumed. While the differentiation of science from the commercial/cosmetics sector assumes that such distinction is not problematic, the implicit complaint is that the sceptical public has an illegitimate tendency to confuse scientific and commercial animal experimentation. Thus, this public is portrayed as epistemologically naive (the public is ignorant of the facts that distinguish scientific from commercial practice – it is, in effect, unqualified to draw parallels) and ethically biased (political commitments predispose it to seeing the similarities as opposed to the differences). In relation to agriculture, the differential utility argument does not apply: here, in pointing to the relative humanitarianism of the British scientists, the sceptical public is criticized for being unfairly concerned with practices of the latter when it should place agriculture under equal scrutiny. Once again, the epistemological and ethical shortcomings of the public are being implicitly invoked. Where pet-keepers comprise 'others', the sceptical public is directly derogated, for not only are they lacking in critical judgement, but they are also the owners who so dismally fail their pets. Finally, as a vicarious experimental animal, the layperson would realize how fortunate she or he is compared to the clinical patient. Thus, even the empathic faculties of the public are questioned when placed in the wider comparative context of experimental versus clinical procedure and policing.

These negative 'others' demarcate the positive space inhabited by British scientific animal experimentation. To the extent that the readership of the

New Scientist, represented by the interviewers, is being invited into this space it must choose contrasting qualities. On the one hand, there are such positive characteristics as the capacity to think hard and clearly about the relevant issues, the ability to treat animals with appropriate and consistent respect, and the willingness to recognize the historical superiority of British biomedicine's treatment of animals. On the other hand, it must decline to indulge in sloppy thinking and overgeneralized moralizing. In tracing out such a contrast between 'good' and 'bad' publics, sympathetic and antipathetic audiences, the scientists also tacitly draw upon their membership of the 'good' public. This is explicitly instanced in the way that some of the respondents occasionally underlined their own ethical stance by referring to their pets at home.

In sum, this 'socio-ethical domain' insulates British animal experimentation from these nefarious 'others'. But, more vitally, and in parallel, it represents those members of the audience that are aligned with the sceptical public as cognitively, critically and morally lackadaisical – something they should, as 'reasonable people', be concerned to remedy. We thus encounter a superordinate rhetoric that draws upon some norm of the 'inherent good of more reflection'. Just as the 'others' were represented as inferior in their capacity or opportunity to reflect, so is the sceptical British public. Its lapses in logic and its inertia when thinking about these issues are contrasted with the reflexive and incisive thinking of the British scientists, a process which has become even more rigorous and energetic thanks to the routinization wrought by the 1986 Act. The perceived audience, the relatively science-friendly readership of the *New Scientist* (for which the interviews were conducted), is presented with a choice of identities: be 'good' and intellectually and morally diligent, or be 'bad' and intellectually and morally lazy.

Let me now translate the foregoing into ANT terms. As mentioned above, one can interpret these exchanges as processes whereby the interviewers were being situated as intermediaries. The performative strategy is to enrol the interviewers into pro-animal experimentation roles, to predispose them to disseminate, via the pages of the *New Scientist*, the appropriate (identity-)texts to the wider public. By black-boxing a series of 'others', there was a parallel black-boxing of the lay public into two discrete and contrastive identity options. On the one hand, the 'good' public role is a key element in the scientists' projected network: the public 'thinks hard', it looks critically – in sum, it is comprised of 'reasonable people'. On the other hand, the other-ized 'bad' public lacks these qualities and, as such, has no part to play in this network. Or rather, more work needs to be done to make this public 'think harder' and thus become eligible for the projected network of harmonious actors – hardworking scientists, hard-thinking publics, laboratories, animals and biomedical products.

In sum, a network is being delineated which, crucially in this context, includes 'reasonable' lay people. Readers of the *New Scientist* either are already 'reasonable' or, if they are not, are being supplied (via the intermediary interviewers/writers) both with a characterization of their 'unreasonableness' and with the sort of identity they will need to be 'reasonable'. However, as the next section will show, the quality of 'thinking hard' is only one dimension in that identity. There are other, more flexible, aspects which, while they do not demand enrolment, at least provide the grounds for some sort of *rapprochement* or *modus vivendi* between those who are pro- and anti-animal experimentation.

Before going on to the next section, the above account needs some reflection. The representations of 'others' were not derived from single scientists, but from a sample. This sample, nevertheless, can be seen as constituting a singular actor, but it is a singularity that is born of the network itself. Over and above the impact of common legislative actors, these different scientific voices cohere as a unitary actor by virtue of the shared broad socio-ethical domain to which each lays claim. However, having noted this, this actor is also an artefact of the interview process and the network building of the interviewers (or rather, the analysts) themselves. I shall return to consider this process in the last section of the next chapter.

Flexible Identities

The duality of identities proffered by the scientists to the audience is backed up by another set of discourses. As indicated at the start of this chapter, animal experimentation scientists are not simply concerned to demonstrate their humane treatment of animals. They are also interested in showing that they are reasonable people, willing and able to enter into dialogue with their critics. In this respect, scientists demarcate at least the minimal characteristics of a critical lay public with which the scientists are ostensibly willing to enter into negotiation. As such, this minimal identity, and the flexibility it incorporates, does not simply serve to 'enrol'. This is because the aim is not to achieve an undiluted consensus with recalcitrant actors by clearly delimiting their identities. Rather, the purpose is to set up the conditions of possibility, rendered in terms of identity, for argumentation and dialogue. Based on the work of Michael and Birke (1994b), I will now examine this feature of science–public relations in the field of animal experimentation by contrasting ANT with the notion of 'core set'.

For Collins (1981, 1985) the core set is defined as the

> set of allies and enemies in the core of a controversy [who] are not necessarily bound to each other by social ties or membership of common institutions. Some members of this set may be intent on destroying the interpretation of the universe upon which others have staked their careers, their academic credibility and perhaps their whole social identity. If these enemies interact, it is likely to be only in the context of the particular passing debate. This set of persons does not necessarily act like a 'group'. They are bound only by their close, if differing, interests in the controversy's outcome. (1985, p. 142)

Collins documents in rich detail the rhetorical strategies deployed by members of the core set to undermine their opponents. These entail a mixture of technical critiques (referring to the quality of scientific work) and evaluations of reputation (for example, the standing of the opponent's home institution or research team, or opponent's personal character). However, as is common in much sociology of scientific knowledge, while any scientific controversy can be shown to entail 'non-technical' argumentation, what is at stake is an outcome about the facticity of a state of affairs in nature. That is to say, the prize is the truth of this or that version of some natural phenomenon (or the efficacy of this or that technological artefact). In the case of animal experimentation, as we have seen, controversy does touch upon these issues of truth and efficacy, but it also contains, pivotally, an overt and public moral component – whether it is right or just or ethically defensible to use animals in pursuit of scientific knowledge, biomedical technique or medical benefit. On the whole, the typical members of core sets in scientific controversy have been scientists and technologists – those experts who have a more or less elaborated knowledge of the theories, concepts and methods used in the apprehension of the relevant natural phenomenon.

Even in those controversies that have an overt moral or political element which ties up to the prevailing concerns of the public, such as nuclear power, the emphasis is upon a core set rightly composed of what Collins elsewhere has called 'professional experts' (Collins and Pinch, 1994). Thus, Collins (1988) argues that the UK's (then) Central Electricity Generating Board's demonstration of the 'safety' of its nuclear fuel flasks, while represented as an open experiment, was actually a display of post-closure knowledge. The CEGB, in inviting the public to witness an apparent experiment (the crashing of a train loaded with flasks), was implicitly also ascribing membership of the core set to the public. Members of the public were being asked to use their powers of logic and induction to judge an experiment. However, what the public was in fact presented with was a display of virtuosity: a demonstration from only one point of view. An alternative perspective was denied them insofar as the public lack a knowledge of the messiness, indeterminacy and contingency of experiments. By being structured by an over-restricted core set, as well as giving a false impression of the internal workings of science, the display attempts to flatter its lay audience into believing that it can arbitrate over the outcomes of the ostensible experiment. Collins' recommendation is that such displays should be opened out – the public can be represented in the core set by counter-experts (e.g. Greenpeace) who can unpick the parameters and contingencies involved in an experiment/display.

Such a recommendation is possible because the core set is characterized by technical expertise – the technical/expert dimension of the demonstration is Collins' primary concern. The worry is that the demonstration per se will dupe the lay audience. However, if we look at this process from the perspective of ANT, a different set of issues emerges.

In contrast, as we have seen for ANT, scientists must have certain practical political, social and economic skills. Thus, they are viewed as marshalling a range of materials and techniques to extend their influence beyond the laboratory. In all this, the technical is only one aspect of the process of enrolment. If in Collins' CEGB case study the lay audience is invited to adopt the temporary identity of 'experimenter', it is simultaneously asked to take on another range of identities – for example, that of citizen concerned with the UK's economic 'well-being'. Without this complementary identity the demonstration can be resisted – if not on technical grounds, then on political, economic or cultural grounds. This might work on the level of a rejection of the demonstration, not in terms of its technical shortcomings, but on its political, environmental or economic merits. An argument against the demonstration might run as follows: 'Well, I can't dispute the technical demonstration of the safety of the flasks, but so what? What happens when the fuel gets to the power station? What are we going to do with the waste? Are we heading for a nuclear police state?' The adoption of this supplementary identity of 'citizen concerned with the UK's economic "well-being"' is a disassociation from other identities, identities which have at their disposal such critical discourses as the above.

In terms of the concept of core set, when such broader political, ethical and economic issues are also incorporated into a controversy, we find that there is not merely a pseudo-core set manipulated by one faction in a controversy, the core set becomes potentially infinitely extendable. That is to say, the core set is now comprised of those actors concerned with a substantively moral and political controversy. As any citizen can in principle contribute to the debate by stressing the 'non-scientific' aspects, this generalized core set can, theoretically, encompass any member of society with a view on the relevant subject.

The point is that these 'extra-scientific' issues are also of concern to the scientific advocate of this or that technology or knowledge. To convince their target public, they must also get them to accept a range of supplementary identities.

To the extent that the animal experimentation controversy is overtly moral in character, the allied core set is infinitely extended – any person can have a moral stance on the issue. As such, scientists attempt to circumscribe it, to redefine it and, as a corollary, to disqualify certain others from proper membership of it. In sum, scientists wish to demarcate the parameters of the core set. (Indeed, if they can convincingly define the controversy exclusively in scientific terms, they have already excluded a large number of potential critics.)

Collins has recognized the existence of this process, though he has not elaborated on it, seeing it rather as a methodological problem. As he notes, there are certain difficulties in demarcating the core set that derive from the efforts of scientists to determine who is legitimately involved in a controversy and who is not. He writes:

> Thus it is impossible to give a clear definition of who is inside and who is outside the core set. The problem is aggravated because there will be systematic biases in scientists' assessments of who is in, and who is out. This is because scientists tend to underrate the contributions of those whose views oppose their own and vice versa . . . . Systematic discrepancies in scientists' perceptions of who is a member are likely to be more interesting than the exact membership. (1981, pp. 8–9)

The following section shows how ANT can inform the analysis of core set demarcation. As we will see, in the case of animal experimentalists, scientists want to dictate the terms and form of the animal experimentation debate. For them, it needs to have certain minimal characteristics – rationality, non-violence, civility and so on. However, the aim is not simply to enrol co-controversialists into a definitive identity; the issue for scientists is not merely who is right and wrong within the core set, but who can have a legitimate membership of, and voice within, it. As we shall see, these scientists are concerned to maintain dialogue with their opponents and critics – the purpose is to envelop them in a restricted debate, that is, a controlled core set. In the process, scientists define the character of the public – they disaggregate it into component, more or less amenable, fractions. In what follows, I will illustrate some of the ways in which scientists involved in animal experiments attempt discursively to construct the minimal characteristics that an anti-vivisection public must have to be part of what they see as the legitimate moral and technical controversy.

Enrolling the Core Set

As before, I proceed on the assumption that the interviewer is polysemic, and thus represents multiple audiences for the interviewee. Consequently, we can regard the scientists' statements as being, at least in part, directed towards the public which the scientist wishes to be a part of their desired core set – in this case, the relatively science-friendly readership of the *New Scientist*. Clearly, the scientists are not directly engaged in the enrolment of this public; nevertheless, they are articulating an ideal core set that, via the interviewers-as-intermediaries, will be presented to the public.

However, before looking at the attempts to construct the 'appropriate' core set, it is necessary to first show that scientists are indeed interested in entering into dialogue with the public. Usually, this is seen to be highly problematic – the problem primarily arising from the perceived nature of the public (though occasionally also an upshot of the scientists' own shortcomings). For example:

> We've got to stick our heads above the parapets to show we are actually ordinary people trying to do a good job for mankind, talk to the press, the public, all the rest of it.

If there is a spoken desire to engage in debate with the public, it is frequently implied that this is a case of rectifying public ignorance – of increasing education and information. However, over and above this wish is a series of representations which cumulatively limits the public that can properly enter into the debate, that can be 'educated'. There is, in other words, a range of discourses of exclusion and inclusion which form a flexible nexus through which identities are attributed and the core set can be demarcated.

Demonization

This is perhaps the most elementary form of exclusion. Here, scientists eject would-be core set members by pointing to their status as criminals – that is, persons who fall outside of the common limits of civilized society. This is most evident in the representation of the radical element in the anti-vivisection movement. For example, one scientist noted:

> Of course the debate ceased being a debate effectively when the ALF [Animal Liberation Front] became involved. I am not convinced that they are not just a bunch of terrorists who were involved in something else and then found this cause . . .

Demarcating Rationality

The tenor of the above quote suggests reluctance to engage in dialogue because of the threat of abuse and reprisal. However, as the quote that precedes it suggests, this does not preclude a general desire for dialogue. The demonization of the radical anti-vivisectionists suggests that there is also a more conducive constituency of critics (for example, the Royal Society for the Prevention of Cruelty to Animals recast as moderate animal welfarists) with whom debate is, eventually, possible:

> It [the radical anti-vivisection movement] is like the IRA. It contains people who are just members of it to blow people up and it has people who become members because of what it believes . . . . we must not tar everyone with the same brush.

> One of the difficulties we have in this area is trying to address the anti-vivisection lobby as a homogeneous population and clearly they are not. There are some very extreme right-wing people who are apparently politically motivated, and there are other people who have a genuine concern for the suffering of animals. I will put myself in that group.

However, this differentiation between the unreasonable and reasonable has a further implication: it positions the scientists as reflexive and rational. This ability to distinguish different facets of the anti-vivisection lobby can be contrasted with the irrationality of the mass of the anti-animal experiment lobby which has a perceived tendency to conflate the various activities in which animals potentially suffer, actually suffer or die. So while, through the above radical–moderate distinction, scientists can attribute rationality (in relation to the willingness to debate in a reasonable manner) to the moderate faction of the anti-vivisection lobby, they can simultaneously show that very rationality to be compromised by pointing to the critics' various shortcomings. Examples of this were provided above in the section on 'others' (e.g. the distinction between biomedical animal experimentation and the cosmetics industry, and the public's ignorance of this).

Demarcating Expertise

If the above quote suggests that scientists problematize the rationality of the mass of lay critics, and thereby their qualifications for membership of the core set, there are also more subtle ways in which this is accomplished. In particular, the contrast hinges on a range of criteria concerned with expertise. Sometimes this expertise takes the form of intellectual or technological skill; in other cases, it reflects the superior or profounder experiential knowledge and emotionality of practitioners.

Intellectual and Technological Criteria At the most basic level, there is a concern with the emotionality of the lay response to animal experiments which disables proper reflection. Once again, this is intimately tied to the scientists' understanding of the provisions of the 1986 Animals (Scientific Procedures) Act which, as we have seen above, has engendered a general increase in scientists' quantity and quality of thought as regards the reasons for conducting animal experiments in any given instance. Now, this 'thinking harder' serves as another criterion for membership of the core set. As the following quote suggests, scientists question the capacity or willingness of the lay public to 'think hard':

> They [the public] have this vision that you [scientists] are all slightly mad and you are all waiting for the opportunity behind closed doors to inflict pain and misery on animals. It's terrifying that anyone one could think that . . .

This and similar quotes suggest that the public's response is basically irrational: the public is represented as perceiving scientists in simplistic terms – scientists are evil, intent on pursuing biomedical benefits whatever the cost. In sum, the public is represented as resorting to stereotypes rather than engaging in the 'hard thought' that characterizes scientists' efforts.

The necessity for 'hard thinking' (as a parameter of the 'appropriate' core set) is underlined by some scientists' suggestions that there is a need to extend the core set to encompass 'ethics professionals' – that is, people who have expertise in the calm and considered calculation of the value of specific experiments. In the following quote, a scientist remarks on the role and composition of ethics committees which could adjudicate on the necessity of animal experiments:

> Thankfully what goes on in ethical committees in general is reasoned debate. All the ones I've had contact with have worked very effectively. For example, most lay representatives would be members of the clergy or legal profession – in other words they would be people who, as part of their daily lives, were used to judging ethical situations. There are even people who are professional ethicists. That is not inappropriate – judging the ethical position on any given subject is quite a professional activity. You can't just walk in and give a gut reaction to what you are being told. You have to carefully consider the pros and cons. There is a tradition of ethics you really have to be aware of. It is important that lay people are selected so that rational debate can take place.

Here, we have the importation of a stratum of ethics professionals who can argue the issues in accordance with a rationality that is more or less absent from an amateurized lay public. However, it is not emotionality per se that so disables the layperson from rational debate. It is an inappropriate emotionality that reacts to the superficial appearances of animal experiments; that is, an emotionality that is not grounded in an appropriate experience of animals or cannot be properly tempered by an appreciation of the possible benefits.

Rational Emotionality Scientists do not dismiss outright the role of emotions in the controversy. For example, they will point to various species and procedures which they would not be willing to use because they would find it too upsetting. However, this 'subjective' reaction, while authentic insofar as it is an aspect of the constitution of the individual scientist, nevertheless could be marginalized in the bigger scientific picture – that is, while the speaker would not engage in procedure X or use species A, this was immaterial as to whether others should:

> I can't see myself doing experiments on dogs or cats or monkeys . . . I probably accept that somebody has to do it . . .

However, the main concern in this section is that scientists represent their feelings for animals as being based on their long-term contact with animals, both in the laboratory and at home:

> I think there are a lot of people who have lost sight of the realities of our relationships with animals which have developed over the years . . . I have a menagerie at home and I look after them, I have a great respect for the animals that I look after.

> . . . we've killed animals in the past and we will always do so in the future, we've got to do it in a humane way . . . keep them . . . in the most humane environment.

These two quotes (by the same scientist) suggest a quasi-historical representation of human–animal relations in which our treatment of animals is embedded. The feeling for animals, minimally signified by the 'great respect' and in the very keeping of them, is further modulated by a historical realism. By comparison, laypeople's emotionality is rendered dubious in a number of ways. Firstly, though sincere, it can be inauthentic – not a facet of self but a product of fashion, manipulation or some other purpose (e.g. environmentalism):

> . . . it is very easy for one or two [extremists] to manipulate the minds of the whole of the rest of the group, even people who are well educated and able to make up their own minds can still be misled . . .

Additionally, this emotionality can be suspect because it is pathological or excessive:

> I think there is a Zeitgeist feeling concern for animals . . . and I think a lot of those people get sucked into it that are just people who are angry, probably about how they are brought up . . .

Finally, it can overspill the boundaries of good sense or true knowledge. In the next example, this takes the form of ignorance of the habitat into which liberated animals are released:

> I mean, do they [anti-vivisectionists] really live a logical existence? . . . I mean they are often the people who take animals and liberate them in the wild and they are immediately scoffed up by the dogs or something.

This illogicality finds its greatest expression in the attributed hypocrisy of castigating animal experimentalists while consuming the products of medical research, grossly mistreating pets or ignoring other instances of animal abuse (see the discussion above on agriculture and abattoirs).

So, here we see the superficiality of the public's emotional response to animals: it is a sentimentality that has selectively attached itself to laboratory animals while neglecting other cases of cruelty to animals. Yet again, public emotionality is represented as inferior.

The above extracts show that there are a variety of rhetorical means by which to tighten up the criteria for membership of the core set – those who can legitimately contribute to the debate. These parameters, in the context of the animal experimentation controversy, are fairly minimal – they concern non-violence, rationality (e.g. an ability and willingness to properly categorize biomedical science) and an authentic emotionality (e.g. feelings rooted in experience, genuine self, an understanding of the historical status of animals). Nevertheless, they serve to exclude a large number of those who are perceived by the scientists to be most vocal in the controversy. The representation of such a core set can be read as an effort to disconnect this vocal public from what is seen as its 'anti-rationalist' anti-animal experimentation identity.

What we have here is an attempt at a semi-enrolment, in which, within the proffered identities and roles, there is a limited flexibility. These roles and identities are characterized by formal qualities: they concern the basic conditions for controversy and debate to be conducted in what is, from the scientists' perspective, an appropriate and orderly fashion. Thus, while it is advocated that the form of argumentation should be a common one (i.e. logical, authentic, hard-thinking, emotionally modulated), the content of the arguments is left open. It is assumed that the relations or associations between anti- and pro-animal experimentation actors will be agonistic: the expressed desire is that that antagonism should take a 'rational' form.

So, Michael and Birke's interviewees are not attempting to formulate definitively the identity of the anti-animal experiment faction in such a way as to enrol them in their particular projects or their distinct actor-network. Rather, they are setting out a flexible or agonistic association which does not entail the complete severance of other associations. In preference to the term enrolment, we can tentatively suggest that of 'envelopment' where target actors are invited and manoeuvred into an argumentational envelope in which there is space for a limited number of opposing or antagonistic positions. Thus, we see how the concept of the core set can inform actor-network theory.

It follows that the 'core set' concept can be adapted in light of the insights of actor-network theory. As was noted above, the core set in the public domain – the generalized core set – overtly incorporates non-technical or non-professional (economic, political, moral) dimensions. The scepticism about the CEGB 'experiment' can be based on evaluations of the economic and political ramifications of the nuclear industry. Likewise, the, albeit grudging, invitation to join the moral–scientific core set of animal experimentation can be subverted on other grounds (e.g. political – 'Why do we need this medical research in the first place? Surely a better preventive medical policy would be more efficacious?')

However, such arguments are effectively excluded by our interviewees in their efforts to construct a 'rational' core set. Indeed, the comments of our scientists reflect an attempt to disassociate members of the public from the more threatening parts of their networks and to stress other parts. Here, we see an active attempt by our scientific participants to formulate a core set. This draws out the point made by Collins (1981) that scientists actively construct their core sets. It is the form of this construction that actor-network theory can illuminate. So, if 'envelopment' serves as a supplement to enrolment, we might elaborate the notion of the 'core set'. Before there is a core set, there is a 'generalized agonistic set' (all those who would like to have, or potentially can have, a voice in the controversy). The minimal criteria of rationality, rational emotionality and non-violence that have been enumerated above are used by the scientists to determine who can move from the 'generalized agonistic set' into (what they would consider to be) the 'core set'.

There is an additional point to make. Presupposed in the scientists' statements is the vision of the animal experimentation community as a necessary player in any such debate. As such, this community serves as an obligatory point of passage: for critics to have legitimate voice, for their concerns to be aired, indeed, for their identities as authentic critics to be at all feasible, they need to address this community. In sum, while critics may take a number of shapes and sizes, they can only be 'real' critics when they enter into dialogue with the scientists. This is a key dimension of critics' identity that is being surreptitiously purveyed through the above representations.

To summarize the sections on 'others' and flexible identities, we have seen how scientists construct both tacitly and explicitly a range of identities for their critical audiences to step into. In the process, they constitute for themselves a particular matrix of identities characterized by such dimensions as 'thinking hard', authentic emotionality, rationality and so on. Indeed, via the medium of the interviewers and the *New Scientist*, they perform a version of their desired social order: they are network-building.

I have attempted to show how an actor-network analysis may be conducted on discourse (interview) data. This material has been interpreted in the context of the interviews. That interpretation has proceeded by suggesting that the interviewees are oriented towards the interviewers as representatives of the *New Scientist*, and, therefore, potential intermediaries who can channel particular scientific and public identities to the readership. This reflects one of the main themes of the book, namely, that of change in identity. The portrayal of the lay public is concerned to reshape that public's identity – to get its members to take on certain characteristics (rational emotionality, for example). If this succeeds, the public can be said to have been enrolled or enveloped.

Conclusion

Now, these representations, articulated as they are in interview, have their desired impact only by virtue of the interviewers, and their subsequent texts, acting as intermediaries. As this chapter all too readily demonstrates, such social science types are not necessarily to be trusted.

Given the resonance of the animal experimentation controversy in the UK, it comes as no surprise that there are more proactive and organized efforts to put the case for animal experimentation directly to the public via media of various sorts. For example, at the British Association for the Advancement of Science (BAAS) conference in August 1990, widely reported in the regional and national press, and later detailed in the BAAS' own short report in 1993, a pro-animal experimentation declaration, signed by a thousand people, was produced. This stressed that the major advances in the medical treatment of people and animals were the direct result of animal experimentation. As the review of the meeting and declaration in the Research Defence Society's *Newsletter* put it:

> The declaration is not only a statement supporting the need for animal experiments in biomedical research. It also urges the scientists involved to respect animal life, using animals only when absolutely necessary and treating them as humanely as possible. Alternative methods, the Declaration asserts, should be adopted as soon as they are proved reliable. The responsibilities of those involved, to adhere to the legislation governing the use of animals in scientific procedures, and to be sensitive to the needs of animals in their care, are clear. (1 October 1990, p. 1)

At another meeting, organized by the Research Defence Society in April 1991, similar statements were issued. The *New Scientist* reported them thus: "'We must make the public realize the extent to which their lives depend on animal experiments," said Colin Blakemore, professor of physiology at the University of Oxford. ". . . Hubel said that doctors should tell patients every time they prescribed drugs that these products are available only because of animal experiments'" (Vines, 1991, p. 10).

Other similar examples could be cited, but given that these media representations are typical, they will suffice for the point that I wish to make. Here, we find that arguments are framed in very general terms. It is abstractions such as 'medical benefits' and 'animal pain' that are deployed in the defence of animal experiments. Further, these statements are usually embedded in an educational or remedial discourse: the public must be informed and disabused – they do not understand the complex ways in which benefits flow from animal experiments. In sum, the public are being furnished with identities that disqualify them from making any interventions in the process of policing animal experimentation. The network that is being constructed directly marginalizes critics. The proper evaluation of the value of animal experimentation is the preserve of the experts.

If the explicit message of these statements is that the public is ignorant, the implicit message is one of certainty and progress in which the day-to-day, moment-to-moment contingent judgements that characterize the scientific enterprise are absent. However, it might well be just this tacit claim to certainty that makes the critical public more sceptical: lay people are only too likely to understand the contingencies of 'reading' the signals (of pain or distress) produced by animals. This contingency also applies to the implementation of the legislation. Such critics and sceptics might ask the following. To what extent 'The responsibilities of those involved, to adhere to the legislation governing the use of animals in scientific procedures, and to be sensitive to the needs of animals in their care' are clear? Are there grave uncertainties contained in the legislation's demarcation of responsibility and delineation of the means by which cost/benefit calculations are made?

In the next chapter I will consider this strategy of constructing a subordinate role for the public more closely, following through, in the process, the theme of how identities change. In the context of a concern with the status of science-in-general and the 'public understanding of science', I will show how social science is drafted in to substantiate a particular model of the member of the public in terms of scientific literacy and competence as proper citizens in a democracy. Moreover, I will also consider how these identities and networks are variously adopted, adapted or resisted.

6

Science, Knowledge and the Public

Chapter 5 addressed the way that scientific actors, in constructing identities for themselves and others, could be interpreted as attempting to use the interviewers as their intermediaries. In contrast, this chapter is concerned with ways in which the spokespersons of science-in-general (where science-in-general refers to the iconic images, knowledges, institutions and techniques of science) attempt more directly to enrol public constituencies into their desired network. As such, I will look at instances where scientists and their (social science) intermediaries construct a particular identity for the lay public, paying particular attention to the role of questionnaire studies of the public understanding of science. We shall see that not only are aspects of identity such as scientific literacy and expertise constituted by such studies, but that they also serve in the privileging of particular versions of citizenship and democratic participation.

In addition, and as a necessary counterpoint to these projected packages of identity, I will examine the way that target audiences respond to these proffered identities. In other words, this chapter aims to 'complete the circle', moving from the formulation of the public by elite scientific bodies, to their exemplification through social scientific methodology, to the resistance or otherwise of publics to these identities. Finally, by way of a little self-critical reflection, I will consider what network-building I am engaged in when representing the recalcitrance of the public.

Characterizing the Relation between Science and Public

In this section I will briefly narrate some of the relations of science to public available to us. At issue here is the perception that the privileged status of science has been eroded. We can now say such things as: gone are the days when members of the public gazed, wide-eyed with credulity, at the great men of science; lost forever is the era when the layperson listened in silent admiration and humble wonder to announcements of the latest scientific discovery; never again shall we hear the awed gasps of the masses as the covers are removed from the newest shiny technological artefact. The heavy-handed irony of the foregoing sentence is grounded in another series of representations which counterbalance this pretend nostalgia: the icons of 'the great scientist' could always be contrasted with the stereotype of 'the mad scientist'; and any spark that flew from the white heat of technology could be, potentially at least, obliterated by the dark shadows wherein lurked Frankenstein's monster and Kubrick's HAL (cf. Toumey, 1992; Weart, 1988).

Here are some more formal stories of the relation between science and public. According to Shapin (1991), the canonical story of the differentiation between science and public goes something like this: in the past science and public were interwoven; the public influenced not only the direction but also the content of the scientific enterprise. Nowadays, science has shed its public – the intervention of public actors in the doing of science would amount to a corruption of science with its own peculiar rules, procedures, technicalities, etc. The public's current role is one of support only. However, Shapin's prime observation is that this separation is a massive historical achievement and not the result of the evolution of science into an increasingly more esoteric, mathematized, complex enterprise that has progressively excluded the public. Throughout history there have been challenges which, for example, as with Paracelsus and his followers, problematized the increasing mathematization in science. The removal of science and its objects of study from the messiness of everyday life was seen by the Paracelsans to produce defective knowledge – true knowledge would, in contrast, be found amongst artisans with practical experience of particular phenomena: miners, farmers, breeders.

This struggle continues to rage in transmuted forms in recent times. Multiple challenges to science seem to be gathering momentum. We find institutionally framed challenges which attack the science of particular actors – the science of non-governmental organizations versus the science of official institutions. As Eyerman and Jamison (1991) suggest, new social movements not only provide a challenge to scientific institutions but also seem to be becoming producers of scientific knowledge in their own right. A competition of 'more scientific than thou' seems to be one dynamic of this challenge, but one in which the parameters of scientificity are beginning to be challenged as issues of holism and the integration of science, policy and the public good come on to the agenda (e.g. Wynne and Meyer, 1993). If much of this conflict is being conducted on fairly traditional scientific grounds, other challenges are altogether more dangerous for the perceived legitimacy of scientific institutions. Andrew Ross (1991), for example, documents the way that New Age practitioners have been derogated for appropriating science for dubious, commercial ends. According to the orthodoxy, theirs is a pseudo-science where scientific and technological knowledge is opportunistically usurped and spuriously deployed to fashion New Age treatments and technologies such as biofeedback therapies, bowel-assisting toilets, de-ionizers and so on. However, as Ross suggests, it might be the case that the attraction for the users of such techniques is not simply their apparent scientificity, but the willingness of practitioners to render them accessible and transparent. This dimension of communitarianism in the New Age movement opens up the science so that users can contribute to the production of knowledge (though it is important to bear in mind that the New Age is also a marketplace in which expertise needs to be protected if livings are to be made). In reaction, traditional scientific institutions are attempting to wrest the right to scientific, or accredited, knowledge away from such movements, and we see this most plainly in relation to alternative medicine (e.g. herbalism – cf. Whitelegg, 1994a, b).

These stories of public disenchantment with science-in-general find expression in other writings. Take for instance, Lyotard's (1984) grand narrative of the end of grand narratives, including that of science. Here, people have become disillusioned with science: science has failed to deliver its Enlightenment promise – it is now just the technician-servant of industry, uninterested in human political progress. Lyotard's account thus rests on the betrayal of the public by science (as well as on the layperson's increasing awareness of the inherent conflicts within science in which experts bicker in public). In sum, science can no longer sustain a unitary voice; its status as a grand narrative by which we might grasp our lives declines catastrophically. By comparison, Gerald Holton's (1992) apologistic account of the public's negative perception of science is framed in terms of the 'anti-science phenomenon'. Here, it is certain characteristics of the public itself that is the root cause of 'anti-science'. Accordingly, anti-science publics are also anti-modernists – they present symptoms of an intolerance to such putative modernist givens as impersonality, industrialization, calculability, bureaucratization and democracy – symptoms that are the correlates of 'anti-scientism'. If Lyotard celebrates the pluralistic flowering of a spectrum of many little narratives in which science is but one means of apprehending the world, Holton laments the de-privileging of science and the corollary descent into mysticism, subjectivism and, indeed, quasi-authoritarianism.

Lyotard's and Holton's respective versions of the public problematizations of science are quite general – they concern a general public and a general science. In contrast to this image of the epochal disillusionment with science, there are treatments which give a more ambiguous picture, which stress the ambiguity of the public to science in its particularity. Thus, in Harry Collins' (1988) example of the UK's Central Electricity Generating Board's demonstration of the 'safety' of its nuclear fuel flasks (mentioned in Chapter 5), we are shown how the CEGB was implicitly also ascribing to the public honorary membership of the scientific elite or core set. The CEGB's display attempts to flatter its lay audience into believing that it can arbitrate over the outcomes of the ostensible experiment. As we saw above, Collins' response was that such displays should be dissected on behalf of the lay public by appropriate counter-experts such as those of Greenpeace who can expose the assumptions built into the experiment/display. The process of negotiation should be openly visible to the public – they should view science through what Collins (1987) calls the 'window of uncertainty' – otherwise they will end up in a 'flip-flop'. According to this flip-flop model, where science succeeds, it will be perceived, paradigmatically, to have an unmediated access to nature and to be the generator of objective truths; where it fails, this can only be due to conspiracy, corruption, fraud, sheer incompetence or the secret machinations of vested interests. Collins' archetypal point (drawn from SSK) is that science is necessarily pervaded by interests and cultural commitments – for the public to properly respond to science, they should become aware of these.

This flip-flop model, while it takes into account the constructions of the public by science-based institutions and represents the ambivalence of the public as chronic, extends it in time: one is first pro, then anti; enchanted, then disillusioned. By comparison, Giddens (1991) and Beck (1992) construe, as characteristic of lay people's contemporary apprehension of science, a profound ambivalence. Thus lay people in late modernity are deeply anxious about science by virtue of its various 'failures' and 'problems' in the context of, for example, environmental threat. Simultaneously, science is also an abstract system upon which people structurally depend for guidance and in which they must necessarily invest trust. As Beck writes: '. . . the risk consciousness of the afflicted, which is frequently expressed in the environmental movement, and in criticism of industry, experts and culture, is usually both critical and credulous of science' (p. 72). There is a sort of 'integrated' ambivalence towards science in this account – at once a dependency on, and scepticism of, science.

The composite picture I have sketched (or rather stitched together) is one in which there is a contemporary public disaffection with science. But this disaffection – variously theorized in the foregoing – is also something to which scientific elites are keenly sensitized. After all, it constitutes a threat to their traditional standing.

The Public Understanding of Science

In this section, I will explore how the spokespersons of science-in-general in the UK, primarily the Royal Society of London, and its social science allies, have attempted to reconstruct and re-entrench a particular identity for the layperson. As we shall see, this rests on simultaneously defining a particular, desirable social and political world.

In the Royal Society's own words, it is 'the foremost learned scientific society in the country' (Royal Society, 1985, p. 35). As a key representative of science-in-general in the UK, it has been acutely aware that in the country 'Hostility, or even indifference, to science and technology, whether by shopfloor workers, by middle or senior industrial management or by investors, weakens the nation's industry' (p. 9). Moreover, these conditions pervade government and the higher levels of the Civil Service. Without a better understanding of science, public policy is not as good as it could be. As regards the general public, 'Scientific literacy is becoming an essential requirement of everyday life' (p. 10; for a partial review of the meanings of scientific literacy, see Durant, 1993). The document from which these phrases are drawn is the Royal Society's 1985 report on the Public Understanding of Science. This text does many things, not least furnishing identities of such constituencies as the commercial sector and government. However, I will focus on the ways in which the report constructs a particular nexus of identities for the public.

To this end, let us resort to another quote from the report: 'There are many surveys of attitudes towards science and technology both in the UK and overseas, especially in the USA. But there has been much less effort outside the formal education system devoted to assessing the understanding of science and technology' (p. 12). What does this statement signify? I would suggest that it sets out in a very programmatic way that is fleshed out in the rest of the report a means of enrolling the public. The public will discover itself to be interested in a particular version of democratic participation, it will find that it is hampered in this pursuit by a deficiency in relevant knowledge, it will recognize that this knowledge concerns science and technology.

Now, let us consider the Royal Society's programme in a little more detail. In its recommendations section, the report reiterates the observation that there are few surveys 'devoted to assessing the *understanding* of science and technology' (p. 31, emphasis in the original). It recommends that 'the Economic and Social Research Council and other appropriate bodies sponsor research into ways of measuring public understanding of science and technology, and of assessing the effects of improved understanding' (p. 31). Clearly, the implication here is that such methods include the survey form: it is the understanding that is being accessed here. People are treated as essentially repositories of information. The survey (or some other knowledge-accessing methodology) will dip into them, rummage around and resurface with a description of their contents, that is, their 'understandings' of science.

However, this research aim is informed by a specific policy purpose: to encourage and nurture democratic participation. Only by identifying and measuring the gaps in people's understanding can the level of scientific literacy be raised to that required to make informed judgements in contemporary democracies. An understanding of science is important 'for individual citizens, to participate in a democratic society' (p. 31); for such societies 'public opinion is a major influence in the decision-making process. It is therefore important that individual citizens, as well as decision-makers, recognize and understand the scientific aspects of public issues' (p. 10). As such 'the individual needs to know some of the factual background and to be able to assess the quality of the evidence being presented' (p. 10) that are related to the relevant policy decision. Here, then, it is assumed that there can be unproblematic 'scientific aspects of public issues'. Yet, as we will see, it is not only what is to count as 'scientific' that is often contentious; it is also what is to count as the real 'public issue', for the way that that is defined will have implications for what will be perceived as relevant or creditable knowledge.

The Royal Society's argument thus acts to de-problematize the way that people evaluate both scientific knowledge and the sources of such knowledge. Measuring the 'public understanding of science' assumes an abstract, uncontentious, universal knowledge. Thus, where attitude surveys, which have traditionally been used to access the public's view of science, allowed people an, albeit limited, voice to evaluate the status of science, the suggested assessment of the public understanding of science and technology sidelines this evaluation of science by members of the public. In other words, the political and moral value of science is presupposed. The aim is primarily to assess how well people can tap into this necessary and positive knowledge domain. This is all in keeping with Shapin's account of the relegation of the public to the role of 'supporters' of science-in-general. In essence then, this text supplies a configuration of identities for the public: the public comes to be represented as awaiting measurement, but measurement not simply of its 'understanding of science', rather in terms of its intellectual deficiencies as measured against the objective or authoritative body of scientific knowledge. That is to say, this research strategy adheres to what Wynne (1991) has dubbed the Deficit model (see also Layton et al., 1993; Irwin and Wynne, in press; Wynne, 1992a, 1995).

In calling for an investigation of the public understanding of science, the Royal Society draws upon the expertise of social science: social scientists are drafted as the technical intermediaries who will constitute and enrol the public as an ally. In the wake of the Royal Society report, the UK's Economic and Social Research Council instituted a research programme into the public understanding of technology. Key in this enterprise was a survey study of the public understanding of science. Now, there were also qualitative and critical projects encompassed by the programme (the work presented below is one example of this) – but this simply means that the ESRC was an unreliable intermediary for the Royal Society. It had its own associations and identities to maintain; after all, the Public Understanding of Science programme was but one research enterprise out of many. Nevertheless, those projects of the programme that were concerned with the 'measurement' of public understanding served their intermediary role.

If the survey research tends to focus upon the deficits in lay people's understandings as measured against accredited scientific knowledge (see, for example, Durant et al., 1989; Evans and Durant, 1989), it comes as no surprise that the public comes out of the survey as somewhat lacking. In the media we see articles reporting these findings and read such headlines as: 'With more than a third of the population not knowing that the earth goes round the sun, Britain could be in serious trouble' (*Sunday Times*, 19 November 1989). And yet, with prescience and wisdom, the Royal Society had already foreseen such dismal results. Before the ESRC survey, the Royal Society's report was already calling for increases in the amount and quality of science education, in media coverage of science, and in scientists' popularizing input into the public sphere.

Let me reframe this episode in ANT terms: the public is assigned the role of ignorant actors and disenfranchised citizens. Where attitude surveys, in however debased a form, at least seemed to take seriously the autonomous opinions of the public, the knowledge surveys presuppose the right of science as the arbiter of truth and then compare and contrast the public's knowledge against this officially sanctioned stock of 'true knowledge'. Clearly, this translating story goes, if the public wants to be 'proper, participating citizens', then it must attain a certain level of scientific literacy. As such, it needs access to this knowledge. In order to realize itself as 'proper, participating citizens' the public must become knowledgeable and for this it must turn to institutionalized science. Institutionalized science becomes its obligatory point of passage. But up to this point, the projected levels of scientific literacy are only guesses. The public needs, for its own good, some awareness of its scientific literacy. Its spokespersons become the social scientists who measure lay people's understanding of science. The multiple bits of paper generated by the survey become statistics and simplified graphs: they become immutable mobiles. Not altogether surprisingly, these immutable mobiles reveal that the guesses of institutionalized science-in-general were correct all along: the public is indeed dangerously scientifically illiterate (and perhaps, lackadaisical citizens to boot). Press releases are circulated and the immutable mobiles enter into the media. The media tells of pervasive, chronic scientific illiteracy. This is the public's text of identity, now entered into the process of dissemination, now increasingly fixed. The public's only hope – its saviours – are the scientists who will educate, enlighten and, ultimately, re-enfranchise them.

This is the sort of (re-)shaping of identity via a 'political packaging process' that ANT can trace. In the case of the 'public understanding of science', the foregoing can be set out in the form of the quasi-syllogism presented in Chapter 4:

> You want to be participating citizens, yet you are ignorant, scientifically illiterate. (Interressement)
> We, the scientists, are the ones who can educate you, raise your scientific literacy and, in the process, enfranchise you. (Translation)
> Now grant us our autonomy; support us in our endeavours; listen and learn from us. (Enrolment).

However, while this might be the implicit strategy of institutional science in the UK, it does not necessarily work. Lay people's reaction to this representation of themselves as scientifically deficient can be, as Beck and Giddens have pointed out, a somewhat ambivalent one. On the one hand, they seem to accept quite willingly that they are 'ignorant', and will often describe themselves as such. On the other hand, they will also often problematize the need to know such abstract facts as the nature of ionizing radiation (Michael, in press). For science, the tacit goal is to prioritize the need for universal knowledge; for ordinary people, such knowledge is more or less irrelevant to their everyday lives. It is knowledge-in-context (Wynne, 1991, 1992a) that is important to most people: techniques for mending the washing machine rather than the first law of thermodynamics. Furthermore, people also have ample capacity for finding out for themselves the scientific knowledge pertinent to their own needs – witness the flourishing of self-help groups, especially in relation to health (e.g. Arksey, 1994). Moreover, people can also be acutely sensitive not so much to the status of particular bits of scientific knowledge, but to the credibility of the sources of such knowledge. In other words, people (like scientists, indeed) evaluate the source of information: some people are thus more likely to believe the scientists who work for Greenpeace than for British Nuclear Fuels, local farmers rather than the experts of the UK's Ministry of Agriculture, Fisheries and Food (cf. Wynne, 1992b).

What these knowledge surveys do, by emphasizing relatively abstract scientific knowledge, is attempt to bypass these more contextualized knowledges. In terms of ANT, it constitutes an effort to disassociate people from their usual sources of information (friends, alternative practitioners, self-help manuals), and to reinstate 'official science' as the prime repository of 'real knowledge'. As a necessary condition for all this, the actual political nature of 'true science' is occluded. But, in addition to this, there is a more a sinister implication. Not only are versions of the lay public and true knowledge being reinforced and disseminated, so too are particular notions of democratic participation. Thus, in this package, to be scientifically literate is to be capable of participation in centralized debates about public policy – 'democracy' comes to be aligned with Western parliamentary democracy. In the process, other local forms of citizenship are marginalized. The rootedness of local knowledge in local community and the ways in which this ties in to forms of local participation and citizenship are rendered invisible. In effect, what this representational matrix of accredited knowledge, parliamentary democracy and scientific literacy does is occlude its opposite: local knowledge and local participation. Central to both the Royal Society's text and survey methodology is a valorization of one dimension of the lay public's identity, that concerned with citizenship in relation to parliamentary democracy and with expert-accredited knowledge. Local variations, local identities, knowledges-in-context and so on are rendered invisible in such representations, and, in the process, the central political and social positioning of such organizations as the Royal Society is reinforced. However, as I noted above, lay people can be ambivalent to representations of themselves as deficient. In the next sections, I will explore this ambivalence by considering how people variously accept and resist these general identities.

Accepting, Tolerating and Resisting Identities: The Meanings of Ignorance

The following sections draw upon research carried out at Lancaster University between 1987 and 1990 as part of the ESRC's research programme into the public understanding of science. The initial aim of the research was to uncover people's 'mental models' of particular scientific phenomena, especially their understandings of ionizing radiation, while embedding these in local exigencies and concerns. It is important that our conceptual and methodological focus on mental models be fully recognized, for this approach served, in part, to set the interviewers in a particular role – as representatives of science-in-general. This has major implication for the present ANT analysis of interviewees' responses (though, of course, it is also possible to provide a more strictly discourse analytic reading of the extracts presented below – see Chapter 2).

Developed by cognitive psychologists, mental models are the representations, pictures, metaphors and so on that people have of scientific or technological phenomena. Thus, we have studies of motion (McCloskey, 1983), electricity (Gentner and Gentner, 1983), home heat control (Kempton, 1987) and evaporation (Collins and Gentner, 1987). Quinn and Holland (1987) have suggested that mental models of physical processes can be picked up and put down at will: they serve as tools. In sum, this approach attempts to get at the ways in which people model, for example, electricity: do they see the movement of electrons in a wire as water flowing through a pipe or as crowds of people progressing through a corridor? When one asks the respondent what happens if the wire becomes thinner at a given point, the metaphors yield different answers.

The emphasis is thus on the instrumental use of such models and as such there has, typically, been little examination of the social and cultural contexts of these models (though this is changing – cf. Lave, 1988). The main point I want to raise concerns 'familiarity'. If we are to conceptualize mental models as 'tools', we would also expect that expertise in their use would be dependent on some sort of practice, and incremental familiarity, with the relevant knowledge domain. The studies mentioned above deal with respondents who have a considerable familiarity with, and sometimes a profound practical understanding of, the knowledge domains being studied by the investigator. In those more typical cases in which people have only sporadic or fragmented contact with the relevant knowledge domain, it is difficult to see how mental models could have been derived. Thus, in our research, when we attempted to get at the mental models of ionizing radiation by using the standard technique of posing various puzzles (for example, what is more dangerous, low prolonged doses of radiation or short high doses?), what we found again and again was a peremptory attempt to answer appropriately followed by a comment on the status of that answer. In other words, despite people's initial willingness to play the game, they found they could not do so convincingly and resorted to glossing that 'inability'. As such they were shifting from 'helpful respondents' to 'reflexive critical commentators' and in the process drawing upon a much broader context and array of social identities.

In particular, under such a regime of questioning, however friendly or relaxed it might ostensibly seem, it is likely that the interviewees will feel that they are being 'tested'. Despite our best intentions, the use of the mental model method of question-and-answer is liable to be experienced as a way of comparing the understandings of the respondents with accredited scientific knowledge (as embodied by the interviewers).

So, the starting point of this section is the observation that people do not simply possess knowledge (or mental models) about scientific 'facts' and scientific procedures and processes, they can also reflect upon the epistemological status of that knowledge. In addition, this active reflection can directly affect their responses to science and scientific experts. In reflecting upon the uncertainties about their understanding of science, or in identifying a 'lack' in their knowledge, people are making tacit judgements in relation to the authoritative source or sources of that knowledge. Thus, people can review the standing of their scientific and technological knowledge in relation to some more or less expert source such as scientists, the media, friends and relatives and so on. As such, identity is deeply implicated. Conversely, the ways in which people regard themselves and the value they place upon their scientific knowledge affect the ways in which they understand science. We have, therefore, a sort of representational jigsaw in which identity, the status of lay scientific knowledge, and scientific expertise are delimited. This is effectively a nexus of representational elements that imply a network which directly parallels that to be found in the Royal Society's report.

Before considering the way that public 'ignorance' is constructed, I will differentiate my approach from two others in the field. I will depart from Ravetz's (1987) analysis of 'ignorance' in the area of science policy. Ravetz's main interest concerns the effects of 'ignorance' in the decision-making process. As he states: 'A decision problem involves "ignorance" when some components which are real and significant are unknown to the decider at the crucial moment' (p. 82). For Ravetz, decision-makers only discover such 'ignorance' retrospectively (an 'ignorance' inheres in the application of technological systems). By comparison, Smithson (1985) develops the following definition of 'ignorance': 'A is "ignorant" from B's viewpoint if A fails to agree with or show awareness of ideas which B defines as either actually or potentially factually valid' (p. 154). According to Smithson, this subjectivist formulation avoids 'confounding judgements by the social scientist about the validity of the cognition being studied' (p. 154). Smithson fully recognizes that A and B can be one and the same person to the extent that an individual can ascribe 'ignorance' to him- or herself. Smithson's overarching aim in this essay is to elevate 'ignorance' to the status of a *bona fide* topic for social theory and, to this end, he reviews a broad range of roles that 'ignorance' might play in the process of social. For example, he points to the following contexts in which 'ignorance' operates: norms against knowing (e.g. as evidenced in politeness phenomena); 'ignorance' strategies and games (e.g. in the courtroom questioning of expert knowledge); the particular settings and occasions of 'ignorance' (e.g. confessions); the roles, scripts and identities associated with 'ignorance' (e.g. the requirement of selective inattention or 'ignorance' for the successful performance of specific duties). In sum, Smithson provides a very useful survey of array of social contexts in which 'ignorance' is constructed, deployed and ascribed.

In contrast, in the present context, I am more interested in taking up and elaborating just one strand from Smithson's wide-ranging and subtle survey. That is to say, I will endeavour to explore the way that people use particular discourses to reflexively comment upon manifest 'ignorance' (in relation to science and ionizing radiation), and thereby tentatively to position themselves in relation to the relevant institutions and groups, both expert and lay. In so doing, these lay people simultaneously instantiate particular identities and formulate corollary relations of power with regard to science. They are constructing a network in which, in relation to science, they are variously located in subordinate or acquiescent positions, within functional associations or in a state of superiority in which science itself is rendered marginal. Now, these 'discourses of ignorance' also have a more mundane role to play in my narrative. They can serve to critique the methodology of survey or questionnaire studies (or, more generally, those approaches that attempt to measure or map the public understanding of science). Such techniques of investigation, where the 'knowledge content' of the individual is investigated through questioning ('Does the earth go around the sun, or vice versa?'; 'Do antibiotics destroy viruses?'; 'What are the more dangerous, alpha-particles or gamma-rays?'), are likely to yield the following response: 'I don't know.' This 'admission' of ignorance is not, however, a reflection of simple deficit. It can encompass a multiplicity of meanings that such knowledge measuring techniques have a tendency to miss. Moreover, as the story in the preceding sections implies, this neglect is not merely an artefact; it is instrumental in reproducing the impression that accredited scientific knowledge is context-free and value-neutral. When people reflect on their 'ignorance', they are able to reinstate an alternative political and social backdrop, and assert, or, rather, perform, an altogether different network, which can not only 'excuse' or 'warrant' this ignorance but also actively promote it.

The account of discourses of ignorance that follows draws heavily on Michael (in press) which in turn is derived from a series of interviews from three pieces of fieldwork carried out with Rosemary McKechnie and Brian Wynne. Semi-structured interviews that attempted to access the mental models of ionizing radiation were conducted in the following contexts (see Michael, in press for more details): 1. Volunteers in a Radon survey carried out by the City Council Environmental Health Office of Lancaster (a small city in the Northwest of England). Radon is generally regarded to be a natural radioactive gas that comes from the breakdown of uranium that is present in rocks and soils. It is possible that it might collect in relatively high concentrations in poorly ventilated properties. Volunteers kept a small plastic Radon detector in their homes for six months. They were also provided with sheets of instructions and details on Radon and the rationale behind the survey. 2. Interview panel of residents of Lancaster and environs. 3. Some 20 time-served electricians working at the Sellafield nuclear reprocessing plant who were interviewed en masse while attending evening classes at a local college of further education.

Discourses of Ignorance

Unconstructed Absence

Firstly, it was often the case that where people were manifestly lacking in specific types of knowledge, this did not occasion further commentary on their part. That is to say, they made no attempt discursively to reconstruct this evident absence or lack. Thus, in many instances, even where they ostensibly had some direct interest in the topic under discussion, in probing their understandings about ionizing radiation, people's responses would take the form of 'I don't know' or 'I never thought about it'. It seems that absence was only brought to people's attention by virtue of the interviewer's questions about ionizing radiation, and that the absence of an answer was simply a fact of life, neither worthy of further elaboration nor meriting special explanation. It would appear that people were tending to treat absence as an irrelevance or, at the very least, peripheral to their primary concerns. However, in many cases, an answer of 'I don't know' would be followed up with a request for the correct answer, for example, 'Well, what does Radon do?' or 'What are alpha particles?' This suggests that the deficit or absence is recognized and the interviewer converted into a potential source of information, and the interview reconstituted as an opportunity to rectify 'ignorance'. Indeed, the subsequent question is used to pre-empt a negative impression, namely, that the respondent is prone to lack of interest or curiosity, indolence or some other failing. The implication is that, for some unspecified reason or circumstance, the interviewee has not been in a position to seek out the relevant information and assimilate it. Here, then, the ignorance so exposed does have some significance for the respondent. In this instance, requests for information at once tacitly demarcate absence and signify that the interviewee is, at minimum, an interested and responsible 'member of the public'. In the following subsections, I explore the way that absence is explicitly constructed.

'Ignorance' as a Reflection of Mental Constitution

Some interviewees explicitly recognized this absence as an entrenched, global scientific 'ignorance' or as a 'not-knowing', a lack of education. It might be the case that this self-characterization is a defensive strategy, deployed in the course of the interview to avoid or mitigate responsibility for specific perceived mistakes. For example:

> MM: Any idea why it [Radon] should bubble up, rather than things like carbon dioxide . . .
> AW: Probably a light gas, just a gas . . .
> MM: I'm not sure it does actually . . . [*Laughs*]
> AW: Oh yeah. . . . My knowledge of science is zero . . .

Subsequently, this participant, a museum director, describes how he thinks Radon is detected through the magnification of fission tracks in the strip of perspex that is contained in the monitoring devices. Further, he mentions that he knows about fission track data analysis through his background in archaeology – yet he has already claimed that his 'knowledge of science is zero'. It seems, in this instance, that here there is a bracketing of scientific knowledge as 'other'. The knowledge that this speaker possesses cannot conceivably (in his own estimation) be a part of 'science'. It might be the case that he considers his knowledge insufficiently detailed or arcane to be counted as science (and perhaps here he is drawing parallels with the more familiar criteria of archaeological expertise which reflect similar rigour, specialist training and so on). Thus, the criteria of what constitutes scientific knowledge are so strict or so obscure that he is not really able to aspire to them.

The metacommentaries of other speakers upon their (lack of) scientific knowledge, however, entail a more forthright characterization of self, namely the 'lack of scientific mind'. Thus:

> MM: Do you think of it [Radon] as er . . . as er rays or gas?
> LG: Erm . . . gas . . . probably . . .
> MM: Any idea how it gets produced in the ground?
> LG: No idea . . . [*Laughs*]
> MM: Have a guess.
> LG: Erm . . . I'm not very scientifically minded . . . I don't know . . .

> MM: Any idea what the processes are by which this gas is created?
> PC: No . . . I would imagine it's just a gas created by the natural breakdown of the various components of the soil. I mean that's just an assumption really. . . . I'm not very scientifically minded. . . . I know there are these things happening in the earth . . .

Here, the interviewees are not merely engaged in differentiating themselves from science per se. Over and above this, they are saying that they are not constitutionally, or mentally, equipped to fathom or grasp the mysteries of science. It appears there is, then, a 'genetic' differentiation between self and science. In the context of the interview, speakers who have recourse to this discourse situate themselves in a position of dependency relative to science. Nevertheless, in stressing one's lack of scientific mind, one can also draw attention to one's own worthy or specialist attributes or functions. This process of favourably comparing one's own skills to those of scientists is nicely captured in the response of a Lancaster Town Hall receptionist (Radon survey volunteer). When talking about scientists in the guise of Lancaster City Council Environmental Health Officers, she noted: 'They couldn't do my job and I couldn't do theirs.'

If we relate this to the preceding Royal Society representation of the public as 'deficient' here we have what appears to be an even more extreme version. People seem not only to accept this deficiency, but also to reify it as a constitutional incapacity. Where the Royal Society at least was interested in encouraging scientific literacy through educational programmes and the like, interviewees who adhere to this discourse seem to refute this possibility. However, there is also, seemingly, a rejection of the offer of a participant citizenship that, according to the Royal Society, this literacy would bring in its wake.

'Ignorance' and the Division of Labour

In contrast to the above discourse that frames 'ignorance' in terms of a constitutional shortcoming, there is a discourse that embeds 'ignorance' in a context in which difference between science and other spheres of action or expertise is functional. That is to say, absence is here conceptualized as a more or less necessary constituent of the division of labour. I will present two examples of this.

> MM: What's strange was when I started reading all this stuff I was dumbfounded about how much I didn't know . . . really . . . and a lot of it is still sort of dodgy especially the biological stuff . . .
> DM: Well, I read quite a bit of it but . . . but it's not my job.

The respondent in the above extract is a statistician. He is denying the necessity to know 'this stuff' because it is not part of his job. In glossing DM's statement, we can remark on the way that straddles the duality of structure and agency (cf. Giddens, 1984) – of the requirements imposed by the social order on the one hand, and personal volition on the other. Absence is accounted for through a dual rhetorical strategy: on the one hand, absence is facilitated by external conditions or demands ('I am not required to know this stuff'); on the other hand, it is the result of personal choice ('I don't need to know this stuff'). In sum, this speaker seems discursively to exploit the ambiguity of the 'my job' construct, as simultaneously implying agency (or volition or 'subjecthood') and social structure (or necessity or 'objecthood') when accounting for his 'ignorance'.

A similar strategy is instanced in the following exchanges between Wynne, McKechnie and Michael and some twenty time-served electricians from the Sellafield nuclear reprocessing plant. Unfortunately, conditions were such that it was impossible to tape-record them: the following is not therefore verbatim and is derived from field notes written immediately after the exchange. The following talk arose in the context of describing what they, as electricians in the course of their daily work practices, needed to know about ionizing radiation. One electrician stated that: 'We're not employed to do what the monitors do . . .' The only woman electrician present followed this with: 'People [i.e. the electricians, and possibly other blue-collar workers] don't have to know too much, you've got to trust someone somewhere, and they're [the health physicists] trained for it.' Subsequently, she added: 'If people knew too much, they would panic in an emergency because they know just how dangerous it really was . . .'

In the former quotes, there is a formulation of absence in positive terms: the absence of knowledge amongst the electricians is compensated for by other functionaries in the organization – i.e. those specialists, such as the health physicists, who possess the correct, relevant knowledge and who deploy it for the benefit of, amongst others, the electricians. But the absence is also formulated positively: to be ignorant can be good insofar as it can preclude panic under certain circumstances. Accordingly, it is functional to be ignorant if one wants to remain clear about proper procedures (too much knowledge would be a distraction).

Now, this contrast and complementarity is evoked in the peculiar circumstances of the nuclear industry. However, in a somewhat less articulated way, some lay people also seem to view their relation to science in terms of the division of labour. (That it is less articulated is only to be expected in light of people's relative paucity of contact with scientists.) For example, in our Radon survey sample, the complementarity between scientists (environmental health officers) and volunteers was framed by interviewees around the common goal of 'doing good'. That is to say, the scientists (with whom the volunteers had little contact) and the interviewees-cum-volunteers were functioning together to conduct a survey of Radon levels in Lancaster and its environs for, on the one hand, the benefit of the inhabitants of Lancaster, and, on the other, for the collective welfare (and understanding) of the nation. Thus, a common goal bound scientist and layperson together as a collaborative unit; the function of the volunteer was as a sort of guinea pig, or perhaps as concerned citizen, that enabled scientists to do their good work. There was no reason to go beyond this sense of collaboration, and there was no need to find out about Radon and its properties. (This is despite the fact that a Radon measuring device had been sitting in one's living room for six months.) Superficially, it is possible to imagine that the monitor might act as an irresistible stimulus to find out more about Radon, even if the knowledge so gained was at best elementary. However, it is also possible to argue that, in the context of a division of labour, the device came to signify or symbolize one's more or less passive role as volunteer: one could say that it actually spurred the volunteer not to find out. In support of this, one might note that a great many of the volunteers, though they expressed to us an interest in finding out more, in practical terms expended little if any energy seeking out information on Radon and the issues surrounding it. I shall return to this feature below.

Suffice it to say, that in ANT terms, the network is formulated so as to incorporate a positive role for a delimited ignorance. As an electrician or a Radon survey volunteer, what one finds is a positive recasting of 'ignorance' which from without seems to be strange, but from within the network, so formulated, seems to be perfectly reasonable. Thus, while a general survey approach would have 'measured' this as ignorance in the context of the network 'parliamentary democracy', the identities of 'participant citizen', and the enabling role of accredited scientific institutions, these participants represent themselves as actors in a relatively local network within which ignorance is functional or, at worst, immaterial. In other words, knowledge is not abstracted, but embedded in local circumstances which encourage particular characteristics and functions.

This formulation of absence as a positive, functional characteristic is echoed in the final broad discourse of ignorance. Whereas the preceding discourses have attributed absence to constitutional disposition or to a localized role/function, the next discursive form entails an ascription to the agential self.

'Ignorance' as a Deliberate Choice

In other interviews scientific knowledge was consciously bracketed, ignored, jettisoned or avoided because it was perceived as essentially peripheral to, or a distraction from, the real issue at stake. Here, 'ignorance' is constructed as a deliberate choice.

For example, panel interviewee DM characterized scientists as 'people who have an incredible faith in science'. When subsequently asked whether he thought radiation could possibly have any positive effects, he remarked: 'There must be one or two, but I can't be bothered thinking about them . . .' This apparent self-imposed limitation on knowledge-seeking is also illustrated in the extract below. Just prior to this, the conversation had centred on the varieties of radiation and subatomic particles and their respective properties. When the interviewer asked how X-rays fit into the discussion, the interviewee responded:

> BW: I'm not sure . . . I know that the net effect of the whole damn lot is that if you get an overdose it's curtains and I don't really need to know any more.

These two cases both suggest that, for the respondents, there is good reason for not wanting to know more: extra scientific knowledge is redundant, or a distraction from the key issue – that radiation is dangerous. As such, knowledge of the processes and uses of ionizing radiation is represented as having little relevance. 'Ignorance' or deficit is now construed as a positive choice. We have seen that the state of 'ignorance', signalled by the lack of a scientific mind, suggests the elevation of the status of science to a necessary and perhaps unavoidable authority. We have also noted that 'ignorance', when accounted for in terms of the division of labour, implies a social and practical functionality and a collaborative relationship with (the practitioners of) science. In the present instance, the expressed determination to curtail scientific knowledge can be viewed as linked with an effort to establish independence from science and, possibly, to challenge the authority of actors using 'science'. This tacit critique is conducted by altering the intellectual register: it is no longer a matter of understanding particular bits of science or better marshalling scientific arguments. Rather, science is rendered peripheral to the substantive, crucial issues. This reading contrasts with Smithson's (1985) account that 'intended ignorance usually performs defensive social functions' (p. 156). While this can no doubt be the case, the above interpretation identifies a rhetoric wherein intentional 'ignorance' is mobilized in order to challenge, or attack, the relevance of a given body of expert knowledge to what the speaker perceives to be the 'real' issue at stake.

The above discourse of ignorance diverges from more obviously antagonistic postures towards science. Here, I have in mind discourses which directly derogate the actors who generate given bits of scientific knowledge. For example, one Radon survey volunteer questioned the reasons underlying what he saw as the current, unjustified popularity of the Radon issue:

> JM: I don't really know why they're having such a push on a national survey. It's the fashion to do surveys on radiation because it's a popular issue. People like yourself and people in science can go and get doctorates . . . . you'll certainly never cure background radiation. It's just job creation . . .

The scepticism expressed in this quote perhaps reflects the fact that this respondent is an ex-physics graduate. Certainly, he seems confident in his view that Radon is not an issue of prime importance: both in itself and relative to what he considers to be more urgent problems (such as the possibly debilitating effects of overhead power cables) the study of Radon is of spurious value. Perhaps ironically, he settles upon job creation as an explanation for the prevalence of the 'Radon issue'. Our second example shows an interviewee formulating the Radon issue as a deliberate distraction, concerted by the nuclear industry, from what should be the key concern, namely, the dangers posed by the nuclear industry:

MM: What do you think of as natural sources [of radiation]?
PD: The sun . . . erm . . . you which is . . . erm you know . . . which is dangerous but
we're living on this planet and er have our ionospheres and our stratospheres and
all these things which appear to protect us so we can get the benefits of it without
the dangers of it. Well, one of the natural radiations which . . . radioactive substances which the [nuclear] industry's jumped on recently is this Radon gas, which
is naturally occurring, so that they can divert people's attention from them [the
nuclear industry] so that they can say, 'Oh, look, well, you know, we'll be able to
seal [nuclear waste] . . .'

What this respondent seems to be advancing in this fragment is the view that
the Radon survey is not an innocent enterprise. Rather, it has specific political spin-offs for the nuclear industry. By embedding the Radon issue in a
larger political context, he effectively argues that it has become a resource for
the nuclear industry. Indeed, it is almost as if Radon as an issue has been constructed, or, at the very least, exploited, by 'bad' science (scientific institutions
with suspect interests). To deploy an ignorance-as-choice discourse is to dispute the usefulness of 'understanding' the scientific knowledge pertinent to
the Radon issue: to come to grips with the science in its arcane detail, would
be to miss the political point (and, possibly, to acquiesce to those institutional
actors to whom he is opposed). Once again, a different network is being
implicitly represented in relation to which the sort of scientific knowledge that
is being 'measured' (say, through our mental models or survey methodology)
ends up being irrelevant, indeed, dysfunctional. Here, a self-identity as a
'maverick' or 'refusenik' is enacted within, and emergent from, a network in
which science is seen as dangerous or problematic. What seems to be going on
here is the tacit ordering of an alternative network in which the key actor is
not accredited science but other actors concerned with, for example, the 'eco-
nomics' or 'politics' of the nuclear industry. It is these that are given priority.
Now, they might be no less centralized than accredited science, but the
implicit claim is that the respondent has a more direct access to them. As with
the generalized agonistic set mentioned above, an expanded network is being
invoked – one which overspills the confines of the narrowly scientific, indeed,
one which undermines the elevated status of those scientific actors associated
with the accredited knowledge of ionizing radiation.

We can systematize the three discourses of ignorance in the following way.
The non-scientific mind discourse constructs a relation of dependency.
Speakers subordinate themselves to the prime actors of science-in-general
represented by the interviewers. In contrast, in the division of labour discourse, ignorance signifies functionality as located within a more local
network – that of the Radon survey or the Sellafield nuclear reprocessing
plant (I will be exploring this in more detail in the next section). Finally, in the
ignorance-as-deliberate-choice discourse, the network associated with science-in-general is rejected or challenged. The negative identities that attach to
the ignorance of ionizing radiation are derogated, and knowledge of such specific phenomena is represented as a distraction from broader political and
economic actors and associations. Within this larger network, the actors of
science-in-general are reconstituted as relatively minor, indeed, marginal,

players. Rather, the expanded network being evoked by such talk 'concretizes' scientific knowledge (in contrast to the abstract scientific knowledge promoted by the Royal Society). By attaching it to particular interested actors such as the nuclear industry, the Government and activist groups, scientific knowledge is divested of its universality and objectivity. It becomes one form of knowledge amongst others – such as economic and political knowledge – in a network also populated with (admixtures of) economic and political as well as scientific actors. These speakers, despite, or, rather, because of, their avowals of scientific ignorance, do not suffer from political quiescence: this questioning of the relevance of abstract scientific knowledge reflects their very participation in the democratic process.

Doing and Undoing the Division of Labour

In this section, I am interested in addressing the way that the associations rendered between science-in-general and the public are themselves woven into the fabric of other networks and other identities which might supplement or undermine them (see Michael, 1992b for more details). I examine in more detail the different identities mobilized within the Radon network and its interactions with science-in-general. Before this, however, it is important to provide a more contextualized account of the study. After a national Radon survey conducted by the National Radiological Protection Board (NRPB) in 1985, local council Environmental Health Officers (EHO) throughout the country began intensive regional monitoring. In 1987, after the publication of the NRPB's report, Lancaster city council embarked on a survey to monitor Radon in over a hundred households. Of these, 22 volunteers were interviewed, 20 of whom were council employees. All but one of these had been approached by a council EHO who explained that, in participating, they would be required to keep a small plastic Radon detector in the home for six months. This came with instructions and an information sheet describing the nature of Radon and the survey. Not all our interviewees could recall receiving the information sheet; in contrast, most were still very clear about the instructions they had had to follow. Our semi-structured interviews covered a variety of topics, including their reasons for volunteering; their knowledge about and perceptions of Radon; ionizing radiation and associated technologies (as before, we were aiming to derive mental models); their sources of information about ionizing radiation; their views on scientists and the council.

Above, it was suggested that participants saw themselves as contributing to the overarching goal of the Radon survey. This involves a discursive construction of an association with both science and the council. We can access this through considering two broad categories of talk: 1. About 'volunteering'; 2. About one's (lack of) knowledge about Radon. I will suggest that the former reflects an identification with the council's science-in-particular and its broader civic aims, while the latter involves a process of differentiation (in the

form of admissions of 'ignorance') from science-in-general. These two identities, I will propose, reinforce one another in a way that diverts any potential
criticism of the survey, especially those criticisms aimed at the possible
ideological or political uses to which it might be put.

As regards the volunteer identity, interviewees' accounts that described
participation in the survey seemed to have two components: firstly, why individuals were considered and asked by the council; secondly, why they
accepted or volunteered.

Firstly, dealing with why the volunteers were asked to participate in the
Radon survey, this concerns volunteers' perceptions as to the reasons they
were approached and how they were chosen. In other words, it relates to
how they were characterized by others in the council. In some cases people
saw this process of selection as reflecting the requirement for appropriate
sampling in the survey. Here, there are few implications for identity or for
their social relation to the council. More interesting, in this context, are those
accounts which stressed that people were approached because of a specific
relation to the council hierarchy. For example, council staff were asked to participate because it was assumed that they would not panic. Less flatteringly,
some respondents suggested that they were obvious choices because of their
social positioning within the council (e.g. as a 'low status' receptionist one is
a 'convenient choice'). Both of these accounts imply a perceived mutual familiarity between self and council. The council officers 'know' one sufficiently
well (whether that be in terms of one's character or one's organizational
standing) to approach one. Likewise, the speaker 'knows' the council well
enough to be receptive to its requests for volunteers.

Secondly, if we look at why the volunteers accepted, the accounts volunteers provided for agreeing to assist the council sheds further light on their
implicit perceptions of their relation to the council.

1. If you 'get volunteered', it is prudent not jeopardise yourself by being
   uncooperative. Here, there is an ambiguous combination of passivity
   (being ordered) and volition (the wily decision to follow the exigencies of
   bureaucratic life).
2. About half of the people we talked to expressed interest in finding out
   the Radon levels for their own home. Here, the volunteers seem to be
   constructing themselves as consumers of the council's services.
3. 'Do-gooding'. This seemed to include two elements: helping out the
   council EHO and contributing to the general good.
4. Some people expected more specific, personal benefit from the survey –
   what might be called 'techno-interests. For example, one interviewee, a
   surveyor, thought that he would derive some insight into how building
   regulations might be affected by the Radon issue.

To summarize the foregoing volunteer accounts: 1. The council does good: a.
for you personally as a volunteer (it discovers the levels of Radon in your
home); b. for the community in general. 2. You as a volunteer do good: a. by
contributing to the survey, you might benefit the community; b. by aiding

EHOs, you enable them to do good for the community; c. as a consumer of council services, you yourself benefit (sometimes this self-interest takes the form of techno-interests).

These volunteer discourses can be interpreted as constructing a positive role – 'the survey volunteer' – which is a cardinal component in the process of knowledge production about local Radon levels. As such, the volunteers contribute both to advances in knowledge (and science-in-general) in some abstract way and to the due protection and care of self and the local population. Now, this volunteer discourse is interwoven with the discourse of ignorance outlined above in the following way. While the discourse of volunteering furnishes an identification with the science of the council (science-in-particular), the discourse of ignorance (especially, that of unscientific mind) serves to distance the volunteers from science-in-general. This pattern of discourses allows the speaker to support the goal of the survey research while simultaneously professing ignorance of its techniques and processes. Let me explain.

The form taken by discourse on the relation of volunteer to council entails self-subjectification – that is, people constitute themselves as subjects (agents). Volunteering is constructed in terms of their intention to contribute to the 'good'. But this subjectification is also present in their accounts of the council: the council's practices are represented as those of an agent intent on administering the Radon survey for the purposes of doing good. Here the dual subjectification of self and institution works to produce a functional agential whole (or actor) geared towards the end goal of 'doing good' – science-in-particular and the volunteer are purposive elements in the division of labour that pursues the realization of the collective 'good'. By comparison, in relation to science-in-general and the discourse of unscientific mind, dual objectification seems to be in operation. Firstly, there is self-objectification in that 'unscientific mind' refers to a missing faculty that is not open to volitional intervention. Secondly, science-in-general is also represented as an object – a sort of impenetrable thing-like entity. Where the complement of volunteer/council is articulated in terms of interests, wills and goals, the layperson/science contrast rests on the relative possession of such properties as capacity to assimilate scientific knowledge. Science 'contains' knowledge, the volunteer does not.

We can juxtapose these two discursive strands by considering the following volunteer's talk. Firstly, there is an example of the 'do-gooding' discourse; secondly, the 'unscientific mind' discourse is illustrated:

MM: And why did you think it was a good idea [the survey]?
MC: Why did I think it was a good idea? Well . . .
MM: You didn't get paid, did you? [*Laughs*]
MC: [*Laughing*] No . . . If you want to help other people, why not?

MM: Do you know what they were . . . measuring?
MC: Radioactivity, weren't they?
MM: Do you know what sort?
MC: No . . .

MM: You don't and they didn't say . . .
MC: I didn't know whether they . . . as I say, I'm not science minded . . . technically minded, anything like that . . .

These two self/institution combinations – volunteer/council (science-in-particular) and layperson/science-in-general – to the extent that they entail, respectively, subjectification and objectification, do not simply co-exist. Rather, they interact in a way that precludes a deeper interrogation of the meanings that can attach to the Radon survey in the context of the broader political environment. One might say that there is a self-reinforcing circle in which a given set of associations is reproduced: arcane science-in-general 'enters into' and underpins the council's expertise; the council's civic responsibility means that the Radon survey is indeed an important and valuable exercise even if it does remain largely incomprehensible to the volunteers. To differentiate oneself from the science-in-general is to insert oneself more securely in the lay network of the council; to identify more closely with the council is to render oneself more firmly at the disposal of science-in-general.

We have already remarked that such a relation can be subverted by asserting the importance of a different network in which the Radon issue is a distraction to key alternative knowledges and actors. The council Environmental Health Office also represents science-in-general, yet it is not interested in gauging the scientific literacy of the volunteers. Rather, it is primarily concerned to collect Radon data under standardized conditions. As such, it is more interested in disciplining the bodies of the volunteers – ensuring that they site the Radon monitor appropriately, in not interfering with it and so on. In order to do this, the identity of 'willing volunteer' has to be available. When the volunteers are confronted with interviewers who quiz them about their understandings of ionizing radiation in order to uncover their underlying mental models, who make salient the abstracted knowledge of science-in-general and its embedding network (however hazy such a network might be to the volunteers), these are not challenged. The volunteer identity is mobilized in order to accent the local network, but this network is then effectively nested within the science-in-general network. And here, it is the Environmental Health Office which serves as the representative of the volunteers – it constitutes the actor into which they are subsumed – a hybrid which includes scientists and volunteers, the knowledgeable and the ignorant. It is this actor that humbly contributes to that great network composed of scientific 'elites', governments, representations of democracy and citizenship, social science intermediaries and so on.

However, it is important to note that the division of labour discourse does not necessarily imply complementarity between lay and scientific actors – chronic conflict can also characterize these relations. An illustration of the latter is Brian Wynne's (e.g. 1992b) study of the responses of the Cumbrian sheepfarmers to the Chernobyl fallout. During May and early June 1986, in the wake of heavy rainfall that deposited the fallout from the Chernobyl nuclear power station explosion, confident ministerial and scientific statements were issued reassuring farmers that the problem would clear up within a few weeks. However, by 20 June restrictions on movement and slaughter of sheep were implemented, though it was also announced that these would be temporary. Most worryingly, on 24 July the ban was extended indefinitely.

The main point to be made here is that, partly in light of these changes in policy, the credibility of the scientists of the Ministry of Agriculture, Fisheries and Food (MAFF) was severely dented. The farmers' scepticism was aggravated in a number of ways. For example, the solutions offered by MAFF scientists tended to neglect the constraints on farmers' practices; scientists manifested unseemly ignorance of basic farming knowledge; scientists' pronouncements were often couched in terms of certainties (although cf. Campbell, 1985) that ran contrary to farmers' own experiences of the contingencies and uncertainties of farming. For instance, Wynne found that the government scientists' unreflexive use of randomized and standardized areas of fell to measure radioactive levels could be contrasted with farmers' knowledge of the uncertainties of the terrain, including the location of pools at certain sites which were the favourite drinking places for sheep. These standardized measures were presented as the 'right' way to measure radiation levels. In the eyes of the farmers, they had little relevance to the realities and uncertainties of the fells and the sheep. The ramification of these disparate perceptions was that the farmers, in problematizing the certainty entailed in the scientists' assessments, began to see them as part of a conspiracy or cover-up. Because they were denied access to the underlying uncertainties involved in the scientific evaluations of the longevity of radioactivity on the Cumbrian hills, they tended to view the changes of mind (policy and scientific assessment of conditions) made by MAFF and its scientists as responses to other political factors (such as the need to cover up the levels of radioactivity released from the nearby Sellafield nuclear reprocessing plant).

Wynne argues that the scientists' expertise encroached upon and often denied the farmers' own local knowledge. Though ostensibly deploying their skills in the farmers' interests, the scientists failed to complement fittingly the comparable skills of the farmers. Now, it might be possible to formulate the association of MAFF scientists with the sheepfarmers in terms of a division of labour – each actor contributing whatever expertise or facilities it possessed in order to address the problems posed by the Chernobyl fallout. But, from the farmers' perspective, it rapidly became evident that scientists were imposing a particular view that was not only inappropriate but also sometimes downright wrongheaded. While the farmers gained some knowledge about ionizing radiation, they generally recognized that it was the proper domain of scientists. However, what most irritated them was that this knowledge, and the accompanying scientific techniques, was applied without entertaining, let alone recognizing, the relevance of their local non-scientific craft knowledge. This wholesale, unreflexive transplantation of scientific knowledge into the Cumbrian fells devalued the farmers' hard-earned, less formally organized knowledge. Where the Sellafield electricians and the Radon volunteers saw this scientific knowledge as, more or less, complementing their own roles, the Cumbrian sheepfarmers came to see it as posing a threat to their local networks which valued craft knowledge. Indeed, the scientists were regarded as being more concerned to uphold MAFF's good name than to assist the farmers (though this impression was allayed when farmers eventually witnessed the actual practices of scientists which, like their own practices, entailed contingency and uncertainty).

In sum, it seems that scientific knowledge can be downgraded by the farmers because it both conflicted with local knowledge and, in view of the form it took, effectively marginalized the farmers' own local craft expertise. The goal ostensibly shared by MAFF and the farmers did not just concern the scientific (and economic) aim of accurately establishing the levels and longevity of the Chernobyl fallout. For the farmers, such a goal also incorporated social and cultural elements: at the very minimum, this goal should not be threatening to local identities and forms of knowledge. Insofar as MAFF ignored these elements, it was very difficult for the farmers to see themselves contributing to the task at hand. There was a divergence rather than a division of labour. In terms of enrolment, MAFF would fail by virtue of not attending to those dimensions of the farmer identity that were most important in the local network.

To the extent that there was a division of labour in this case study (ensuring the safety of sheepfarmers and sheep), it was one fraught with misunderstanding and suspicion partly based on the lack of commonly agreed criteria of expertise. To the extent that the scientists served as intermediaries for science-in-general and the Government, they failed by refusing to take into account the contingencies and uncertainties of their own knowledge and, therefore, the potential value of the local craft knowledge of the farmers – a knowledge intimately tied to an understanding of contingency and uncertainty. Wynne (1991) calls the Government's tacit, unreflexive privileging of abstract scientific knowledge the 'body language' of the institution. It was resisted by the sheepfarmers because they had available to them relevant and potent counter-identities and counter-knowledges. That is to say, in place already were a range of workable, tried and tested, local knowledges and practices that were embedded in, and constitutive of, the Cumbrian sheepfarming network. These served as narrative resources and texts of identity with which to resist would-be network-building and enrolment by MAFF (through its production of immutable mobiles of standardized, unproblematical, scientific data and texts; through engaging in forms of displacement by participating in local meetings with farmers, farming union representatives and local officials; through – perhaps by default – problematizing the existing identities of the farmers). In comparison with the sheepfarmers who were characterized by a counter-identity and counter-network that facilitated resistance (or scepticism or ambivalence) towards the institutions of science, for most of the participants in the Radon survey no such resources were available.

A Moment of Reflection

Before going on to review some of the points made in this chapter, it is important to inject a little reflection into the above account – an account which
seems to entail a contrast between the 'suspect' constructed universal science
of the scientist against the 'authentic' local knowledge of the layperson. How
does this narrative work?

It should, hopefully, by now be clear that what the survey approach at
once embodies and projects is a model of the intellectual deficiencies in
people's understandings as measured against some objective or authoritative
body of scientific knowledge. As it is cast above, this is a 'bad' thing. It is part
of the scientific establishment's (and its social science lackeys') view of the
public as somehow lacking the wherewithal to understand science. If the
deficit model stresses what is missing in the layperson's understanding of science, another way in which scientists and science policy makers regard the
public understanding of science is as a corruption of proper scientific knowledge. According to this, people by virtue of their lack of training, their
cultural embeddedness and their animation by vitiating interests have only
distorted knowledge.

The dichotomy at the heart of this apprehension pans out as follows. On
the one hand, from the science/policy faction's (and the 'bad' social scientists') perspective, the public are 'bad': they are either deficient or corrupted
by the 'cultural', or they are prone to subjectivity. In comparison science is
objective. On the other hand, from the 'good' social scientists' perspective, it
is science which is 'bad'. It is science's knowledge that is structured by laboratory culture, cognitive interests, professional standards of proof,
disciplinary assumptions and the like – yet, scientists and their institutions
resolutely refuse to acknowledge this. In contrast, the public is 'good': it can
recognize the uncertainties and contingencies built into any knowledge. Such
a public sensibility rests on: a. its culture (as in the case of the Cumbrian
farmers); and/or b. its actual, real and objective experience of uncertainty and
contingency.

What is happening here? Well, there is a reversal of status: from the 'good'
scientists versus the 'bad' public ('objective' scientists versus 'subjective' public), to the 'bad' scientists versus the 'good' public (scientists are tainted by
the cultural whereas the public have direct or authentic experience of their
natural world; to put it another way, scientific knowledge is contingent while
the public have an unmediated knowledge of uncertainty). This reversal seems
to me to be perfectly understandable when recast as a case of doing politics.
Just as the 'bad' social scientists attempt to mediate the 'goals' of the natural
scientists by furnishing and disseminating a particular nexus of identities for
the public and for science around such issues as knowledge, democracy, participation and scientific literacy, so we 'good' social scientists set up another
identity nexus, one which perhaps goes something like this.

Firstly, when we are being critical, tactically fighting the corner of a specific
public engaged in a particular dispute with an identifiable scientific body, we

champion the knowledge of the public as superior. In this respect we are not being symmetrical in David Bloor's (1976) sense of applying the same style of explanation to the two opposing knowledges (e.g. socio-cultural–interest-laden). One is seen as culturally contingent (science); the other as a direct access to the real world (public). The same goes for the representation of each other: thus, the public-as-deficient is seen as a culturally laden representation socially constructed by science and its 'bad' social science intermediaries; whereas the body language of scientific institutions is viewed as a real phenomenon, directly accessed by the public.

Secondly, when we are engaged in more strategic or long-term, or even utopian, critique, where our main aim is to advocate particular institutional arrangements and media of consultation, or to promote a generalized scientific accountability thereby laying the basis for a more pluralistic context for knowledge generation, then the symmetry tenet is upheld. We see that all knowledge, both that of the public and that of science, is contingent. The aim is therefore to open up the process of negotiation, extend the core set, take in more social worlds, bring multiplicity and marginality into the network.

The point of all this is that this is a pretty fine line that we tread. Obviously, it is politics that we are practising. We variously construct science and public actors to fit particular roles. We pattern our contingent and empiricist repertoires (Gilbert and Mulkay, 1984) like scientists do; only our 'objects of study' are public and science and their inter-relations, not brain peptides and proton pumps. So, it goes without saying that I have done the same in the present text, reifying 'bad' social scientists and 'good' publics like the sheepfarmers. It seems to me that we are in a genuine dilemma advocating two differing orderings and projecting two divergent networks.

Conclusion

In this chapter I have tried to examine, perhaps not altogether cogently, the specific deployment of identities and how these are implicated in the ordering of networks. Thus, for example, I referred to the way that the social scientific intermediaries of science-in-general generate a set of identities for the lay public, and how members of that public attempt to generate counter-identities when faced with the perceived representatives of science-in-general in the form of the interviewers (myself included). This conflict of representations and orderings was set in the historical context of an ongoing association between science-in-general and the lay public, an association that is in constant need of repair and reproduction. However, into this contested network flow other representations and identities drawn from other networks that concern gender, class, schooling, community and so on. To trace these network resources is beyond the scope of this volume. Nevertheless, as the discussion of the division of labour suggested, identities that are part of local networks also feed into the associations with science-in-general, either supporting it (Radon survey volunteers) or undermining it (Cumbrian sheepfarmers).

However, for all the potency of the discourses of identity that I have (re)constructed in this chapter, they are but one facet of social ordering and the construction of identity. As we noted in the last chapter, the most durable identities are those inscribed by technologies prescribing as they do regularities in action/behaviour. These are the 'hard' facets of the network. But, as I have remarked throughout this volume, these are not the only nonhumans to influence identity – there are also 'natural' nonhumans. How actor-network might theorize the roles of these actors in the production of identity is the subject of the next chapter.

7

Actors, Identities and 'Natural' Nonhumans

In the preceding chapters, we saw how identity was resourced by particular actors attempting to generate the sorts of associations that would best serve their desired network. However, in Chapter 4, it was noted how ANT was also concerned to overcome the privileging of the social in any account of the production of social order and, by extension, of identity. In this chapter, we take up this 'radical symmetrism' (Callon and Latour, 1992) in order to suggest, tentatively, ways in which we might theorize identity as the construction of both human and nonhuman, particularly 'natural', actors.

To date, detailed work on this particular facet of ANT has been confined, primarily, to the role of technological artefacts such as door grooms and key weights (see Chapter 4). As we have seen, technological actors can be traced back to the activities of human actors who are themselves the partial products of the pre-/pro-inscriptions of technological nonhumans (and so on *ad infinitum*). In the context of encounters between human and technological entities, it is possible to attribute, albeit circumspectly, agency to the latter by virtue of the fact that they have been partly constructed by humans. As such, the wills, desires and goals of those humans can be said to reside in, to be embodied in, those technological nonhumans as they go about their routines of disciplining human bodies. Indeed, as Latour argues, technological artefacts are the most moral and moralizing of characters, structuring human action/behaviours in all sorts of ways. In contrast, it is, at this point in history, considerably more difficult to do the same for 'natural' nonhumans like animals and local environments. In a sense, the status of 'natural' nonhumans is more opaque in our current Western networks (though historically the 'agential' status of the 'natural' has, in the past, been more readily accepted). Below, I will explore some (strictly limited) ways in which it might be possible to narrate the roles of such 'natural' nonhumans in the construction of human identity.

To this end this chapter is structured in the following way. Initially, I will consider some social constructionist positions on 'nature' – mainly those which articulate nature as a 'construct' or representation that fulfils certain social functions. Usually, this construct has the form of 'nature-as-object-with-certain-properties'. In contrast, one can seek out other historical representations of 'natural' nonhumans which attribute to them something like agency or personhood. I will then briefly enumerate some of the discourses which construct the relations between humans and 'natural' nonhumans, especially through the dichotomy of subject/object. In so doing, and by pointing to efforts to recover the agential status of 'natural' nonhumans, I aim to suggest that the capacity of 'natural' nonhumans to intervene in social ordering and in the (re)production of identity as something like an actor is on the historical increase. The networking by 'natural' nonhumans, that is, their impact upon the constitution of human identity, will be illustrated with regard to two actor/entities: animals and local environments (bioregions).

'Nature' as Functional Construct

I have neither the competence nor the space properly to cover all the social constructionist approaches to 'nature'. As such, I will merely introduce a number of examples to illustrate, or, rather, give a flavour of, this broad and eclectic perspective. We have already had a skirmish with SSK and its typical analysis of the ways in which scientists constitute nature, natural processes and their own supposedly unique and direct access to these. So, I will attend to other bodies of literature which, while they have oblique connections to SSK, have rather different lineages. For example, Mary Douglas and her followers have elaborated their radically Durkheimian grid/group theory. In grid/group theory it is assumed that risk and uncertainty are identified as being located in certain parts of the natural world in such a way that the internal structure of the group to which individuals belong, and its relation to other collectivities, is reproduced (e.g. Douglas, 1970; Schwarz and Thompson, 1990; Thompson et al., 1990; but see Johnson, 1987). Grid/group theory presents us with two dimensions: group defines the degree to which a boundary is drawn between members of a group and outsiders. Strong group thus implies exclusivity, weak implies individual autonomy. Grid addresses the differentiation between individuals. High grid suggests an explicit set of institutionalized classifications which keeps individuals apart and regulates interaction. Low grid refers to those instances where such distinctions have broken down and people negotiate as in a free market. The combination of these two dimensions leads not only to characteristic social configurations, but also to allied perceptions of nature and its inherent uncertainties. Drawing upon Schwarz and Thompson (1990), the following illustrate two of the group/grid configurations, with their concomitant conceptions of nature and uncertainty. High grid, high group is hierarchist and bureaucratic, there is a reliance upon rules and procedure, and nature is perceived as perverse and/or tolerant. By comparison, low grid, low group is individualist and entrepreneurial with a commitment to an ethos of the 'bottom line' (get out and do it); as such, nature is regarded as highly resilient.

In these instances, constructed nature 'legitimates' those social activities of group members and as such serves in the social reproduction of the group configuration. To behave in a certain way towards nature (itself conceived and constructed as a particular type of entity) means that there are norms and rules that structure that behaviour and can therefore be used to judge the (belonging-ness of the) actions of others within one's group. For example, Thompson et al. (1990) give an account of the low grid, low group individualists as holding to a vision of nature as benign – it 'encourages and justifies bold experimentation. As long as we all do our exuberant, individualistic things, a "hidden hand" . . . will lead us to the best possible outcome' (p. 27). But this is allied to a vision of human nature: 'For individualists, human nature, like physical nature, is extraordinarily stable. No matter what the institutional setting, individualists believe, human beings remain essentially the same: self-seeking. By making man (sic) self-seeking, individualists can justify a way of life that attempts to channel human nature rather than change it' (p. 34). It is through this representation that other visions of nature, human nature and political system are (negatively) evaluated, and the desired form of social interaction reproduced.

But, if representations of nature serve as means towards (particular models of) social cohesion, there are other instances in which nature, in the way that it is differentiated from society and science, serves to warrant a particular relation to nature and a corollary political posture. Thus Michael (1991), in his analysis of interviews with respondents about their understandings of ionizing radiation, derives two ideal typical discourses which situate nature in relation to society and science. In the first ideal type, nature is dangerous, science subjugates and controls nature, lay society is subordinated to the expertise of science. Without science nature is uncontrolled and a dire threat to humanity and civilization. An example of this discourse is where the ionizing radiation produced by technological sources (nuclear industry, medical radiography) is seen as less of a risk because it is more open to control than radiation that is derived from natural sources (e.g. Radon, cosmic rays). In the second ideal type, nature is essentially good and relatively amenable to human desires. Science should be at the command of society which is able to constrain scientific excess. Nature can be used, but in a respectful, cooperative spirit. Were science allowed a free hand, it would disrupt the balance of nature and bring about all manner of catastrophes. An example of this is the idea that while X-rays are nature harnessed – science-in-the-service-of-society – radiation from nuclear power stations is nature abused – science-working-for-itself.

However, in addition to these ideal types, there were also more nuanced discourses which contain a version of society as a political construct. Here are two examples of such implicit political stories contained within representations of ionizing radiation. JM is a physics graduate. Up to this exchange we have been talking about his involvement with the Lancaster City Council Radon survey.

> MM: 'Do you draw any distinction between artificial and natural radiation?'
> JM: 'It's all natural really . . .'

While this is a minimal quote, Michael assumes that, as a physics graduate, by 'natural' JM is referring to the microphysical processes of radioactive decay. (This microphysical view is supported by a passage elsewhere in the transcript where he says that no radiation is safe, presumably referring to cellular damage caused by radiation.) This interpretation highlights a discursive abstraction: the different types of ionizing radiation with their disparate isotopic, and thus environmental and institutional, sources are 'reduced' to natural subatomic physical processes. This can be said to be equivalent to a sort of a de-differentiation. All ionizing radiations are dangerous and all ionizing radiations are products of natural processes of radioactive decay: there is nothing else – the social and political context of such radiations is rendered invisible. The risks of ionizing radiation are simply and naturally part and parcel of living in the world: society is discursively subsumed by nature. The function of this de-differentiation seems to be the diffusion of the causal social loci of danger or risk. Of course, this is a version of the classic ideological form of 'naturalization' but one where the historicity of the social is occluded – not by naturalizing the social directly but by naturalizing a nature (ionizing radiation) that is through and through social.

Against this, there is the discursive form of hyper-differentiation. For example, consider the following exchange:

> MM: I assume that as it [ionizing radiation] increases, it's getting more dangerous . . .
> ML: Well, and then I presume it will depend on the actual host if you can call it that.
> MM: So you think there's differences between people?
> ML: You know, erm . . . not immunity, but something similar, you know, whether your cells were, you know, that sort . . .

What ML is referring to here are individual differences in susceptibility to the dangers of ionizing radiation. Society is hyper-differentiated into its constituent individuals each of which has their own peculiar natural cellular responsivity to ionizing radiation. Once again there is a diffusion of the causal locus that shifts emphasis from the particular component social institutions to the necessary condition of individual susceptibility. As with de-differentiation, society is bracketed in favour of natural processes. If de-differentiation implies dimensions of nature such as inevitability and pervasiveness, hyper-differentiation implies the dimensions of luck (of the draw) and fate.

In both cases, we see that talk about ionizing radiation and its associated dangers, when translated into a representation of mechanism – the process of radioactive decay and individual genetic predisposition – reflects and mediates a particular representation of society wherein political action is seen to be futile. In the context of the interview, it renders a particular impression of the speaker – as warrantably passive or indifferent to the political conditions under which ionizing radiation is generated. One could also add that the microsocial construction of 'nature' can fulfil other functions: for example it can be instrumental in the deflation of relativist arguments (Edwards et al., 1995), or can promote or undermine arguments for developing particular environmental policy (MacNaghten, 1993).

While the above examples impute a functionality to various constructions of nature, the following accounts place such representations in a more diffuse and epochal social and cultural context. Here, representations of nature have emerged in the process of broad, complex historical changes. For example, Collingwood (1960) describes the conceptions of 'nature' that have developed from the period of the ancient Greeks to the rise of modern science. According to Collingwood, the Greeks conceived of 'nature' as a rational, mindful organism: it was saturated with mind which orchestrated the ceaseless movement of bodies and elements to yield orderliness and regularity, and hence the possibility of science. By the Renaissance period, the order of 'nature' was thought to be imposed from without and 'nature' was conceived as a machine – a configuration of parts designed, wrought, assembled and animated by an intelligent mind (God). By the end of the eighteenth century, partly derived from the study of human affairs, 'nature' was no longer seen to be cyclical, but evolving.

If Collingwood provides us with a broad outline of the cosmological construction of 'natural', other authors have studied historically more nuanced changes in our conception of 'natural'. Thus, Williams (1980) notes that the Elizabethan and early Jacobean representation of 'nature' as singular, abstracted and personified as God's minister and deputy instructing humankind as to its duties was transformed into a sort of constitutional lawyer by the seventeenth century. By the nineteenth century attention effectively had moved from this law-giver to the details of the laws (of nature) and their interpretation. Other scholars (e.g. Merchant, 1980; Berman, 1981) have reconstructed the changing conception of 'nature' with the express aim of recovering a more 'environmentally-friendly' formulation, or of mapping out the historically variable valuation of various 'natural entities' such as animals and wilderness. These authors argue that the agency that was once seen to be integral to natural nonhumans has been historically superseded by representations which render them objects (see also Thomas, 1984; Tester, 1991). Beck (1992) has considered the emergent contradictory reconceptualization of 'nature' under the conditions of what he calls the 'Risk Society'. 'Nature' is no longer the antithesis of society – where once a 'pure nature' was directly accessed by the layperson now it is mediated by experts who inform us of the risks that lurk in every part of a thoroughly 'corrupted socialized nature'.

However, all these approaches have constituted 'nature' as a construction, as opposed to some external given. The analytic purpose is to expose the discursive, rhetorical, practical, historical, political, etc. resources that serve in the construction of an ostensibly unproblematic (or rather, unproblematizeable) 'nature'. In the present context, while accepting the importance of the above perspectives, and on the basis of the critique of social constructionism outlined in Chapter 3, I want to consider some of the ways in which 'nature' is beginning to be reintroduced into social theorizing, in particular, as an independently effectual actor. To rephrase the central issue outlined at the beginning of this chapter, one might ask: how could we possibly justifiably treat 'natural' nonhumans as autonomous participants, whether agential or not, in the world as opposed to 'merely' the social constructions of human discursive collectivities?

Such an intellectual query is, of course, not altogether novel. Indeed, we find it appearing in several sub-disciplines such as sociological theory, feminist theory, SSK and environmental ethics. We have already noted in Chapter 3 how it is possible to problematize the differentiation between the 'natural' and the 'social' in social anthropology (Horigan, 1988), and we have noted Benton's account of the re-emergence of 'nature' on the social science agenda. Horigan and Benton have produced programmatic analyses of the (possible) return of 'nature'. Dickens (1992), on the other hand, attempts to formulate the broad outlines of a coherent (social) theory that encapsulates the roles of both the 'social' and the 'natural'. Drawing upon the young Marx, he elaborates a critical realist account of society that hinges on 'nature' that is at once socially constructed but also 'transcendental'. The latter refers to 'causal powers', that is, the way that 'organisms are seen as having necessary, latent or potential ways of acting . . . but [these] critically depend on contingent circumstances' (p. 178). Thus, 'nature' is constitutive of people insofar as they have 'particular kinds of latent tendencies and potentials (natural and species being) which may or may not be realised in their association (or lack of association) with the natural world' (p. 64).

But, contrary to Dickens, we might argue that these contingencies – or rather these positionings in networks – are exactly what we should be interested in. It is these that at once constitute and mediate these natural actors. But, of course, these networks – in part social and technological – are, in turn, constituted and mediated by 'natural' nonhuman actors. The point is not to lay some abiding, if slippery, foundation or to point to a transcendental grounding. Rather, it is a question of finding a way of narrating the role of 'natural' nonhumans that shows that their interventions are always a matter of contingency – that any properties or impacts they might have are effects of a network. In sum, these properties and impacts are relational in the sense that what these actants can 'do', and what can be known about them (how they might be constructed) depends on the state and configuration of actors around them. I shall return to this important issue below.

By and large, the approaches mentioned above tended to regard 'nature' as a mechanistic component in the (re)production of the social. It is as an, albeit contingent, causal influence on social processes that 'nature' is to be reappropriated and theorized. In contrast, there are alternative perspectives that attempt to reintroduce 'nature' as a semiotic player. Here, 'nature' adopts the part of another interlocutor in the discursive/practical community that (re)constructs both the 'social' and the 'natural' or 'technological'. This can take various forms. For example, there are efforts to recover the agential status of 'nature' or to retrace its fall from the heights of personhood (Adorno and Horkheimer, 1979; Berman, 1981; Merchant, 1980).

Perhaps the most elaborated accounts of treating 'nature' as a subject in interaction with humans can be found in the burgeoning field of environmental ethics. Much of the intellectual effort expended in environmental ethics seeks to find a philosophical (e.g. Heideggerian, aesthetic, phenomenological) or theological (e.g. Christian, Native-American) basis for 'ecological consciousness' (cf. Rodman, 1983). As such these projects are proactive and normative: they serve as warrants and justifications for encouraging a jaded and corrupted Western consciousness to reorient itself to nature in an ethically responsible mode. In some treatments, 'nature' is elevated to a 'Thou' – a full participant, equivalent to a human interlocutor, in conversation with the human 'I' (e.g. Buber, 1970; Tallmadge, 1981; however, see also Kultgen, 1982; Reed, 1989; Michael and Grove-White, 1993). In this latter case, 'nature' is merely 'humanized': 'nature' is attributed characteristics typical of humans conceived in humanistic terms. The agential status of 'nature' is here assumed or argued for (as is that of humans). As we will see below, such 'semiotic' (broadly defined) interactions need not trade on pre-existing agents – indeed, agency may be an emergent element in the interaction. Certainly, the production of agency, as with the production of 'society' or 'nature' can be seen as an accomplishment. In sum, these efforts by some humanistic environmental ethicists are essentially attempts to articulate what it might mean to broaden the 'linguistic' and 'responsible' collective to include the 'natural'.

Now, following Michael and Grove-White (1993), I want tentatively to formalize some of the possible associations between humans and nonhumans and the discourses that are connected with them. The purpose is to avoid an overly humanistic account of 'natural' nonhumans (though, it should be mentioned, as Soper, 1986 has pointed out, humanism does have strategic political force). As such, while the relation of humans to nature has been formulated, apprehended or articulated in a multitude of ways, the present analysis provides a somewhat more abstract schema with which to comprehend previous approaches to human–nature relations. On this score, I use as my starting point Martin Buber's (1970) contrast between I-it and I-Thou.

The following schema is thus an attempt to arrange the ways of 'knowing nature' in terms of the relative subject-ness (personhood) or object-ness (thing-likeness) which is ascribed respectively to humans and nature, whether this ascription is discursive (linguistic formulation) or practical (in the 'handling of nature'). For the moment, though I will return to this nexus of issues below, it will suffice to note that my approach expands the version of human to incorporate a notion of the human-as-object, which I will call 'me' (and here I must extend my apologies to Mead, 1934) that parallels the 'it' of nature-as-object, and is differentiated from the 'I' of the human-as-subject, as the 'it' is differentiated, in Buber's scheme, from the 'Thou' of nature-as-subject.

Finally, before presenting the typology, I must note that it is taken as read that the following schema is itself a particular, historically situated reading of these forms of knowing, not least because the very dichotomies of human and nature, and subject and object, are themselves constructs. We have already encountered Horigan's documentation of the way that the early champions of social anthropology, in their attempts to constitute their practices as an independent discipline, free from its historical roots in biology and natural philosophy, overstated the primacy of social factors and neglected the role of the biological upon human behaviour. What counted as 'natural' or biological, and what counted as social or 'human', was influenced by the exigencies of constructing and maintaining institutional and disciplinary boundaries. With respect to the latter dichotomy, subject and object have been shown to be both linguistically mediated (Harré, 1989) and historically contingent in the sense that the emergence of the human subject, and its maintenance in particular forms, has been associated with the large-scale historical transition of the Enlightenment and before (e.g. Adorno and Horkheimer, 1979; Merchant, 1980; Berman, 1981), but also to the microprocesses of institutional surveillance and normalization exemplified in Foucault's germinal historical studies (1979b, 1981; see also Donzelot, 1979; Rose, 1989b). On the issue of the historicity of the subject/object divide, I will follow Smart (1982) and resign myself to the view that, under the prevailing 'episteme', these categories are inescapable. Nevertheless, we can distinguish ideal types of ways of 'knowing nature' that embody the most unalloyed versions of these combinations of subject/object, nature/human.

In what follows, I formulate what is effectively a 2 x 2 matrix in which the four permutations of object/subject and human/nature are outlined. In each combination of human (as either subject/I or object/me) and nature (as subject/Thou or object/it), I refer to the more or less institutionalized or articulated textual forms (in the broadest sense) through which these apprehensions have been fashioned – that is, the sorts of academic, or lay, discursive work that is done in the construction and mediation of this relationship. In order to illustrate the discursive/practical forms through which these four human/nature relationships have been formulated, three examples will be presented: the planting of a tree; the death of a human individual; the destruction of the ozone layer. These three have been chosen primarily because they address three different 'proximities' of nature (the body; an individual plant; a macro-ecological entity).

1   Human-as-object (me)/Nature-as-object (it). In this permutation, both nature and humanity are viewed as objects in material interaction, for example, exchanging bio-energy. The interaction is purely mechanical. This is the domain of science (e.g. academic ecology) and it is the discourses of objectivity, universalism, lawfulness and so on that investigate this relation. The planting of a tree in this instance is formulated as a sequence of mechanical procedures; a person's death is documented as a series of physiological, biochemical and physical processes; the destruction of the ozone layer is likewise formulated in terms of a combination of chemical, atmospheric and physical processes.

2   Human-as-subject (I)/Nature-as-object (it). Here, humans are conscious, volitional subjects whereas nature is an object or resource to be studied or exploited. The accompanying discursive repertoires address the respective status of human intervention (for example, in the form of science and technology), and nature. This differential status can be formulated in terms of the 'control over', or the 'responsibility for', nature, and the formal accounts of this relation range from the scientifically triumphalist (technological fix) to the humble calls for a revivified ethos of stewardship (e.g. Passmore, 1974). Ethics, epistemology and accounts of the politics of science all address this

relation. Within this array of discourses, to plant a tree is to engage with the motives and reasons of the planter: are they merely instrumental (for harvesting) or do they reflect a 'responsible' attitude to nature? In addition, the relationship can also be formulated, not in terms of morality, but in terms of knowledge: how can we know nature? With regard to our examples, we can see that a 'natural' death can be cast as both a 'positive' (time to 'move on') and a 'negative' ('live fast, die young') 'choice'. Finally, the destruction of the ozone screen can likewise be viewed as a choice; alternatively, the register in which the issue is framed may change from the ethical to the epistemological – do we have accurate measurements? can we monitor and model the change? is there really a change? – in the effort to diffuse responsibility and waylay practical effort (e.g. Yearley, 1991).

3   Human-as-object (me)/Nature-as-subject (Thou). This combination addresses the reverse configuration in which humans are the objects and nature is the subject. The questions that are enjoined by the related knowledge forms include: 'what is the wider meaning of death?' or 'is there a higher agent (God, Spirit, History) who controls our destinies and what are her/his/its purposes?' These questions are tied to attempts to grasp the fate, destiny or telos of individuals and collectivities. For example, in Greek Orthodox theological accounts, it is the very ambiguity or hybrid-status of humans as both object (like animals) and subject (like angels) that makes humans special in the scheme of God (Ware, 1987). Thus, the knowledge forms that attend to these issues include the likes of metaphysics, mythology and eschatology. An individual's death can be viewed as part of a deity's purpose; the planting of a tree can be seen as a part of Gaia's plan of regeneration; the destruction of the ozone layer can be viewed fatalistically as the playing out of some millenarian apocalypse.

4   Human-as-subject (I)/Nature-as-subject (Thou). The final inter-relation entails that both humans and nature are subjects/agents. That is, both are viewed as cognizant, reflexive, volitional beings. The interaction between these persons takes the form of an 'authentic' (in the sense of subjectively felt) exchange, that is to say, a communication between two subjects. Here, discourse addresses the content and form of statements passing back and forth between interlocutors – human and natural actors. These can range from individual communion to collective ritual. The planting of a tree is thus an actual communication, say in the conversational mode described by Roads (1987) in which dialogues take place between the author and the various natural entities such as trees. However, this is only one, rather literal, form of 'talking with nature'. Other modes can be somewhat more extended in time (e.g. Berger, 1979), or more 'diffuse', that is to say, less linguistically mediated (e.g. Evernden, 1985; Harrison, 1986; Mabey, 1984). As regards a human death, this would be understood through the rituals that surround the dying person and through which the dying and his or her relatives communicate with gods or ancestors. The destruction of the ozone layer comes to be grasped as an outrage against the earth, in which talk and ceremony are directed to the appeasement and strengthening of the earth.

The above model serves the heuristic purpose of allowing us to trace the movements and sedimentations in the knowing of 'knowing nature'. However, as the categories 'subject' and 'object' suggest, this typology can serve to classify, at the most abstract level, the inter-relation between 'self' and 'other'. In the present case, the roles of self and other have been played by humans and nature; in other instances these positions might have been allotted to man and woman, white and black or bourgeoisie and proletariat. Indeed, these dichotomies are not altogether separate from the human/nature couple we have examined (e.g. Ortner, 1976; Hoch, 1979). Of course, there is also a fifth position which rejects the above typology altogether by delineating some relation to nature that transcends the subject/object dichotomy. I do not rule out this alternative. However, as noted above, on the assumption that this dichotomy comprises a primary and entrenched feature of contemporary Western thought, both professional and lay, it is important, if not imperative, to explore how it structures human/nonhuman relations.

It was noted above that much environmental ethics has been engaged in trying to legitimate, and sometimes legislate, the shift from I-It to I-Thou. Against, variously and in combination, the technocratic, Christian, patriarchal, capitalist, scientistic, Western objectification of nature is counterposed a more authentic, better or deeper relation between humans and nature, that of 'I-Thou'. My point is that all four permutations make up part of our relationship with nature. We, like nature, are both subject and object – and these are effects of the network. As such, the aim is not to valorize subject-hood over object-hood – neither of these is seen to be *a priori* superior over the other. Just as subject-ification (and the I-Thou relation) is not assumed to be unproblematically 'good' – witness, for example, the critiques of humanist psychotherapeutic subculture and of 'technologies of the self' (Fairclough, 1992; Rose, 1989b) – so too object-ification is not held to be uniformly 'bad'. Rather, it is a question of pursuing these categorizations, tracing how they are accomplished and how this accomplishment through discourse and material interactions has effects, serving to mediate, in the context of given network configurations, the interactions and enrolments between humans and 'natural' nonhumans (which, in turn, affect the (re)production of these interactions).

The Role of 'Natural' Nonhumans: Media of Communication and Enrolment

But how are we to theorize the media through which interactions between the social and the non-social, humans and 'natural' nonhumans, are conducted? ANT, as we have seen, while it ascribes autonomy to 'nature' and to technological artefacts, nevertheless conceptualizes these as historically contingent entities which can, with further analysis, be shown to be constructed out of further 'technological', 'natural' and 'social' entities (or actors or actants) that make up the network. As a corollary, the object or subject status of 'natural' entities, technological artefacts or humans is emergent from the network and therefore is one topic of analysis. In relation to the construction of identity, the questions that we are faced with can be phrased in the following way: how might 'nature' intervene in the construction of identity? Here, I focus upon the way that the 'natural' serves to enrol human actors, and how its resistance – a resistance that, as I have framed it here, is always already historically contingent – begins to shape the construction of a social identity. However, such resistances as they are expressed in the micro-situational interaction need not always be linguistic. Indeed, to capture the range of the media through which the interactions between humans and nonhumans are conducted, one needs an expanded definition of semiotics. Fortunately, Akrich and Latour (1992) provide just such a definition. Semiotics is:

> The study of how meaning is built, [where] the word 'meaning' is taken in its original nontextual and nonlinguistic interpretation: how a privileged trajectory is built, out of an indefinite number of possibilities; in that sense, semiotics is the study of order building or path building and may be applied to settings, machines, bodies and programming languages as well as texts . . . . (p. 259)

What concerns us here is the notion of 'building a privileged trajectory out of an indefinite number of possibilities'. The point is that the 'natural' can play a part in such structuring. Through a variety of media, the natural can enrol humans by giving them (or getting them to accept) particular identities. In the process, order (behavioural as well as linguistic or narrative) comes to be generated out of an indefinite number of possibilities. However, in suggesting such a project, in keeping with the problematic of agency mentioned above, we would need to address the issue of how to ascribe the status 'subject' or 'object', or, rather, how to trace the emergence of 'subjects' and 'objects' within a given network. The typology I have developed above, albeit tentatively, serves to illustrate Akrich and Latour's re-articulation of semiotics, fleshing out the notion of building order and regularity in the interaction – whether through mechanical or communicational media or through some hybrid of the two. In a very schematic way, what follows is an attempt at instanciating some of the forms of subject/object, human/nonhuman determinations that we find in various discourses and networks; in keeping with Callon and Latour's (1992) radical symmetrism (in which what is to count as subject/object, human/nonhuman is the product of network-building, not its basis), the combinations of subject/object, human/nonhuman should be seen as options or trajectories (and perhaps, sometimes, strategies) in the process of network-building and identity production. In the section that follows, I will look in more detail at some of the possible enrolments or associations that two 'natural nonhuman' actors can construct with human actors.

ANT, 'Nature' and Identity

This section deals with two examples of the way that ANT might be used to theorize the construction of identity in which nonhumans play a relatively autonomous part. Rather than press this claim to the limit and look for the

most difficult cases, I have been somewhat cowardly and opted for compara-
tively easy illustrations where the conduits of communication or semiosis are
relatively unmediated. Thus, I deal with those nonhumans whose interactions with humans are traditionally thought to fall within the limits of human
perception: animals rather than viruses; immediate environment rather than
the cosmos. In keeping with the focus upon the microsocial context of construction (see above), it is at this locus that 'conversation', however
formulated, can take place (though of course, there is no guarantee that it
will). At all other levels, some mediation must presumably take place.

Nice Animals

In regard to the role of the 'natural' in the constitution of identity, we can
draw one final time upon Callon's classic (1986a) study of the scallops,
researchers and fishing community of St Brieuc Bay mentioned above. This
we can reinterpret in terms of the production of identity that was partially
shaped by the intransigence of both social and, especially in the context of the
present discussion, natural entities. The researchers attempted to construct an
actor-network in which they narrated the roles of the component actants:
local fishermen, the scallops and the relevant scientific community. The identity the three researchers had constructed for themselves could only be
sustained as long as each of these three 'populations' continued to fulfil their
assigned roles. In particular, when the scallop larvae 'refused' to be cultivated and levels became hopelessly low, the stories the researchers could tell
about themselves as scientists and cultivators were catastrophically undermined. In terms of the microsocial context, the biologists' interactions with
the larvae produced a certain outcome, namely that non-cultivation of the
scallops and, as a result, the identity that the researchers had created for
themselves, grounded as it was in the behaviour of scallop larvae, became
insupportable. Now, this example relies on an access to the scallops mediated
through the scientific techniques of measuring the successful anchoring and
development of the larvae. The scallops' recalcitrance had to be observed
through the mechanical interventions of the biologists and, as such, falls
within the I-it category of interaction advanced above. However, there are
other animals, interaction with whom lends itself to other sorts of characterizations, where the media of communication are more plural, and where the
subject/object status of both nonhuman and human actors is much more
fluid.

   In this respect, an amenable example of human–nonhuman interactions
can be found in accounts of interactions with putatively 'more overtly respon-
sive' (i.e. interactive) animals. Animal companions (sometimes known as pets)
have long been said to have therapeutic effects upon their owners, though
obviously this will depend on the precise nature of the relationship. In particular, owners say that 'their animals are sensitive to their [the owners'] moods
and feelings' (Serpell, 1986, p. 114; cf. also Sanders, 1992). The processes of

communication that are evident here are clearly not linguistic, but vocal, visual and tactile. However, animals' lack of linguistic capacity may be one of their prime assets. As Serpell (1986) puts it:

> Lacking the power of speech, animals cannot participate in conversation or debate but, by the same token, they do not judge us, criticize us, lie to us or betray our trust. Because it is mute and non-judgemental, their affection is seen as sincere, innocent, and without pretence. It is essentially reliable and trustworthy. (p. 114)

Sanders (1992) echoes this point when he says that the

> chief pleasure they [owners] derived from the animal–human relationship was the joy of relating to another being who consistently demonstrated love – a feeling-for-the-other which was honestly felt and displayed and not contingent upon the personal attributes or even the actions of the human-other. (p. 16)

However, this intimacy does not preclude humans from 'speaking for' their animal companions. As Sanders notes:

> Because the animal is 'mute,' caretakers often find themselves in situations in which they must 'speak for' their nonhuman companions. In so doing, they make use of a rich body of knowledge derived from an intimate understanding of the animal-other built up in the course of day-to-day interactional experience. Dog owners commonly give voice to what they perceive to be their animals' mental, emotional, and physical experiences. (pp. 6–7)

Such patterns of 'speaking for' suggests a process of re-narration by humans of their own and their animals' experiences with the aid of more or less familiar stories. These stories, which imply that companion animals communicate with humans in certain non-linguistic ways, both to give comfort to their owners and to express their own inner states, tend to anthropomorphize the animals. In other words, these narratives can be said to attribute human qualities to animals – animals which are essentially 'other'. For me to take such accounts seriously, and then further to argue that companion animals enrol their owners in various ways, is to practice a double anthropomorphism. In general, then, any such account which regards animal companions as autonomous co-conversationalists (albeit outside the medium of language) will neglect to give due weight to the discursive trajectories by which such animals are constructed as autonomous actors by owners and ethnographers/sociologists alike for their own particular interactional/social ends. However, in response, we might paraphrase Latour's (1992) counter-queries: What role does the accusation of anthropomorphism have for the critical social constructionist? Should we not follow this communicative process seriously (not via some pure empiricism as Latour occasionally seems to suggest), but through an analytic posture that aspires to agnosticism as to the form of the interaction and attempts to remain sensitive to extra- or quasi-linguistic shaping of human identity?

However, though a convincing social constructionist account of pet owners' anthropomorphizing of animals can no doubt be provided, it is also easy enough to derive another story. It is possible to detect in owners' accounts a view of the animal as an 'Other World'. Noske (1989), in her critique of the

social sciences' neglect of the animal (as anything other than 'symbol'), suggests that the 'otherness' that the social anthropologist confronts and respects
in her ethnographic endeavours, should be extended to animals. If social
anthropology is 'the science of the other', then social scientists need to
immerse themselves in contexts that contain animal others to understand
the what and how of animal–animal and animal–human interactions while
retaining a sensitivity to animals' otherness. This point is underlined by
Haraway (1992) in her meditation on Noske's book (amongst others). In
addition to not being objectified, Haraway suggests that:

> The last thing 'they' [animals] need is human subject status, in whatever cultural-
> historical form . . . . We need other terms of conversations with animals, a much less
> respectable undertaking. The point is not new representations, but new practices,
> other forms of life rejoining humans and not-humans. (pp. 86–7)

Out of this emerges, Haraway hopes, a new form of human being:

> Once the world of subjects and objects is put into question, that paradox concerns
> the congeries, or curious confederacy, that is the self, as well as selves' relations with
> others. A promising form of life, conversation defies the autonomization of the self,
> as well as the objectification of the other. (p. 90)

What (I think) Haraway is getting at here is that to engage in those non-linguistic processes of communication with animal others is to diffuse one's
self – to admit of its multiplicity and dispersion. It is perhaps just this dimension of 'dissipation' that enrols the human actor to its animal companion.
The identity that is thus generated is one that no longer follows the linearities
of narrative, but is one mediated by and realized in the many channels of
human–animal communication. Thus, over and above the identities that are
reflected in owners' narration of the animal–human dyad, it is the form of
non-linguistic communication that becomes the content of human identity in
the association between human and animal companions. So, animals, in all
their other-worldliness, enrol humans; but the identity that they offer them is
of a different order from the typical modes of the human social self. (As
Noske notes, babies and disabled people can offer similar identities.)
Constructed but not socially constructed, micro-situationally negotiated but
not linguistically mediated, these human identities serve the animal's network which is none other than the dyad itself. In terms of ANT, the network,
the obligatory point of passage and the identity begin to fuse into a whole: the
animal–human dyad. However, the human identities present here differ from
those found in the stories of ANT in another respect too. In contrast to the
(to be sure, productive) shapings and constrainings of human identities in the
sociotechnical network, here we have an expansion of identity. For humans
who venture into associations with animal companions, horizons are enlarged
and variety is enabled.

However, it would be naive in the extreme to assume that this account
exhausted the networks between, say, human and dog: as ever the story is not
so simple. The process of enrolment wherein human's identity becomes, via
animal companions, 'expanded' (e.g. there is a 'loss of self', an unabashed

tactility, uncontingent love and so on) also has a more mundane side in which other identities are furnished for humans. Humans are also 'pet owners' with responsibilities for feeding and caring for their animals. In consequence, they find themselves pivotal in other networks which include pet-food manufac-turers, veterinary surgeons, animal trainers and animal cruelty inspectors. And if these actors find themselves so minded to form associations with the 'pet owner', it turns out that the actor 'pet owner' is a network – the very dyad we described above.

Now, this is merely one story that could be told about human/animal relationships. At its core is an issue of sensitizing ourselves to the possibility and mechanics of non-linguistic 'conversation' with animals, of allowing them free entry into our conversational communities. Contrary to Serpell and Saunders, we can say that animals are mute only if we remain deaf. As Smart (1993) shows, dogbreeders do indeed believe themselves to be in conversation with their animals. Moreover, they consider themselves to be under scrutiny, even under surveillance, by their dogs, adapting their actions in response to these interactions. However, how have these animal entities come to be inter-locutors? How have they come to be elevated to the status of potential, if not actual, enrollers? What are the cultural conditions (or, rather, the broader net-works of actors, identities and associations) which have enabled them to enter into a human conversational community? As noted, in comparison to ANT studies which narrate the emergence of human identities in terms of con-straint upon the opportunities to act, my reading of human–animal dyad can be read as an expansion of human identities and potentialities. And yet, humans need to have in place discourses and identities that predispose them to engage in such interactions. These pre-identities can be historically located in different ways. Thus, one might trace the social and cultural shifts in the representation of animals. One could, for instance, point to the rise of Cartesianism with its view of animals as machines, and the subsequent romanticization of rural life that arose with the decline of routine contact between humans and 'natural' nonhumans wrought by increasing urbanization in the eighteenth century. Indeed, one could seek authority in the following quote by Thomas (1984):

> The growth of towns led to a new longing for the countryside . . . . economic inde-pendence of animal power and urban isolation from animal farming had nourished emotional attitudes which were hard to reconcile with the exploitation of animals by which most people lived. Henceforth an increasingly sentimental view of animals as pets and objects of contemplation would jostle uneasily alongside the harsh facts of a world on which the elimination of 'pests' and the breeding of animals for slaughter grew everyday more efficient. (p. 301)

But if such historically novel identities predisposed humans to apprehend their animals in complex ways and facilitated the modern-day human–animal dyad, one can also weave a story that places the animals at the active core of this relationship and the formation of human identities. But to do this, one needs to narrate some origin story about the prehistory of human/nonhuman relations, as, indeed, many dogbreeders are only too willing to do. Without such a story, say about the entry of dogs into early human communities, about the growth of mutuality and dependency between the two species, about the selective breeding of dogs in the context of local economic and environmental circumstances, it becomes very difficult to see how dogs could have attained their ascribed position. For, as such an account might allow, in the process of this intertwining in the deep, dark historical past, humans become enrolled, as well as enrollers. If dogs were initially enrolled as some sort of tool, through history, humans became dependent upon this tool (just as they become dependent upon technological tools, their networks becoming modified to better accommodate them). By virtue of this human dependency, dogs found their voice. Complete human deafness to dogs, if it ever existed, has long been dispelled. Now, this portrayal, for all its naivety (after all, there are extensive networks that do not share this apprehension of dogs, let alone other species of animal), nevertheless serves as a provisional model for addressing the above questions, and for showing how animals become actors through the shifts and changes in human networks which, as an unforeseen consequence, open up a space for the agential interventions of 'natural' nonhumans. As ever, agency and actor-ship (this time of 'natural' nonhumans) are effects.

And yet, this story still rests on a view of humans as initially – or, rather, originally – being the active, agential actors in the forging of the relationship with animal nonhumans. Budiansky (1994) contends, in contrast, that this is a manifestation of human hubris: animals 'chose' us and a life of domestication, for a number of reasons. Thus, animals were attracted to human communities by virtue of the shelter, food and protection they offer. It is the case, argues Budiansky, that the domestication of animals such as dogs 'is an evolutionary phenomenon rather than a human invention . . .' but this 'is not to argue that humans were mere pawns in some grand preordained plan. Human choices and ingenuity clearly must have a played a part – but only a part, insufficient in itself' (p. 50). Part of that evolutionary phenomenon, Budiansky goes on to suggest, is that of neoteny – animals arrested in the juvenile stage who nevertheless breed. Neoteny allows certain youthful traits to be passed on, traits such as 'curiosity about . . . surroundings, an ability to learn new things, a lack of fear of new situations, and even a nondiscriminating willingness to associate and play with members of other species . . .' (pp. 77–8). It is these traits that attracted animals to humans and vice versa, and which was key to the domestication of a whole range of species.

Now, this origin story, sketchily told here, performs an important function in my particular version of the human–animal relation. It begins to displace the recourse to social constructionism, mediated by accounts of the social and cultural history (as related by, for example, Thomas), and the attendant pre-identities of humans that dispose them to entering into the dyadic relationships I described above. Rather, there is an evolutionary story in which animals, for all their other worldliness, feature as actors, instrumental in the laying down of the necessary conditions for their historical situation as domesticates. The point about this story, however, extends beyond finding a suitably agential role for animals. It also reminds us that the assiduous avoidance of origin stories in social constructionist accounts of identity and/or nature deny us an insight, however circumspect or fanciful, into the relation of social constructionist processes to 'nature' – whether that be the moving body (Varela, 1994), animals or the environment. That is to say, it exemplifies one way of narrating a role, in this case originary (and in the case of the dyad, localized), for nonhumans in the very processes of constructing human identities and social ordering.

Nice Environments

In this section, I once again look at some of the ways that we might consider 'nature' – this time in the guise of the local environment – as a contingently independent player. In keeping with my cowardly strategy of choosing the easiest cases, I will focus on the environment in its more conducive incarnation – the sunny scenario, so to speak. The reason why will become clearer below.

Above, we saw how various accounts of 'nature' as a co-conversationalist – a Thou – explicitly tried to construct 'nature' as a subject. This was implicitly criticized for its humanist stance. Given the short but glorious and renowned history of post-structuralist critiques of the centred subject, I will not rehearse its arguments against humanism, and instead turn to an account that aims to broaden 'community' to include 'nature' but which does not, in the process, attribute subjecthood to 'nature'. Here, we turn to the work of the environmental ethicist Jim Cheney. Cheney (1989) attempts to articulate an environmental consciousness, and a relation between humans and 'nature', that draws upon the postmodern project of avoiding the essentialization of the self. His solution is to develop a notion of bioregional narratives grounded in geography:

> Narrative is the key then, but it is narrative grounded in geography rather than in a linear, essentialized narrative self . . . . Totalizing masculine discourse (and essentializing feminist discourse) give way to a contextualized discourse of place. (p. 126)

Thus,

> Within the geography of the human landscape the contextual voice can emerge in clarity and health only through a 'constant recontextualizing' which prevents the oppressive and distorting overlays of cultural institutions . . . from gathering false, distorting and unhealthy identities out of 'the positive desire for unity, for Oneness'. (p. 128)

Clearly, Cheney is wary of essentializing discourse. His partial answer is to:

> expand the notion of a contextualizing narrative of place so as to include 'nature' – 'nature' as one more player in the construction of community. . . . that we extend these notions of context and narrative outwards so as to include not just the human community, but also the land, one's community in a larger sense. (p. 128)

The medium through which this could be achieved is, according to Cheney, myth. If 'bioregionalism can "ground" the construction of self and community'

(p. 134), it will proceed through the narratives and metaphors of mythology which are derived from the landscapes and the localities themselves. Obviously, this begs a lot of questions as to how such a process of derivation might come about. While it expresses an albeit normative hope (this is ethics, after all) that 'nature' can be regarded as a voice in the community that constructs such social psychological staples as identity, the way in which 'nature' actually intervenes in such a community remains painfully vague.

In the terms of ANT, 'nature', qua bioregional locality, is an actant. Elsewhere, I have suggested that Cheney's 'nature' is an actant that is not given to the coherence of a unitary entity:

> Rather, its very diversity and richness serves to disaggregate the texts of identity of its human inhabitants. Again, in terms of actor-network theory, we might say that it has enrolled human actors who begin to formulate, that is to say, narrate themselves in like fashion – they are dispersed and decentred – in short, they are 'postmodern selves'. The obligatory point of passage is one in which the core texts of identity are those of fracture, of the forgoing of 'coherence, continuity and consistency' (Cheney, 1989, p. 126). In the process, the power of 'nature' does indeed take the form of an association in which the human actants give up their stories of unitary self if they wish to 'carry on'. (Michael, 1992a, pp. 83–4)

However, in retrospect, how this process of fragmentation is conveyed remains somewhat opaque. Once again, in terms of ANT, how 'nature' 'interresses' and eventually enrols the human actor – the semiosis by which this is mediated – is left uncomfortably obscure.

Drawing on Latour's (e.g. 1992) recent work on the social intervention of technological artefacts, we observe that door grooms and hotel key weights take on their supposed moral standing by acting against the body of the human actor. The aim, in true Foucauldian form, is to discipline the human actor by delegating certain functions to nonhuman actors. Door grooms – the hydraulic mechanism which both offers resistance when opening a door and then slowly closes it – discipline humans who must exert additional energy when opening the door (the point of the groom is to avoid slamming and broken noses). Let us remind ourselves of Latour's (1992) point cited in Chapter 4: '. . . neither my little nephews nor my grandmother could get in unaided because our groom needed the force of an able-bodied person to accumulate enough energy to close the door later . . . . these doors discriminate against very little and very old persons' (p. 234).

As noted previously, this quote draws our attention to the role of technological artefacts in the shaping of the capacities of the body and in the disciplining of the human actor – that is, in the construction of human identities. The physical constraints that come about when technological artefacts interpose themselves between humans and their goals, while not constituting major, or even noticeable, barriers for many humans, comprise major obstacles for others. Those 'disadvantaged' humans, who cannot pass unhindered through the spaces and against the forces mediated by technologies such as door closers, are obliged to persuade others to do their door-opening for them. They must enrol other actors, human or nonhuman, who can reduce the forces or reshape the spaces around such technologies so that their bodies and capacities can once again become connected to their goals. If these relatively 'disabled' humans succeed in such enrolments, they have, in an almost literal sense, grown bigger. Nevertheless, the centrality of the capacities of the body to Latour's story remains. In what follows, however, I want to draw out some of the ways in which 'nice nature' interacts with the body to recover previously suppressed possibilities, where the environment – 'natural' instead of 'technological' – potentially enables, rather than constrains, the movement of the body in light of the body's capacities.

Drawing on Gibson's (1979) notion of 'affordance', Michael and Still (1992) suggest that the interface between organism and environment generates behavioural options for the individual with which to challenge power-knowledge (in the Foucauldian sense). 'Affordance' refers to the way in which the (optic) array of surfaces and structures in environment specify a range of possible actions for the organism. A flat horizontal surface thus affords sitting on, lying across, rolling out dough and so on. As such, there are a range of options that are implicit within a physical milieu and this implicitness is directly connected to the bodily capacities and limits of the organism. It is important here to stress the optionality of afforded actions: the environment does not determine what happens, it implicates a repertoire of possible happenings. This non-determination by the environment brings to mind Deleuze's (1988) treatment of Foucault's distinction between the discursive and the non-discursive. The former is constituted by statements and is determining, whereas the latter is visible, is constituted by visibilities and is determinable. These visibilities 'are not the forms of objects . . . but rather luminosities which are created by the light itself and allow a thing or object to exist only as a flash, sparkle or shimmer' (p. 52). Deleuze firmly historicizes these visibilities such that the 'visibilities of one epoch become hazy and blurred to the point where "self-evident" phenomena cannot be grasped by another age . . .' (p. 57). However, while these visibilities are 'determinable' by discourse, they are not determined: as Deleuze argues, there is a rift between what we see and what we speak, between the visible and the articulable. As such there is a potential slippage between what we 'see' – in Gibson's terms, what is afforded – and what the discourses of power-knowledge dictate (or pro-/pre-scribe). In a sense, affordance serves to map out some of the corporeal resources for resistance against Foucauldian discipline. Thus, always immanent in the technologies that Latour narrates are other practical options that outstrip the moralities and prescriptions embodied by those technologies.

Returning to my effort to constitute the local 'natural' environment as a semiotic player in the micro-situation, we can make the following tentative observations. Firstly, such an environment incorporates a variety of affordances for the human individual. The discourses and narratives that the individual brings to bear within such a physical milieu are potentially subverted or challenged by the affordances and visibilities of local 'nature'. Now, such discourses can be highly pro- and pre-scriptive. As MacNaghten (personal communication) has noted, in Britain, policy documents and tourist/user guides produced by such institutions as English Nature, the English Tourist Board and the Countryside Commission serve as manuals that impart techniques and technologies of the self (cf. Martin et al., 1988). The implicit instructions contained in these documents serve to locate the countryside visitor as a particular sort of entity who must regulate themselves (be contemplative, enjoy the aesthetics of the landscape, comport themselves respectfully). The corollary of this is a parallel representation of nature: as an entity that demands respect, deserves contemplation, facilitates aesthetic bliss. Yet, that tree in the local wood is not just an object of beauty and contemplation; it is also a thing to climb, to scratch oneself against, to sleep under and so on. None of these options might be realized; however, in being afforded in relation to bodily capacities and limits, these serve potentially to challenge particular disciplined views of the tree and the human identities which attend these.

The point here is that nice local 'nature' (like nice animal companions) enrols by virtue of opening up behavioural vistas – that is, by expanding the potential range of identities for an individual. In contrast to Latour's view of enrolment by nonhumans/technology in which limits are placed upon the enrolled actor, here limits are potentially removed and repertoires implicitly revealed.

As noted above, this story rests on the sunny scenario of 'nature'. 'Nature' is represented as benign and its prime narrative role is as a world of surfaces. (As such it is no different from the built environment – nevertheless, the point holds: affordance still operates in 'non-natural' or technological environments.) However, 'nature' (again like animal companions) can also be nasty: it can serve up its own resistances – rain, cold, mud, etc. – which in the context of bodily capacities serve to constrain options. Moreover, throughout this account, I have mostly focused upon the individual human. Missing from the storyline is a vision of the expanded or collective physical individual. This expansion can involve both humans and nonhumans. Thus, the affordances offered by a local 'nature' can multiply in the company of some humans (e.g. friends) or decrease in the company of others (e.g. wardens). Likewise, affordances can be expanded with the aid of some technologies and natural nonhumans (e.g. horses, Landrovers, boots, grappling hooks), and reduced by the presence of others (e.g. electric fences, barbed wire, walls).

Nonetheless, the central argument holds, namely, that 'local nature' can potentially enrol through the expansion of identity, formulated in physical/behavioural terms: this is part of its attraction for humans. For humans who wish to expand their identities, to become liminal perhaps (cf. Michael, 1992a), it can be said to be an obligatory point of passage. Like animals, the 'local nature' of the situational interaction is an 'other world' – its motives and purposes remain obscure. However, it can still be treated as an actor or actant that, in the above story, enrols and the medium through which it does so is not linguistic or symbolic but corporeal/perceptual. However, in all this, certain conditions need to be fulfilled. Firstly, there is the need to recover and invent a set of circumstances which predispose the body to such interactions with bioregions – in other words, an appropriate network needs to be in place. These circumstances can be social or technological (as I have suggested in the previous paragraph). But also, these dispositions are realized through new sets of representations and discourses which can narrate 'natural' non-humans as 'proper participants' or as actors which can do certain things to one. What these discourses do is set up a responsivity in human actors that allows nonhumans to enter into the network. One might thus re-frame the work of some environmental ethicists, animal rights activists and writers on human–animal interactions as a series of political interventions. These attempt to put into circulation within the existing network representations of nonhumans which contribute a less objectifying relation to 'natural' nonhumans: their purpose is, of course, to alter the constituent actors in that network and therefore its character.

Conclusion

This chapter has advocated, or at least told a story about, a form of construction of identity that adds to the typical conduits of communication: parallel with the linguistic are other semiotic modes. I have attempted to tell a tale about what we might call a 'corporeal semiotics' (or inter-corporeality). This is a medium that, as with its linguistic counterpart, falls within the compass of individual human perception (which I have left largely unproblematized). It is the human body, with its capacities and faculties, that sets out the parameters for such communications (and thereby the constitution of identity and enrolment). Such an individualistic account is, inevitably, contentious, especially in light of some of the recent writings on cyborgs (e.g. Haraway, 1991) which reformulate the 'individual' as an entity extended across space by virtue of its integration with technological systems. This point has already emerged in relation to the above considerations of human–animal dyads and affordance. Both of these reflect a process by which the unity and integrity of the human individual are broken down, and out of which emerges a distributed self (physically, as well as in the post-structuralist sense or in Giddens' (1991) high modernist context). The actor becomes a collective one; the unit of analysis is broadened to encompass the human-other (animal/local environment) complex. At such a point, as with Haraway's cyborgs – which she clearly states are historically novel entities – we might say that enrolment by the 'other' has been successful, and the actor that was the animal or local environment has grown bigger. In terms of ANT, the association is (albeit temporarily) secure, appropriate human identities are in place, the enroller has enlarged and, in relation to the human, black-boxed its network: the network so produced is the new actor.

In sum, the present chapter has been a tentative and elementary attempt to map out one possible means of theorizing the role of natural nonhumans in the production of identity. However, there are certain glaring problems with this account. Firstly, I have concentrated on more tangible nonhumans – where are the microbes and the galaxies? – where interactions with humans are relatively sensorially unmediated. But, here, I must stress the 'relatively'. For even the senses are caught up in the network – they are trained, expanded and reduced by neighbouring human, natural and technological actors as Gifford (1990) illustrates so well (see also Shilling, 1993; Classen, 1993). Moreover, it is not only the 'senses' that are so moulded – it is also the parameters of the body that come to be contingent on the network. Do we still have bodies? Or are we now cyborgs? Or have we always been hybrids? At this point, the notion of 'human' identity I have been trying to tie to ANT comes under severe pressure. Where in the network should we assign an 'identity'? How do we draw its borders? Why focus on the 'humans' when the regularities that we see function at another level, in some admixture, configuration, or better still network, of 'human', 'technological' and 'natural' actors? Could we speculate on what gets missed out? And finally, how, in the process of such demarcations and assignments, do we analysts, function in our own network? It is to these issues, amongst others, that I turn in the next, concluding, chapter.

8

Conclusion

This book has been written with the express aim of explicating some of the implications of ANT for the 'new wave' social psychological study of identity. To do this, some of the cherished assumptions and routine practices of social constructionism have been scrutinized and found incomplete. The theorization of historical change, the demarcation of agency, the identification of key generative actors, the role of nonhumans – all these have been raised with the view to contributing to a 'new improved' new wave social psychology. However, hopefully I have not been too slavish in my exposition of ANT; it has not been my intention to hold it up as some sort of sacrosanct theoretical framework which can readily and unproblematically embrace, indeed, consume, the new social psychology. ANT is a heuristic, as all theories should be. It raises interesting questions and suggests fruitful avenues of investigation. As we have seen, 'classical' ANT can always be supplemented. The uses of ambivalence, the construction of flexible identities, the accommodation of antagonism, the deployment of 'others', the problematic status of 'natural' nonhumans – each of these pushes ANT in new directions. But there are other trajectories available to us and it is to some of these that the present chapter is devoted. So, in this chapter, my aim is to identify a number of critical concerns that will arise spontaneously, and no doubt virulently, in the mind of any reader. In addition to this defensive function, there is also another, namely, to explore future research agendas that pursue some of the issues that have emerged in the foregoing chapters.

What about All Those Other 'Natural' Nonhumans?

As mentioned in Chapter 7, my examples for illustrating some of the possible ways in which an ANT perspective might incorporate 'natural' nonhumans into an account of the (re)production of identity and of the parallel processes of social ordering were rather cowardly. Or, to put it in less confessional terms, they were 'meso-natural', referring to 'natural' entities (animals and bioregions) which could be accessed, more or less technologically unmediated, by the human complement of senses. Obviously, there are a range of such entities which fall outside this spectrum, ranging from subatomic particles and viruses to ecosystems and galaxies, entities which need a variety of technologies to be 'observed' (or, according to SSK, socially constructed). How are these to be encompassed by the ANT approach?

The first and obvious point to make is that these are social constructions; their reality, according to SSK, is the upshot of negotiation and enrolment amongst scientists and non-scientists alike. Yet, these mediated phenomena and entities are also based on technologies which have an, albeit historically contingent, autonomous effectivity of their own. As Latour has shown us (see Chapter 4), technologies enrol – they shape human (in this case, scientific) identities and practices. If social processes reify the scientific instruments through which we 'observe' or 'detect' micro- and macro-natural entities, and to the extent that scientists are able to enrol wider lay constituencies, then such technologies allow us to formulate those phenomena that impact upon us. Thus, these phenomena are effects, but they also, by virtue of their prominence in networks, come to have an identifiable effect upon us. I say 'identifiable effect' because entities which we cannot identify, while they might have an effect upon us, remain beyond our knowledge and, as such, do not enter into the network. In consequence, we can say that these phenomena can be actors insofar as they derive their potency from the network. Thus, for example, the effectivity of the HIV/AIDS virus rests on our prevailing popular understanding of the virus which entails a, more or less concerted, suppression of alternative aetiologies (see Grinyer, 1993 for a review).

But such a vision sidesteps the possibility that such entities might have an autonomous impact – uninterrupted by our knowledge of them. After all, bodies go wrong, buildings fall down in earthquakes, the biosphere undergoes catastrophic changes, to get crassly realist about it. However, these 'icons of the real' do not represent unproblematic loci of physical causality. This is simply one historically contingent way of understanding the decision to get ill and die, the anger of the gods, the realignment of Gaia. Each of these 'reals' can be reviewed as failures of enrolment on the part of social actors: if only we made the right decisions, if only we appeased the gods, if only we paid our dues to Gaia. If that is not far-fetched enough, here is another extreme argument about the network-ness of such 'reals'. These phenomena and entities exist by virtue of a lack. We are enrolled into having such identities as 'mortal bodies' and 'insignificant beings in the great scheme of things' because we do not yet have the means of fighting back, of resisting. Who knows what technologies (in the broadest sense) will arise to allow us to problematize these 'reals' and expose them as effects. It is simply the case that the current state of the network militates against this. Whether this is a good thing or not is another matter.

How Heterogeneous is Heterogeneous?

So far the notion of a heterogeneous network has addressed humans and nonhumans, where the category of nonhumans has encompassed technological artefacts and 'natural' entities. Yet, in many cultures there are other actors which do not fall easily under either rubric. Here, I have in mind actors such as ancestors, spirits, gods and astrological configurations. If social constructionism has been resolute in its neglect of the non-social and nonhuman, and if ANT has subverted this by introducing nonhuman actors into constructionist accounts of social ordering, ANT has nevertheless remained determinedly secular. Again the question that arises is: how does ANT accommodate these 'mystical' entities?

Once more, these entities are effectual insofar as they are rendered pivotal in the network by appropriately situated spokespersons, that is, those who can convincingly lay claim to having a special access to, or affinity with, these entities (much as scientists lay claim to having a special access to 'natural' phenomena by virtue of their scientific training). As such, these 'mystical' actors do not formally differ from the micro- and macro-natural entities mentioned above. Nevertheless, it is a matter of interest to pursue the role of the non-secular in the generation of networks and their associated identities. At the very least such a project would begin to throw into relief some of the contingencies that make up our trusted repertoire of analytic categories.

A Trifle Individualistic?

Following ANT, I have tried to problematize the notion of identity, extending it beyond its application to the individual person in order to encompass hybrids. However, I have not really dealt with the interactions, associations or enrolments between collective actors. In other words, missing from this book is a proper consideration of identity as collective regularity. If a network maintains a certain resilience, if the actors within it are aligned in more or less predictable ways, then that network can be regarded as a cogent actor. This is similar to the ANT point about agency being a property of any size of actor if it is successfully so imputed. As long as the integrity of an actor remains unproblematized (likewise agency), then it acts within the network as a unitary actor. What then of the interactions of collective actors, say between societies or species?

Well, the sorts of intermediaries that pass between these actors can be of various sorts, as we saw in the last chapter. They might be in the form energy of one sort or another – say food. As Noske (1989) points out in relation to the dependency of modern societies on certain animal products (and their associated commercial and industrial sectors), it is possible to imagine that certain human societies can be characterized as – that is, be ascribed the identity of – routinely dependent upon certain animals and modes of consumption. However, at this level of abstraction where we derive certain macro-regularities, we are nevertheless, as analysts, importing such representations into a network populated by other like actor units for the purposes of building/realizing our own networks. As we use these representations of the macro as the currency with which to enrol others, we find ourselves operating at the level of individuals-in-micro-situations. These representations, as with those representations of institutions and societies, occlude the multiple micro-interactions and associations between particular animals and humans.

Having restated this point, it is still important to note that the relations between these macro-entities, however much social constructionism might be averse to engaging directly with these, can nevertheless be narratively woven into accounts of identity of micro- as well as macro-entities. Thus, for example, when we consider Western society's associations with certain species, we can point out that these associations entail not only certain modes of consumption, but also certain modes of knowledge and internal relations of power. Where animal species, say, are primarily objects of study and consumption, this reflects the primacy of particular discourses and institutions (e.g. the subject/object dichotomy, the hegemonic positioning of biomedical and pharmaceutical concerns). In sum, while the micro-interaction between actors (humans and nonhumans) takes analytic priority, it is nonetheless possible to give accounts which demarcate larger actors and macro-identities, though when one does, one necessarily brackets the multiplicity that is present at the level of the micro (as we saw in relation to Callon's early case studies of the scallops and the electric vehicle).

What about the Body, Nonhumans and Phenomenology?

If human identity emerges from associations with a heterogeneity of other actors, one form of impact of technological nonhumans tends to be upon the human body. Thus, the human actor is variously constituted by nonhumans in ways which accord with the capacities of the human body. In Latour's examples of the door closer and the hotel key weight, these put up resistances to the body of one sort or another. This suggests that there is an aporia at the heart of ANT: the phenomenological preconditions that shape the nature of this impact upon the human body, which underpin the transformation of these impacts into the regularities that make up identity. The questions that arise in the wake of this point are: How do we incorporate a sense of the diversity of interactions (intersubjective, intercorporeal or some mixture of the two) when we render our representations of macro-actors? Is this necessarily a good thing – narratively, politically, analytically?

Yet, there is no simple or necessary relation between the nonhuman actor and human body, for, as we saw in the previous chapter, the capacities of the body can be modified in various ways by importing the resources of other humans or nonhumans, technological (e.g. mechanized vehicles) or 'natural' (e.g. horses). The point is that phenomenologically certain nonhuman–human associations proceed unremarked: they are invisible so that to problematize these associations would require extreme effort – the construction of a counter-network wherein one's bodily facilities were effectively extended or modified. That such counter-networks do not even appear phenomenologically as options attests to the fact that technological nonhumans emerge within a pre-existing network in which certain human identities are already in place, identities which militate against their problematization (for example, the clothed body in relation to the 'hostile' environment). The same holds for 'natural' nonhumans; as we have seen, their influence is likewise mediated by the pre-existing heterogeneous networks in which human actors are located.

It strikes me that this issue of 'invisibility' is an important one to explore. Though beyond the scope of the present volume, the ways in which the body is delimited – its apparent capacities, and the ways these are taken for granted, predisposing human actors to certain enrolments – are desperately in need of mapping. Under what historical/network circumstances have given bodily capacities, and their corollary nonhumans, been assumed or been problematized? In other words, what are the preconditions which allow this or that technological artefact or 'natural' entity to phenomenologically disappear – as it were, to associate with a human actor so that a hybrid is produced (e.g. the clothed body)?

Where is Big Culture?

In my critique of social constructionism, I was particularly damning of what I called the 'cultural ether' out of which discourses are somehow distilled in micro-situations. My elementary aim in making these remarks was to try to force us to think about the particularities of 'culture' and raise to prominence the issue of the mechanisms of change. In other words, I have wanted to draw attention to the importance of examining those concrete points where certain significations and artefacts are innovated, transformed and imparted. Yet, while we might pursue specific instantiations of cultural factors, say the mind/body or subject/object dichotomies, we might also ponder how it is exactly that we analytically link these back to networks. ANT cannot claim to be especially adept at excavating these 'big' cultural factors – they are embedded in a whole series of events, and permeate hugely extensive networks.

But what we have here is an issue of convenience: these cultural conditions are effects too, but the networks out of which they have emerged and through which they have been mediated are often too far removed from the immediate concerns of the narrative account rendered by ANT. For example, how do we incorporate those background presuppositions about mind/body duality when investigating the production of women's identities in the cycles of objectification that Cussins (in press) has found to take place in infertility clinics? We do so by resort to a notion like cultural backdrop. In principle, these could be excavated by ANT, tracing back the associations that have reflected and mediated the rise of particular motifs, dilemmas, commonplaces, discourses, metaphors and the like. However, in the context of a typical ANT case study, such a project would be a narrative luxury. Rather, it is possible to focus upon these big cultural factors as they are realized in the identities of actors. The generality of these elements of identity (after all, we are talking about cultural dimensions that characterize very large networks) means that they serve as the common backdrop against which specific associations and negotiations are played out – they constitute the basic units of discursive intercourse. Very occasionally these, let us call them cultural grounds, get problematized. Of course, sometimes such problematizations are immanent, in the sense that there are already contradictions within them. For example, the efforts to (re-)establish animals as agents reflect the ambiguities in the categorization of animals in, say, British culture or in the culture of horse training (e.g. De Cock Bunning, 1993). More usually, these cultural resources are simply assumed, running through from broader networks (populated by bigger actors such as communities) into particular networks, automatically manifested in specific interactions and associations. The harshness of my criticisms of the likes of Gergen as well as Muhlhausler and Harré was thus not so much directed at their focus on culture per se, but towards their reification of culture, disembodying it from the networks that reproduce and, more importantly, render changes in culture.

'Hybrids', 'Cyborgs' and Boundaries

At the end of Chapter 7, I promised I would return to the issue of where we should draw the boundaries around 'identity'. To reiterate the key question: is the analytic category of identity concerned with the individual human, or can it be extended to some configuration of humans and nonhumans? For example, in the case of Latour's door closer and its human users, should we be speaking about the impact of the door closer in pre-/pro-scribing human action and identity, or should we consider the human door closer an entity or regularity in its own right? Inevitably, this depends on our own network-building activities. If, by showing how constraints and enablements are entailed in technologies, we furnish fellow humans with the resources to excavate the ways in which their routine behaviours could have taken some other form, then our network analysis 'empowers' (while also enrolling people to our ANT network, of course). It serves in the 'defence' of human agency and 'rights' by facilitating reflections upon the way such agency and 'rights' are mediated by the nonhumans that populate the social world. However, if we suggest that the unit of analysis is some human–nonhuman configuration, then we project a different sort of network and politics. Haraway (1991) suggests a mythic apprehension of the cyborg as a political identity that resources the transgression of the great totalizing and dualistic theories of the West; the cyborg becomes the locus of a 'powerful infidel heteroglossia' (p. 181). The upshot is an aggravated fluidity in the givens that make up the West: cyborg imagery 'means both building and destroying machines, identities, categories, relationships, space stories' (p. 181). Here, then, rather than attempt to recover the human agent from its entanglements with technology, such a network would promote a breakdown in the subject/object dichotomy (amongst others) and an ongoing critical immersion and re-immersion of humans and technologies.

Haraway's mythologizing still seems to require a 'social' – collective humans (specifically, women) intervene in order to destabilize the representations that have, in the West, traditionally mediated those humans. But this intervention is only enabled by virtue of humans' (women's) integration into networks in which the boundaries between human and nonhuman have collapsed. It is this cyborg-being that allows such destabilizations to be a possibility. Haraway's stories stand in marked contrast to Latour (1993) who argues that hybrids have always been around, but that in modernity we have consistently paid them scant attention (whereas premodern cultures were obsessed with policing them). The result has been a dangerous proliferation. Latour suggests that we now need a heightened awareness of the role of hybrids, and a means of properly scrutinizing them so that we can duly welcome some while rejecting others. The implication is that human identity cannot be separated from these associations with nonhumans – it is more a question of learning to decide which are the 'best' associations and the most valuable hybrids. In this scheme, hybridity per se does not yield multiplicity and heteroglossia – it is just as likely to close down options, to reassert old dualisms. But who does the learning and the deciding? Is it humans or hybrids? How can we speak of hybrids with such capacities as 'learning' and 'decision-making'? At this point our vocabularies seem to get exhausted. However, this should be the spur for rethinking our categories of identity and (social) ordering. But that is another book.

Too Linear? Not Enough Fluidity?

The networks I have considered, despite interjecting with such concepts as ambivalence and envelopment, have tended to be about enrolment – the distribution of more or less clearly demarcated identities by key focalized actors to others. However, not all interactions between actors and networks are of this form. In some cases, there is a 'calibration' of networks. That is to say, certain networks in their interactions mould themselves to one another in such a way that they maintain pre-existing identities. One tradition that has been particularly concerned with these processes of social calibration and coordination is social worlds and social arenas theory (e.g. Clarke and Fujimara, 1992; Clarke and Montini, 1993). According to this perspective,

> Social worlds form fundamental 'building blocks' of collective action and are principal affiliative mechanisms through which people organize social life. A social world is an interactive unit, a 'universe of regularized mutual response,' communication or discourse. . . . 'Society as a whole,' then, can be conceptualized as consisting of a mosaic of social worlds that both touch and interpenetrate. (Clarke, 1990, pp. 18–19)

This might proceed by way of a 'boundary object' – a suitably flexible signifier that allows members of different social worlds to interpret a given entity according to the character of their own social world (thus reproducing that social world), but nevertheless facilitating coordination. Thus, according to Star and Greisemer (1989), a boundary object is

> an analytic concept of those scientific objects which both inhabit several intersecting worlds and satisfy the informational requirements of each of them. Boundary

objects are objects which are both plastic enough to adapt to local needs and the constraints of the several parties employing them, yet robust enough to maintain a common identity across sites. (p. 393)

(However, see also Fujimara, 1992 for a form of interfacing intermediate between enrolment and boundary object, namely, standardized packages.) Here, then, rather than any one social world (or network) enrolling another by sending out intermediaries to shape the other's identity, calibration proceeds by mutual use of objects that allow each world to retain its typical character.

More recently, Mol and Law (1994) have highlighted that networks are but one metaphor (or topological assumption) for articulating the processes of social ordering. Firstly, there is the metaphor of regions in which 'objects are clustered together and boundaries are drawn around each cluster' (p. 643). In contrast, networks describe connections on the basis of 'similar sets of elements and similar relations between them' – proximity or similarity is a function of the success of those intermediaries or immutable mobiles that cross boundaries, giving other regions a like identity. However, in some cases networks fail and mobiles become mutable. Mol and Law construct this sort of scenario in terms of a fluid space in which 'there are often, perhaps usually, no clear boundaries. Typically, the objects generated inside them – the objects that generate them – aren't well defined' (p. 659). As such objects (Mol and Law are particularly interested in 'anaemia' as it moves from the Netherlands to Africa) flow from one setting to another, they change but nevertheless stay the same, transforming themselves 'from one arrangement into another without discontinuity' (p. 664). The point of all this is that the network metaphor does not exhaust the modes by which identity is generated. Texts, technologies, bodies need not be 'sent' out into the world by key focalized actors, they can flow changing 'in shape and character' (p. 664). In the process, the humans they encounter may have their identities shaped by them – maybe a little, possibly a lot, perhaps not at all. Such fluidity is hard to encompass in a singular, linear network narrative.

But Why Identity?

And finally, in scouring the navel of ANT, I have to turn to the very issue of why identity should be such an issue – or why I have made it so. There seems to be, at least anecdotally, an increasing interest in the social sciences in 'identity' and this book is a twig in the logjam of texts that address the construction of identity and its relation to the production of innumerable phenomena ranging from the magnificently macrosocial (e.g. postmodernity) to the pre-eminently psychological (e.g. memory, emotions). But why has 'identity' taken on the narrative mantle that once adorned such concepts as 'spirit', the economic infrastructure in the last instance, and the collective? I cannot pretend to be able to answer this question (though I have some rather semi-formed and semi-informed ideas about how this question might be approached). I raise this issue here simply to start a self-critical discussion about why we, as 'academics', have formulated a series of problems in terms of 'identity' and what ramifications such a formulation might have both for us and for the people/collectives/social processes we believe we are 'engaging with'. So, to end, we might ask: Into what networks are we analysts being enrolled when we pose our questions in terms of 'identity'? Whose (where 'whose', naturally, need not refer to a human agent) networks do we begin to mediate? How might we think beyond 'identity' while doing justice to the sorts of political/intellectual concerns that drive us? What 'identity' do we perform when we talk of 'identity'?

References

Adorno, T. and Horkheimer, M. (1979) *Dialectic of Enlightenment*. London: Verso.

Akrich, M. (1992) The de-scription of technical objects. In W.E. Bijker and J. Law (eds), *Shaping Technology/Building Society* (pp. 205–24). Cambridge, MA: MIT Press.

Akrich, M. and Latour, B. (1992) A summary of a convenient vocabulary for the semiotics of human and nonhuman assemblies. In W.E. Bijker and J. Law (eds), *Shaping Technology/Building Society* (pp. 259–63). Cambridge, MA: MIT Press.

Anderson, P. (1983) *In the Tracks of Historical Materialism*. London: Verso.

Animals (Scientific Procedures) Act. Public General Acts and General Synod Measures. 1986. London: HMSO.

Aries, P. (1962) *Centuries of Childhood*. Harmondsworth: Penguin.

Arksey, H. (1994) Expert and lay participation in the construction of medical knowledge. *Sociology of Health and Illness*, 16, 448–68.

Arluke, A. (1990) Moral elevation in animal research. In G. Albrecht (ed.), *Advances in Medical Sociology*. Greenwich, CT: JAI Press.

Arluke, A. (1991) Going into the closet with science. *Journal of Contemporary Ethnography*, 20, 306–30.

Armistead. N. (ed.) (1974) *Reconstructing Social Psychology*. Harmondsworth: Penguin.

Ashmore, M. (1989) *The Reflexive Thesis: Wrighting Sociology of Scientific Knowledge*. Chicago: Chicago University Press.

Atkinson, J.M. and Drew, P. (1979) *Order in Court*. London: Macmillan.

Austin. J.L. (1962) *How to Do Things with Words*. Oxford: Oxford University Press.

Barnes, B. (1977) *Interests and the Growth of Knowledge*. London: Routledge and Kegan Paul.

Barnes, B. (1981) On the 'hows' and 'whys' of cultural change. *Social Studies of Science*, 11, 481–98.

Barthes, R. (1972) *Mythologies*. London: Paladin.

Baudrillard, J. (1983) The ecstasy of communication. In H. Foster (ed.), *The Anti-Aesthetic: Essays in Postmodern Culture* (pp. 126–34). Port Townsend, WA: Bay Press.

Beck, U. (1992) *The Risk Society*. London: Sage.

Benedict, R. (1935) *Patterns of Culture*. London: Routledge.

Benton, T. (1991) Biology and social science: Why the return of the repressed should be given a (cautious) welcome. *Sociology*, 25, 1–29.

Berger, J. (1979) *Pig Earth*. London: Writers and Readers.

Berger, P.L. and Luckman, T. (1966) *The Social Construction of Reality*. Harmondsworth: Penguin.

Berman, M. (1981) *The Reenchantment of the World*. Ithaca, NY: Cornell University Press.

Bhaskar, R. (1989) *Reclaiming Reality*. London: Verso.

Billig, M. (1987) *Arguing and Thinking: A Rhetorical Approach to Social Psychology*. Cambridge: Cambridge University Press.

Billig, M. (1988a) Methodology and scholarship in understanding ideological explanation. In C. Antaki (ed.), *Analysing Everyday Explanation* (pp. 199–215). London: Sage.

Billig, M. (1988b) Social representations, objectification and anchoring: A rhetorical analysis. *Social Behaviour*, 3, 1–16.

Billig, M. (1991) *Ideology and Opinions*. London: Sage.

Billig, M. (1992) *Talking of the Royal Family*. London: Macmillan.

Billig, M. (1994) Repopulating the depopulated pages of social psychology. *Theory and Psychology*, 4, 307–35.

Billig, M., Condor, S., Edwards, D., Gane, M., Middleton, D. and Radley, A. (1988) *Ideological Dilemmas*. London: Sage.

Bloor, D. (1976) *Knowledge and Social Imagery*. London: Routledge and Kegan Paul.

Bourdieu, P. (1984) *Distinction: A Social Critique of the Judgement of Taste*. London: Routledge and Kegan Paul.

Bowers, J. (1988) Review essay: Discourse analysis and social psychology. *British Journal of Social Psychology*, 27, 185–92.

Bowers, J. and Iwi, K. (1993) The discursive construction of society. *Discourse and Society*, 4, 357–93.

Brannigan, A. (1981) *The Social Basis of Scientific Discoveries*. Cambridge: Cambridge University Press.

Brown, R.H. and Hewstone, M. (eds) (1986) *Contact and Conflict in Intergroup Encounters*. Oxford: Blackwell.

Buber, M. (1970) *I and Thou*. New York: Scribner's.

Budiansky, S. (1994) *The Covenant of the Wild*. London: Weidenfeld and Nicolson.

Button, G. (1993) The curious case of the vanishing technology. In G. Button (ed.), *Technology in Working Order: Studies in Work, Interaction and Technology* (pp. 10–28). London: Routledge.

Callon, M. (1986a) Some elements in a sociology of translation: Domestication of the scallops and fishermen of St Brieuc Bay. In J. Law (ed.), *Power, Action and Belief* (pp. 196–233). London: Routledge and Kegan Paul.

Callon, M. (1986b) The sociology of an actor-network: The case of the electric vehicle. In M. Callon, J. Law and A. Rip (eds), *Mapping the Dynamics of Science and Technology* (pp. 19–34). London: Macmillan.

Callon, M. (1991) Techno-economic networks and irreversibility. In J. Law (ed.), *A Sociology of Monsters* (pp. 132–61). London: Routledge.

Callon, M. and Latour, B. (1981) Unscrewing the big Leviathan. In K.D. Knorr-Cetina and M. Mulkay (eds), *Advances in Social Theory and Methodology* (pp. 275–303). London: Routledge and Kegan Paul.

Callon, M. and Latour, B. (1992) Don't throw the baby out with the Bath school: A reply to Collins and Yearley. In A. Pickering (ed.), *Science as Practice and Culture* (pp. 301–26). Chicago: Chicago University Press.

Callon, M. and Law, J. (1982) On interests and their transformation: Enrolment and counter-enrolment. *Social Studies of Science*, 12, 615–25.

Campbell, B. (1985) Uncertainty as symbolic action in disputes among experts. *Social Studies of Science*, 15, 429–53.

Cheney, J. (1989) Postmodern environmental ethics: Ethics as bioregional narrative. *Environmental Ethics*, 11, 117–34.

Clarke, A.E. (1990) A social worlds research adventure: The case of reproductive science. In S.E. Cozzens and T.F. Gieryn (eds), *Theories of Science in Society* (pp. 15–42). Bloomington, IN: Indiana University Press.

Clarke, A.E. and Fujimara, J.H. (eds) (1992) *The Right Tools for the Job: At Work in Twentieth-Century Life Science*. Princeton, NJ: Princeton University Press.

Clarke, A.E. and Montini, T. (1993) The many faces of RU486: Tales of situated knowledges and technological contestation. *Science, Technology and Human Values*, 18, 42–78.

Classen, C. (1993) *Worlds of Sense: Exploring the Senses in History and across Cultures*. London: Routledge.

Clegg, S.R. (1993) Narrative, power and social theory. In D.K. Mumby (ed.), *Narrative and Social Control: Critical Perspectives* (pp. 15–45). Newbury Park, CA: Sage.

Collingwood, R.G. (1960) *The Idea of Nature*. New York: Galaxy.

Collins, A. and Gentner, D. (1987) How people construct mental models. In D. Holland and N. Quinn (eds), *Cultural Models in Language and Thought* (pp. 243–65). Cambridge: Cambridge University Press.

Collins, H.M. (1981) The place of the core-set in modern science: Social contingency with methodological propriety in science. *History of Science*, 19, 6–19.

Collins, H.M. (1985) *Changing Order*. London: Sage.

Collins, H.M. (1987) Certainty and the public understanding of science: Science on television. *Social Studies of Science*, 17, 689–713.

Collins, H.M. (1988) Public experiments and displays of virtuosity. *Social Studies of Science*, 18, 725–48.

Collins, H.M. and Pinch, T. (1994) Representativeness and expertise: A response from Harry Collins and Trevor Pinch. *Public Understanding of Science*, 3, 331–7.

Collins, H.M. and Yearley, S. (1992a). Epistemological chicken. In A. Pickering (ed.), *Science as Practice and Culture* (pp. 301–26). Chicago: University of Chicago Press.

Collins, H.M. and Yearley, S. (1992b). Journey into space. In A. Pickering (ed.), *Science as Practice and Culture* (pp. 369–89). Chicago: Chicago University Press.

Coulter, J. (1979) *The Social Construction of Mind: Studies in Ethnomethodology and Linguistic Philosophy*. London: Macmillan.

Cussins, C. (in press) Ontological choreography: Agency for women patients in an infertility clinic. In M. Berg and A. Mol (eds), *Differences in Medicine*. Harvard: Harvard University Press.

Danto, A.C. (1985) *Narration and Knowledge*. New York: Columbia University Press.

Davies, B. and Harré, R. (1990) Positioning: The discursive production of selves. *Journal for the Theory of Social Behaviour*, 20, 43–53.

De Cock Bunning, T. (1993) Three types of man–horse relationship and the parsimony maxim. In E.K. Hicks (ed.), *Science and the Human–Animal Relationship* (pp. 95–104). Amsterdam: SISWO.

Deleuze, G. (1988) *Foucault*. London: Athlone Press.

Deleuze, G. and Guattari, F. (1984) *Anti-Oedipus: Capitalism and Schizophrenia*. London: Athlone Press.

Deleuze, G. and Guattari, F. (1988) *A Thousand Plateaus: Capitalism and Schizophrenia*. London: Athlone Press.

Derrida, J. (1976) *Of Grammatology*. Baltimore, MD: Johns Hopkins University Press.

Derrida, J. (1978) *Writing and Difference*. London: Routledge and Kegan Paul.

Derrida, J. (1982) *Positions*. London: Athlone Press.

Dickens, P. (1992) *Nature and Society*. Hemel Hempstead: Harvester Wheatsheaf.

Dittmar, H. (1992) *The Social Psychology of Material Possessions*. Hemel Hempstead: Harvester Wheatsheaf.

Donzelot, J. (1979) *The Policing of Families*. London: Hutchinson.

Doran, C. (1989) Jumping frames: reflexivity and recursion in the sociology of science. *Social Studies of Science*, 19, 515–31.

Douglas, M. (1970) *Natural Symbols: Explorations in Cosmology*. New York: Pantheon.

Douglas, M. (1986) The social preconditions of radical skepticism. In J. Law (ed.), *Power, Action and Belief* (pp. 68–87). London: Routledge and Kegan Paul.

Durant, J.R. (1993) What is scientific literacy? In J.R. Durant and J. Gregory (eds), *Science and Culture in Europe* (pp. 129–37). London: Science Museum.

Durant, J.R., Evans, G.A. and Thomas, G.P. (1989) The public understanding of science. *Nature*, 340 (6 July), 11–14.

Edwards, D. and Mercer, N. (1987) *Common Knowledge: The Development of Understanding in the Classroom*. London: Methuen.

Edwards, D. and Potter, J. (1992) *Discursive Psychology*. London: Sage.

Edwards, D., Ashmore, M. and Potter, J. (1995) Death and furniture: The rhetoric, politics and the theology of the bottom line arguments against relativism. *History of the Human Sciences*, 8, 25–49.

Evans, G.A. and Durant, J.A. (1989) The understanding of science in Britain and the USA. In R. Jowell, S. Witherspoon and L. Brook (eds), *British Social Attitudes* (pp. 105–15). Aldershot: Gower.

Evernden, N. (1985) *The Natural Alien: Humankind and Environment*. Toronto: Toronto University Press.

Eyerman, R. and Jamison, A. (1991) *Social Movements: A Cognitive Approach*. Cambridge: Polity Press.

Fairclough, N. (1989) *Language and Power*. London: Longman.

Fairclough, N. (1992) *Discourse and Social Change*. Cambridge: Polity Press.

Farr, R.M. (1978) On the varieties of social psychology. *Social Science Information*, 17, 503–25.

Fay, B. (1990) Critical realism? *Journal for the Theory of Social Behaviour*, 20, 33–41.

Featherstone, M. (1991) *Consumer Culture and Postmodernism*. London: Sage.

Fee, E. (1983) Women's nature and scientific objectivity. In M. Lowe and R. Hubbard (eds), *Women's Nature* (pp. 9–27). New York: Pergamon.

Feyerabend, P. (1975) *Against Method*. London: Verso.

Fleck, L. (1979) *Genesis and Development of a Scientific Fact*. Chicago: University of Chicago Press.

Forgas, J.P. (1983) What is social about social cognition. *British Journal of Social Psychology*, 22, 129–44.

Foucault, M. (1965) *Madness and Civilization*. London: Tavistock.

Foucault, M. (1979a) Truth and power: Interview with A. Fontano and P. Pasquino. In M. Meaghan and P. Patton (eds), *Power, Truth, Strategy* (pp. 29–48). Sydney: Feral Publications.

Foucault, M. (1979b). *Discipline and Punish*. Harmondsworth: Penguin.

Foucault, M. (1981) *History of Sexuality*, Vol. 1. Harmondsworth: Penguin.

Foucault, M. (1986) Disciplinary power and subjection. In S. Lukes (ed.), *Power* (pp. 229–42). Oxford: Blackwell.

Freeman, M. (1993) *Rewriting the Self: History, Memory, Narrative*. London: Routledge.

Fuhrman, E.R. and Oehler, K. (1986) Discourse analysis and reflexivity. *Social Studies of Science*, 16, 293–307.

Fujimara, J.H. (1992) Crafting science: Standardized packages, boundary objects, and 'translation'. In A. Pickering (ed.), *Science as Practice and Culture* (pp. 168–211). Chicago: Chicago University Press.

Garfinkel, H. (1967) *Studies in Ethnomethodology*. Cambridge: Polity Press.

Gentner, D. and Gentner, D.R. (1983) Flowing waters of teaming crowds: Mental models of electricity. In D. Gentner and A.L. Stevens (eds), *Mental Models* (pp. 99–129). Hillsdale, NJ: Lawrence Erlbaum.

Gergen, K.J. (1973) Social psychology as history. *Journal of Personality and Social Psychology*, 26, 309–20.

Gergen, K.J. (1982) *Toward Transformation in Social Knowledge*. New York: Springer-Verlag.

Gergen, K.J. (1985) The social constructionist movement in modern psychology. *American Psychologist*, 40, 266–75.

Gergen, K.J. (1991) *The Saturated Self*. New York: Basic Books.

Gergen, K.J. (1992) Toward a postmodern psychology. In S. Kvale (ed.), *Psychology and Postmodernism* (pp. 17–30). London: Sage.

Gergen, K.J. and Davis, K.E. (eds) (1985) *The Social Construction of the Person*. New York: Springer-Verlag.

Gergen, M. (1992) From mod mascu-linity to post-mod macho: A feminist re-play. In S. Kvale (ed.), *Psychology and Postmodernism* (pp. 183–93). London: Sage.

Gibson, E.E. (1979) *The Ecological Approach to Visual Perception*. Boston: Houghton Mifflin.

Giddens, A. (1984) *The Constitution of Society*. Cambridge: Polity Press.

Giddens, A. (1990) *Consequences of Modernity*. Cambridge: Polity Press.

Giddens, A. (1991) *Modernity and Self-Identity*. Cambridge: Polity Press.

Gifford, D. (1990) *The Farther Shore: A Natural History of Perception*. London: Faber and Faber.

Gilbert, G.N. and Mulkay, M. (1984) *Opening Pandora's Box: A Sociological Analysis of Scientists' Discourse*. Cambridge: Cambridge University Press.

Gillespie, B., Eva, D. and Johnson, R. (1979) Carcinogenic risk assessment in the US and Great Britain: the case of Aldrin/Dieldrin. *Social Studies of Science*, 9, 265–301.

Gluck, J.P. and Kubacki, S.R. (1991) Animals in biomedical research: The undermining effect of the rhetoric of the besieged. *Ethics and Behavior*, 1, 157–73.

Goffman, E. (1959) *The Presentation of Self in Everyday Life*. Harmondsworth: Penguin.

Good, J.M.M. (1993) Quests for interdisciplinarity: The rhetorical constitution of social psychology. In R.H. Roberts and J.M.M. Good (eds), *The Recovery of Rhetoric* (pp. 237–62). Charlottesville, VA: University Press of Virginia.

Gramsci, A. (1971) *Selections from the Prison Notebooks*. London: Lawrence and Wishart.

Greenwood, J.D. (1992) Realism, empiricism and social constructionism: Psychological theory and the social dimensions of mind and action. *Theory and Psychology*, 2, 131–51.

Grinyer, A.F. (1993) Science, policy and the public: Constructing the risk of AIDS and HIV. PhD dissertation, Lancaster University.

Halpin, Z.T. (1989) Scientific objectivity and the concept of 'the other'. *Women's Studies International Forum*, 12, 285–94.

Haraway, D. (1989) *Primate Visions*. London: Routledge and Kegan Paul.

Haraway, D. (1991) *Simians, Cyborgs and Nature*. London: Free Association Books.

Haraway, D. (1992) Other worldly conversations; Terran topics; Local terms. *Science as Culture*, 3, 64–99.

Harré, R. (1979) *Social Being*. Oxford: Blackwell.

Harré, R. (ed.) (1986) *The Social Construction of Emotions*. Oxford: Blackwell.

Harré, R. (1987) Social construction of selves. In K. Yardley and T. Honess (eds), *Self and Identity* (pp. 41–52). Chichester: Wiley.

Harré, R. (1989) Language games and the texts of identity. In J. Shotter and K.J. Gergen (eds), *Texts of Identity* (pp. 20–35). London: Sage.

Harré, R. (1992) What is real in psychology? A plea for persons. *Theory and Psychology*, 2, 153–8.

Harré, R. and Secord, P.F. (1972) *The Explanation of Social Behaviour*. Oxford: Blackwell.

Harrison, F. (1986) *The Living Landscape*. London: Pluto Press.

Harvey, D. (1989) *The Condition of Postmodernity*. Oxford: Blackwell.

Heelas P. and Lock, A. (eds) (1981) *Indigenous Psychologies: The Anthropology of the Self*. London: Academic Press.

Heider, F. (1958) *The Psychology of Interpersonal Relations*. New York: Wiley.

Held, D. (1980) *Introduction to Critical Theory*. London: Hutchinson.

Henriques, J., Hollway, W., Unwin, C., Venn, C. and Walkerdine, V. (1984) *Changing the Subject: Psychology, Social Regulation and Subjectivity*. London: Methuen.

Hewstone, M. and Jaspers, J. (1984) Social dimensions of attribution. In H. Tajfel (ed.), *The Social Dimension*. Cambridge: Cambridge University Press.

Hoch, P. (1979) *White Hero, Black Beast*. London: Pluto Press.

Holton, G. (1992) How to think about the 'anti-science' phenomenon. *Public Understanding of Science*, 1, 103–28.

Horigan, S. (1988) *Nature and Culture in Western Discourses*. London: Routledge and Kegan Paul.

Ingold, T. (ed.) (1989) *What is an Animal?* London: Unwin Hyman.

Irwin, A. and Wynne, B. (eds) (in press) *Misunderstanding Science?* Cambridge: Cambridge University Press.

Israel, J. and Tajfel, H. (eds) (1972) *The Context of Social Psychology*. London: Academic Press.

Jardine, A.A. (1985) *Gynesis: Configurations of Women and Modernity*. Ithaca, NY: Cornell University Press.

Jasper, J. and Nelkin, D. (1992) *The Animal Rights Crusade*. New York: Free Press.

Jaspers, J.M.F. (1983) The task of social psychology: Some historical reflections. *British Journal of Social Psychology*, 22, 277–88.

Johnson, B.B. (1987) The environmentalist movement and grid/group analysis: A modest critique. In B.V. Covello and B. Johnson (eds), *The Social Construction of Risk* (pp. 147–75). Dordrecht: Reidel.

Kempton, W. (1987) Two theories of home heat control. In D. Holland and N. Quinn (eds), *Cultural Models in Language and Thought* (pp. 222–42). Cambridge: Cambridge University Press.

Kitzinger, C. (1987) *The Social Construction of Lesbianism*. London: Sage.

Knorr-Cetina, K.D. (1981) *The Manufacture of Knowledge: An Essay on the Constructivist and Contextual Nature of Science*. Oxford: Pergamon.

Knorr-Cetina, K. (1988) The microsocial order: Towards a reconception. In N.G. Fielding (ed.), *Actions and Structure: Research Methods and Social Theory* (pp. 21–53). London: Sage.

Kropotkin, P. (1939) *Mutual Aid*. Harmondsworth: Penguin.

Kuhn, T.S. (1962) *The Structure of Scientific Revolutions*. Chicago: University of Chicago Press.

Kultgen, J. (1982) Saving you for real people. *Environmental Ethics*, 4, 59–67.

Kvale, S. (ed.) (1992) *Psychology and Postmodernism*. London: Sage.

La Boétie, E. de (1975) *The Politics of Obedience: The Discourse of Voluntary Servitude*. New York: Free Life Editions.

Lash, S. (1988) Discourse or figure? Postmodernism as a 'regime of signification'. *Theory, Culture and Society*, 5, 311–36.

Lash, S. and Urry, J. (1987) *The End of Organized Capitalism*. Cambridge: Polity Press.

Latour, B. (1981) Insiders and outsiders in the sociology of science: Or, how can we foster agnosticism? *Knowledge and Society*, 3, 199–216.

Latour, B. (1983) Give me a laboratory and I will raise the world. In K. Knorr-Cetina and M. Mulkay (eds), *Science Observed* (pp. 141–70). London: Sage.

Latour, B. (1986) The powers of association. In J. Law (ed.), *Power, Action and Belief* (pp. 264–80). London: Routledge and Kegan Paul.

Latour, B. (1987) *Science in Action: How to Follow Engineers in Society*. Milton Keynes: Open University Press.

Latour, B. (1988a) *The Pasteurization of France*. Cambridge, MA: Harvard University Press.

Latour, B. (1988b) The politics of explanation – an alternative. In S. Woolgar (ed.), *Knowledge and Reflexivity: New Frontiers in the Sociology of Knowledge* (pp. 155–76). London: Sage.

Latour, B. (1990) Drawing things together. In M. Lynch and S. Woolgar (eds), *Representations in Scientific Practice*. Cambridge, MA: MIT Press.

Latour, B. (1991) Technology is society made durable. In J. Law (ed.), *A Sociology of Monsters* (pp. 103–31). London: Routledge.

Latour, B. (1992) Where are the missing masses? A sociology of a few mundane artifacts. In W.E. Bijker and J. Law (eds), *Shaping Technology/Building Society* (pp. 225–58). Cambridge, MA: MIT Press.

Latour, B. (1993) *We have Never Been Modern*. Hemel Hempstead: Harvester Wheatsheaf.

Latour, B./Johnson, J. (1988) Mixing humans with non-humans? Sociology of a few mundane artefacts. *Social Problems*, 35, 298–310.

Latour, B. and Strum, S.C. (1986) Human social origins: Oh please, tell us another story. *Journal of Social and Biological Structures*, 9, 169–87.

Latour, B. and Woolgar, S. (1979) *Laboratory Life: The Social Constructon of Scientific Facts*. London: Sage.

Lave, J. (1988) *Cognition in Practice*. Cambridge: Cambridge University Press.

Law, J. (1987) Technology and heterogeneous engineering: the case of Portuguese expansion. In W.E. Bijker, T.P. Hughes and T. Pinch (eds), *Social Construction of Technological Systems* (pp. 111–34). Cambridge, MA: MIT Press.

Law, J. (1991a) Introduction: Monsters, machines and sociotechnical relations. In J. Law (ed.), *A Sociology of Monsters* (pp. 1–23). London: Routledge.

Law, J. (1991b) Power, discretion and strategy. In J. Law (ed.), *A Sociology of Monsters*, (pp. 165–91). London: Routledge.

Law, J. (1994) *Organizing Modernity*. Oxford: Blackwell.

Layton, D., Jenkins, E., MacGill, S. and Davey, A. (1993) *Inarticulate Science?* Nafferton, Driffield, E. Yorks: Studies in Education Ltd.

Lukes, S. (1974) *Power: A Radical View*. London: Macmillan.

Lynch, M. (1985) *Art and Artifact in Laboratory Science*. London: Routledge.

Lynch, M. (1988) Sacrifice and transformation of the animal body into a scientific object: Laboratory culture and ritual practice in the neurosciences. *Social Studies of Science*, 18, 265–89.

Lyotard, J-F. (1971) *Discours, Figure*. Paris: Editions Klincksieck.

Lyotard, J-F. (1984) *The Postmodern Condition: A Report on Knowledge*. Manchester: Manchester University Press.

Mabey, R. (ed.) (1984) *Second Nature*. London: Cape.

McCloskey, M. (1983) Naive theories of motion. In D. Gentner and A.L. Stevens (eds), *Mental Models* (pp. 299–324). Hillsdale, NJ: Lawrence Erlbaum.

McGuinness, K. (1993) Gene Sharp's theory of power: A feminist critique of consent. *Journal of Peace Research*, 30, 101–15.

MacKenzie, D. (1981) Interests, positivism and history. *Social Studies of Science*, 11, 498–504.

MacKenzie, D. (1990) *Inventing Accuracy*. Cambridge, MA: MIT Press.

McNaghten, P. (1993) Discourses of nature: Argumentation and power. In E. Burman and I. Parker (eds), *Discourse Analytic Research* (pp. 52–72). London: Routledge.

Martin, Bernice (1981) *A Sociology of Contemporary Cultural Change*. Oxford: Blackwell.

Martin, Brian (1989) Gene Sharp's theory of power. *Journal of Peace Research*, 26, 213–22.

Martin, L.H., Gutman, H. and Hutton, P.H. (eds) (1988) *Technologies of the Self: A Seminar with Michel Foucault*. London: Tavistock.

Mauss, M. (1985) A category of the person: The notion of person; the notion of self. In M. Carrithers, S. Collins and S. Lukes (eds), *The Category of the Person* (pp. 1–25). Cambridge: Cambridge University Press.

Mead, G.H. (1934) *Mind, Self and Society*. Chicago: Chicago University Press.

Mehan, H. (1987) Language and power in organizational process. *Discourse Processes*, 10, 291–301.

Merchant, C. (1980) *Death of Nature: Women, Ecology and the Scientific Revolution*. London: Harper and Row.

Michael, M. (1989) Review of *Texts of Identity* (eds J. Shotter and K.J. Gergen). *British Journal of Social Psychology*, 28, 285–8.

Michael, M. (1991). Discourses of danger and dangerous discourses: Patrolling the borders of 'nature', society and science. *Discourse and Society*, 2 (1), 5–28.

Michael, M. (1992a). Postmodern subjects: Towards a transgressive social psychology. In S. Kvale (ed.), *Psychology and Postmodernism* (pp. 74–87). London: Sage.

Michael, M. (1992b) Lay discourses of science: Science-in-general, science-in-particular and self. *Science, Technology and Human Values*, 17, 313–33.

Michael, M. (1994) The power–persuasion–identity nexus: Anarchism and actor-networks. *Anarchist Studies*, 2, 25–42.

Michael, M. (in press) Discourses of ignorance in the public understanding of science. In A. Irwin and B. Wynne (eds), *Misunderstanding Science?* Cambridge: Cambridge University Press.

Michael, M. and Birke, L. (1994a) Accounting for animal experiments: Credibility and disreputable 'others'. *Science, Technology and Human Values*, 19 (2), 189–204.

Michael, M. and Birke, L. (1994b) Animal experimentation: Enrolling the core set. *Social Studies of Science*, 24, 81–95.

Michael, M. and Grove-White, R. (1993) Talking about talking about nature: Nurturing 'ecological consciousness'. *Environmental Ethics*, 15, 33–47.

Michael, M. and Still, A. (1992) A resource for resistance: Affordance and power-knowledge. *Theory and Society*, 21, 869–88.

Middleton, D. and Edwards, D. (eds) (1990) *Collective Remembering*. London: Sage.

Mol, A. and Law, J. (1994) Regions, networks and fluids: Anaemia and social topology. *Social Studies of Science*, 24, 641–71.

Mort, M. (1994) What about the workers? (Review of G. Spinardi, *From Polaris to Trident*). *Social Studies of Science*, 24, 596–606.

Moscovici, S. (1981) On social representations. In J.P. Forgas (ed.), *Social Cognition* (pp. 181–209). London: Academic Press.

Moscovici, S. (1984) The phenomenon of social representations. In R.M. Farr and S. Moscovici (eds), *Social Representations* (pp. 3–70). Cambridge: Cambridge University Press.

Mouzelis, N. (1993) The poverty of sociological theory. *Sociology*, 27, 675–95.

Muhlhausler, P. and Harré, R. (1990) *Pronouns and People: The Linguistic Construction of Social and Personal Identity*. Oxford: Blackwell.

Mulkay, M. (1985) *The Word and the World*. London: George Allen and Unwin.

Nietzsche, F.W. (1956) *Birth of Tragedy, and the Genealogy of Morals*. New York: Doubleday.

Noske, B. (1989) *Humans and Other Animals*. London: Pluto Press.

Noske, B. (1992) Animals and anthropology. In E.K. Hicks (ed.), *Science and the Human–Animal Relationship* (pp. 79–90). Amsterdam: SISWO.

Ortner, S.B. (1976) Is female to man as nature is to culture? In M.Z. Rosaldo and L. Lamphere (eds), *Woman, Culture and Society* (pp. 67–87). Stanford, CA: Stanford University Press.

Parker, I. (1989) *The Crisis in Modern Social Psychology – And How To End It*. London: Routledge and Kegan Paul.

Parker, I. (1990a) Discourse: Definitions and contradiction. *Philosophical Psychology*, 3, 189–204.

Parker, I. (1990b) Real things: Discourse, context and practice. *Philosophical Psychology*, 3, 227–33.

Parker, I. (1992) *Discourse Dynamics*. London: Routledge.

Parker, I. and Shotter, J. (eds) (1990) *Deconstructing Social Psychology*. London: Methuen.

Passmore, J. (1974) *Man's Responsibility for Nature*. London: Duckworth.

Pinch , T.J. and Bijker, W.E. (1984) The social construction of facts and artefacts: Or, how the sociology of science and the sociology of technology might benefit each other. *Social Studies of Science*, 14, 399–441

Poster, M. (1984) *Foucault, Marxism and History*. Cambridge: Polity Press.

Potter, J. (1992) Constructing realism: Seven moves (plus or minus a couple). *Theory and Psychology*, 2, 167–73.

Potter, J. and Reicher, S. (1987) Discourses of community and conflict: The organization of social categories in accounts of a 'riot'. *British Journal of Social Psychology*, 26, 25–40.

Potter, J. and Wetherell, M. (1987) *Discourse and Social Psychology*. London: Sage.

Potter, J., Stringer, P. and Wetherell, M. (1984) *Social Texts and Contexts: Literature and Social Psychology*. London: Routledge and Kegan Paul.

Potter, J., Wetherell, M., Gill, R. and Edwards, D. (1990) Discourse – Noun, verb or social practice. Definitions and contradiction. *Philosophical Psychology*, 3, 2045–217.

Quinn, H. and Holland, D. (1987) Cultural models in language and thought: An introduction. In D. Holland and N. Quinn (eds), *Cultural Models in Language and Thought* (pp. 3–40). Cambridge: Cambridge University Press.

Ravetz, J.R. (1987) Uncertainty, ignorance and policy. In H. Brooks and C.L. Cooper (eds), *Science for Public Policy* (pp. 77–94). Oxford: Pergamon.

Reed, P. (1989) Man apart: An alternative to the self-realization approach. *Environmental Ethics*, 11, 53–69.

Research Defence Society, *Newsletter*, 1 October 1990.

Roads, M.J. (1987) *Talking with Nature*. Tiburon, CA: H.J. Kramer.

Robbins, D. and Johnson, R. (1976) The role of cognitive and occupational differentiation in scientific controversies. *Social Studies of Science*, 6, 349–68.

Rodman, J. (1983) Four forms of ecological consciousness reconsidered. In D. Scherer and T. Attig (eds), *Ethics and the Environment* (pp. 82–92). Englewood Cliffs, NJ: Prentice-Hall.

Rose, H. (1993) Rhetoric, feminism and scientific knowledge: Or from either/or to both/and. In R.H. Roberts and J.M.M. Good (eds), *The Recovery of Rhetoric* (pp. 203–23). Charlottesville, VA: University Press of Virginia.

Rose, N. (1985) *The Psychological Complex*. London: Routledge and Kegan Paul.

Rose, N. (1989a) Individualizing psychology. In J. Shotter and K.J. Gergen (eds), *Texts of Identity* (pp. 119–32). London: Sage.

Rose, N. (1989b) *Governing the Soul*. London: Routledge.

Ross, A. (1991) *Strange Weather*. London: Verso.

Royal Society of London (1985) *The Public Understanding of Science*. London: Royal Society.

Rupke, N.A. (ed.) (1990) *Vivisection in Historical Perspective*. London: Routledge.

Sampson, E.E. (1981) Cognitive psychology as ideology. *American Psychologist*, 36, 730–43.

Sampson, E.E. (1983) Deconstructing psychology's subject. *Journal of Mind and Behaviour*, 4, 135–64.

Sampson, E.E. (1988) The debate on individualism: Indigenous psychologies of the individual and their role in personal societal functioning. *American Psychologist*, 43, 15–22.

Sampson, E.E. (1989) The deconstruction of the self. In J. Shotter and K.J. Gergen (eds), *Texts of Identity* (pp. 1–19). London: Sage.

Sampson, E.E. (1993) *Celebrating the Other*. Hemel Hempstead: Harvester Wheatsheaf.

Sanders, C.R. (1992) Perceptions of intersubjectivity and the process of 'speaking-for' in canine–human relationships. Paper presented at the international conference on Science and the Human–Animal Relationship, Amsterdam, Netherlands, 5–6 March, 1992.

Schutz, A. (1967) *Phenomenology of the Social World*. London: Heinemann.

Schwarz, M. and Thompson, M. (1990) *Divided We Stand*. Hemel Hempstead: Harvester Wheatsheaf.

Scott, P. (1991) Levers and counterweights: A laboratory that failed to raise the world. *Social Studies of Science*, 21, 7–35.

Serpell, J. (1986) *In the Company of Animals*. Oxford: Blackwell.

Shapin, S. (1988) Following scientists around. *Social Studies of Science*, 18, 533–50.

Shapin, S. (1991) Science and the public. In R.C. Olby, G.N. Cantor, J.R.R. Christie and M.J.S. Hodge (eds.), *Companion to the History of Modern Science* (pp. 990–1007). London: Routledge and Kegan Paul.

Shapin, S. and Schaffer, S. (1985) *Leviathan and the Air-Pump*. Princeton, NJ: Princeton University Press.

Sharp, G. (1973) *The Politics of Nonviolent Action*. Boston: Porter Sargent.

Shilling, C. (1993) *The Body and Social Theory*. London: Sage.

Shotter, J. (1975) *Images of Man in Psychological Research*. London: Methuen.

Shotter, J. (1992) Social constructionism and realism: Adequacy or accuracy? *Theory and Psychology*, 2, 175–82.

Shotter, J. (1993) *Conversational Realities*. London: Sage.

Shotter, J. and Gergen, K.J. (eds) (1989) *Texts of Identity*. London: Sage.

Singleton, V. (1993) Science, women and ambivalence: An actor-network analysis of the cervical screening programme. PhD dissertation, Lancaster University.

Singleton, V. and Michael, M. (1993) Actor-networks and ambivalence: General practitioners in the Cervical Screening Programme. *Social Studies of Science*, 23, 227–64.

Sismondo, S. (1993) Some social constructions. *Social Studies of Science*, 23, 515–53.

Smart, B. (1982) Foucault, sociology and the problem of human agency. *Theory and Society*, 11, 121–41.

Smart, K.R. (1993) Resourcing ambivalence: Dogbreeders, animals and the social studies of science. PhD dissertation, Lancaster University.

Smithson, M. (1985) Toward a social theory of ignorance. *Journal for the Theory of Social Behaviour*, 15, 152–72.

Soper, K. (1986) *Humanism and Anti-Humanism*. London: Hutchinson.

Spender, D. (1980) *Man-Made Language*. London: Routledge and Kegan Paul.

Spinardi, G. (1994) *From Polaris to Trident: The Development of the US Ballistic Missile Technology*. Cambridge: Cambridge University Press.

Star, S.L. (1991) Power, technologies and the phenomenology of conventions: On being allergic to onions. In J. Law (ed.), *A Sociology of Monsters* (pp. 26–56). London: Routledge.

Star, S.L. and Griesemer, J.R. (1989) Institutional ecology, 'translations' and boundary objects: Amateurs and professionals in Berkeley's museum of vertebrate zoology, 1907–39. *Social Studies of Science*, 19, 387–430.

Stenner, P. and Eccleston, C. (1994) On the textuality of being. *Theory and Psychology*, 4 (1), 85–103.

Strum, S.S. and Latour, B. (1988). Redefining the social link: From baboons to humans. *Social Science Information*, 26, 783–802.

Tallmadge, J. (1981) Saying you to the land. *Environmental Ethics*, 3, 351–63.

Taylor, D.M. and Brown, R.J. (1979) Towards a more social social psychology. *British Journal of Social and Clinical Psychology*, 18, 173–80.

Tester, K. (1991) *Animals and Society*. London: Routledge.

Thomas, K. (1984) *Man and the Natural World*. Harmondsworth: Penguin.

Thompson, J. (1984) *Studies in the Theory of Ideology*. Cambridge: Polity Press.

Thompson, M., Ellis, R. and Wildavsky, A. (1990) *Cultural Theory*. Boulder, CO: Westview.

Toumey, C.P. (1992) The moral character of mad scientists: A cultural critique of science. *Science, Technology and Human Values*, 17, 411–37.

Turner, B. (ed.) (1990) *Theories of Modernity and Postmodernity*. London: Sage.

Turner, B.S. (1992) *Regulating Bodies: Studies in Medical Sociology*. London: Routledge.

Turner, J.C. (1987) *Rediscovering the Social Group: A Self-Categorization Theory*. Oxford: Blackwell.

Turner, V.W. (1969) *The Ritual Process*. London: Routledge and Kegan Paul.

UK Global Environmental Research Office (1993) *Global Environmental Change: The UK Research Framework*. Swindon: UK GER Office.

Varela, C.R. (1994) Harré and Merleau-Ponty: Beyond the absent moving body: Embodiments in social theory. *Journal for the Theory of Social Behaviour*, 24, 167–85.

Vines, G. (1991) Researchers rally behind animal experiments. *New Scientist*, 4 May, 10.

Ware, K. (1987) The unity of the human person according to the Greek Fathers. In A.R. Peacocke and G. Gillett (eds), *Persons and Personality* (pp. 197–206). Oxford: Blackwell.

Weart, S. (1988) The physicist as mad scientist. *Physics Today*, June, 28–37.

Wetherell, M. and Potter, J. (1989) Narrative characters and accounting for violence. In J. Shotter and K.J. Gergen (eds), *Texts of Identity* (pp. 206–19). London: Sage.

Wetherell, M. and Potter, J. (1992) *Mapping the Language of Racism*. Hemel Hempstead: Harvester Wheatsheaf.

Wetherell, M., Stiven, H. and Potter, J. (1987) Unequal egalitarianism: A preliminary study of discourses concerning gender and employment opportunities. *British Journal of Social Psychology*, 26, 59–71.

Wexler, P. (1983) *Critical Social Psychology*. Boston: Routledge and Kegan Paul.

White, H. (1987) *The Content of the Form: Narrative Discourse and Historical Representation*. Baltimore, MD: Johns Hopkins University Press.

Whitelegg, M. (1994a) Defence of comfrey. *European Journal of Herbal Medicine*, 1, 11–16.

Whitelegg, M. (1994b) Paradigms and the use of science in alternative and orthodox medicine. PhD dissertation, Lancaster University.

Widdicombe, S. (1993) Autobiography and change: Rhetoric and authenticity in 'Gothic' style. In E. Burman and I. Parker (eds), *Discourse Analytic Research* (pp. 94–113). London: Routledge.

Williams, R. (1980) *Problems of Materialism and Culture*. London: Verso.

Wittgenstein, L. (1953) *Philosophical Investigations*. Oxford: Blackwell.

Woolgar, S.W. (1976) Writing an intellectual history of scientific development: The use of discovery accounts. *Social Studies of Science*, 6, 395–422.

Woolgar, S. (1981) Interests and explanation in the social studies of science. *Social Studies of Science*, 11, 365–94.

Woolgar, S. (1983) Irony in the social studies of science. In K.D. Knorr-Cetina and M. Mulkay (eds), *Science Observed* (pp. 239–66). London: Sage.

Woolgar, S. (1988a) *Science, the Very Idea*. Chichester: Ellis Horwood.

Woolgar, S. (ed.) (1988b) *Knowledge and Reflexivity: New Frontiers in the Sociology of Knowledge*. London: Sage.

Woolgar, S. (1989) The ideology of representation and the role of the agent. In H. Lawson and L. Appignanesi (eds), *Dismantling Truth* (pp. 131–44). London: Weidenfeld and Nicolson.

Woolgar, S. (1992) Some remarks about positionism: A reply to Collins and Yearley. In A. Pickering (ed.), *Science as Practice and Culture* (pp. 327–42). Chicago: University of Chicago Press.

Wynne, B.E. (1989) Frameworks of rationality in risk management: Towards the testing of naive sociology. In J. Brown (ed.), *Environmental Threats* (pp. 33–47). London: Belhaven Press.

Wynne, B.E. (1991) Knowledges in context. *Science, Technology and Human Values*, 16, 111–21.

Wynne, B.E. (1992a) Public understanding of science research: New horizons or hall of mirrors. *Public Understanding of Science*, 1, 37–43.

Wynne, B.E. (1992b) Misunderstood misunderstanding: Social identities and public uptake of science. *Public Understanding of Science*, 1, 281–304.

Wynne, B.E. (1995) The public understanding of science. In S. Jasanoff, G.E. Markle, J.C. Peterson and T. Pinch (eds), *Handbook of Science and Technology Studies* (pp. 361–88). Thousand Oaks, CA: Sage.

Wynne, B.E. and Meyer, S. (1993) How science fails the environment. *New Scientist*, 5 June, 33–5.

Yearley, S. (1991) *The Green Case*. London: HarperCollins.

Index